Raimon Panikkar
Henri Le Saux (Abhiṣiktananda)

The Gift of Friendship

Correspondence and Inner Journeys

Raimon Panikkar
Henri Le Saux (Abhiṣiktananda)

The Gift of Friendship

Correspondence and Inner Journeys

Edited by
Milena Carrara

ISPCK

2023

Raimon Panikkar - Henri Le Saux (Abhiṣiktānanda): The Gift of Friendship - Published by the Indian Society for Promoting Christian Knowledge (ISPCK), Post Box 1585, Kashmere Gate, Delhi-110006.

First edition, translated from the French version Intériorité et révélation. Essais théologiques (published by Présence, Sisteron, 1982).

Online Order: http://ispck.org.in/book.php

Also available on amazon.com

ISBN: 978-81-962033-7-5

Cover Image Credit: Editor

Laser typeset by

ISPCK, Post Box 1585, 1654, Madarsa Road, Kashmere Gate, Delhi-110006 • *Tel:* 23866323/22

e-mail: ashish@ispck.org.in • ella@ispck.org.in
website: www.ispck.org.in

Printed at Saurabh Printers, Noida.

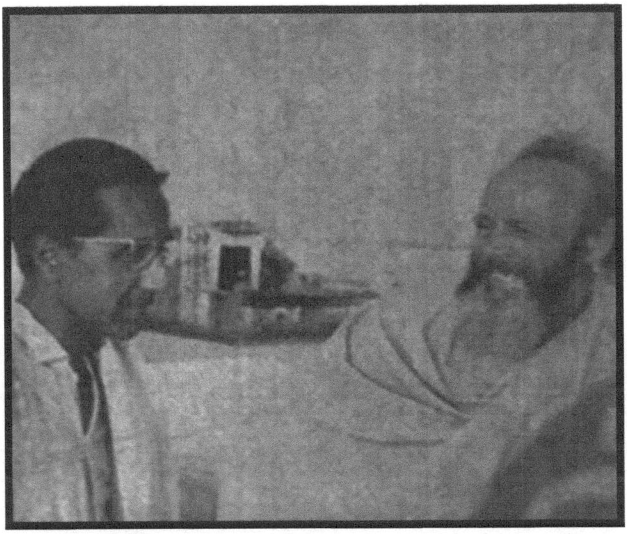

Contents

Prologue to Correspondence between Raimon Panikkar and Abhiṣiktānanda

Javier Melloni

The epistolary genre allows us to have a privileged and very special closeness to people, since it gives us a direct insight into both their everyday life and their most intimate and spontaneous confidences. This is what we find here in these letters between two of the most important men of the 20th Century, not only in the field of dialogue between Christianity and Hinduism but also in that of the mystical exploration of Christianity.

Reading this correspondence, one cannot help but feel great respect and immense nostalgia for the developments that took place between the 1950s and 1970s, a few years after India's independence (1947). This was a time characterised by an open, bold, generous and fruitful exchange between Hinduism and Christianity, though, I should add, generally more on the Christian side than the Hindū side. It was us Christians, in fact, who, after four centuries of western Christianity in India, finally began to realise what treasures the country guarded, which up until then we had treated with contempt. I say "western Christianity" because eastern Christianity has been present in South India since the first century through a tradition that dates back to St. Thomas.

This correspondence is also a historical document, inasmuch as the extended relationships of both, many of which they shared, feature such prominent figures of the day as Bede Griffiths, Murray Rogers (Protestant pastor who founded the Jyotiniketan *āśram*), Patrick de Souza, the bishop of Benares who made Panikkar unconditionally welcome throughout his life, and various Protestant pastors, bishops, Jesuits, etc., all pioneers of interreligious dialogue. The letters also contain references to their respective families, and also to future articles and books in the making, the contents of which they shared and discussed together.

A brief contextualisation

Henri Le Saux arrived in India from his Benedictine monastery in Brittany, France at the age of thirty-eight (1948) and remained until his death in 1973, never returning to Europe. Raimon Panikkar, eight years younger, first arrived in India in 1955, at almost the same age, and died in his native land of Spain in 2010 after many years of travelling back and forth, characteristic of his restless heart and mind. Abhiṣiktānanda died at the age of 63; Panikkar lived to be 91. Here we have two very different personalities who shared the same vibrant *pathos,* the same desire to create a dialogue between Christianity and Hinduism, but sought to achieve it in very different ways, each from his own mystical peak, which for Le Saux was the naked life of monasticism-*saṃnyāsa* beyond all names and forms, while for Panikkar it was the acceptance and celebration of the profusion of names and forms.

The name that Henri Le Saux took on his arrival in India was Abhiṣ iktānanda, "the bliss of the anointed", while Raimon Panikkar simply added a "k" to his Hispanicised surname (Paniker) and changed the "e" to an "a", so that it sounded more like his name in Malayalam. The name Panikkar originated as an honorary title meaning "distinguished servant". The former, therefore, strove to make a synthesis between two cultures and cosmovisions; the latter received it from birth. It is significant, in fact, that in all his letters Abhiṣiktānanda signs his name in Sanskrit.

The diary spans 16 and a half years of epistolary relationship: the first letter we have was written by Panikkar on March 18th, 1957 and the last was written by Abhiṣiktānanda on November 8th, 1973, twenty-eight days before his death. There are 99 letters by Raimon Panikkar and 64 by Abhiṣiktānanda. There is a curious symmetry in the disproportion of the correspondence: at the beginning there are many letters from Panikkar and almost none from Abhiṣiktānanda, while towards the end (1969-1973) it is the opposite.

To the great credit of the editor,

Relationship

When writing to Panikkar, Abhiṣiktānanda always begins his letter with *My dear Raymond*, while Panikkar addresses Abhiṣiktānanda in various different ways over the years: *My dear Father* at the beginning, then *My dear Svāmi* (the equivalent in the Indian world); on many occasions he adds the suffix *–jī*, denoting both respect and affection, i.e. Svāmijī, Abhiṣ iktajī; he also uses other expressions, such as: *My dear friend*, *My dear brother*, and sometimes both: *My dear brother and friend*. This diversity reflects Panikkar's polymorphic nature, while Le Saux's greeting, which remains the same over the years, is typical of his own personality.

The year in which the bond between the two was truly cemented was 1964, when Panikkar returned to India after spending four years in Rome. In that year they went on two pilgrimages together to two of holiest Hindū sites: Gangotrī, at the source of the Ganges in the Himalayas (June 1964), and six months later, between late December and the beginning of 1965, Aruṇācala (Tiruvannamalai, Tamil Nadu, South India), the sacred mountain where Rāmaṇa Mahārṣi (1880-1950) found shelter, and where Le Saux had his founding experiences, shortly after his arrival in India.

In the letters of both there are a few references to these two events, but it is in their diaries, most of all, that we read how immensely important they were to them. Regarding the pilgrimage to Gangotrī, Panikkar wrote in his diary:

> Impossible to be alone and in silence. As things have turned out, I have wasted 10 days waiting for the Svāmi-jī's permit for Gongotri. And yet a wonderful experience, not only getting to know him better but also thiskind of life and its limitations. Now he is coming with me to Gangotri. My health is very bad: stomach trouble, headache, pains in my feet, tiredness, etc. Let us see how I resist.
>
> (Uttarkashi, June 1st, 1964)

And six days later he added:

> We started last Monday at noon and came back this morning. A wonderful pilgrimage, not for me alone, but for thousands of people. Monday slept at Ganganani, Tuesday at Harisal, Wednesday and Thursday at Gongotri, Friday Harisal and Saturday Bhatvali. The route is marvellous. The sight of the mountain inspiring. I was able to spend some time in silence and the talk on the way was generally very good. Mass at all these places and Thursday 3 miles north of Gongotrī, at the side of the Ganges. We brought Christ there. I thank thee, my Lord, for all.
>
> (June 7th, 1964)

The entries that Abhiṣiktānanda makes in his diary were published a little later under the title: *Une messe au sources du Gange.*[1]

On the pilgrimage to Aruṇācala, we read in Panikkar's diary:

> On the 2nd day we went to visit the Tiruvannamalai temple with Abhiṣ iktånanda and on the 3rd we concelebrated on the top of Aruṇācala! Good Sunday! On the 4th day we went to see Gñānānanda at Tapovanam.
>
> My heart and my head are so full of impressions that I cannot summarize them. I was wrong not to write them down here every day.
>
> (January 10th, 1965)

After one of their first meetings, Panikkar noted in his diary: «I spent the afternoon with Le Saux, talking about our projects, but neither he nor I are men of action» (New Delhi, July 25th, 1959). These two experiences sealed the friendship that was to develop between them over the course of sixteen years. Throughout their correspondence we see that three major common concerns and missions repeatedly appear: the transformation of the Church in India, the emergence of a new form of monasticism, and how to live, understand and convey the Christian *advaita.*

The Church in India

The period of this correspondence coincides with the most important years of the Church's renewal around the Second Vatican Council (1962-1965). The reflections and comments that the two exchange before, during and after the Council are a clear example of the prophetic lucidity they had in common. In addition, Panikkar was in Rome for most of this period (1960-1964) and witnessed first hand what was happening, even though

---

1 Paris: Le Seuil, 1967.

The neo-Hinduist movement which has controlled the nation's government since the 1990s severely hampered the progress of the Hindū-Christian dialogue and induced many Indian Christian communities to regard the Christian *aśramic* movement as a pact with Brahmanism. Nevertheless, the *āṣram* founded by Le Saux still exists; associated with the Camaldolese Benedictines, it continues to be a place of formation and reference for Hindū-Christian dialogue.

A new form of monasticism

In 1950, two years after his arrival in India, Henri Le Saux founded the first Christian *āśram* in South India, near the Kavery River, together with Jules Monchanin (1895-1957), a French priest. They called it *sat-cit-ānanda*, a name that incorporates both the Vedānta trinity and the Christian trinity. Abhiṣiktānanda's relationship with Monchanin and the *āśram* was complex from the start, since he was more of a hermit than a monk. The Hindū category of *saµnyasin* (renunciation), nomadic by nature, corresponded more to his vocation. When Panikkar arrived in India, Jules Monchanin had already passed away and Henri Le Saux hardly ever attended the *āśram;* increasingly he made trips to the Himalayas, although his awakening to *advaita* took place on Aruṇācala during his meeting with Rāmaṇa Mahārṣi, whom he only saw once.

Both believed that the only possible form of dialogue with the East would begin from a true contemplative experience, and the place where it would be cultivated would be Christian *āṣrams*. Both took part in numerous meetings in India on this issue. Seeking possible themes, Panikkar wrote to Abhiṣiktānanda from Vārāṇasi (Benares): «A possible theme relating to the idea of the Christian *āśrams* could be contemplative prayer in the context of the apostolate and also in active life» (March 17, 1960).

When Panikkar returned to India after four years in Rome and began to look for a place to work and live, he wrote to Abhiṣiktānanda:

> In Banaras I would have the possibility of a chair in comparative religions, but I am very afraid of the "politics".I don't have a house yet. I would like to get a small *sunyapit* near the Ganges and not far from the University, but it isn't easy. I could then have one room as a library and another as

> a chapel. A real *āśram*, if you will, but without calling it such.I see my theandric journey a little more clearly (a synthesis between action and contemplation, spirit and body, Hinduism and Christianity, etc.).
>
> (Najipur, April 15, 1964)

These lines have great biographical value. As he feared, Panikkar failed to obtain the professorship he sought, on account of him being a Catholic priest and a foreigner. He did, however, find a small house on the banks of the Ganges, which was to become his home for almost twenty years whenever he was in India (the house still exists). At the same time, the elements of his own particular monasticism can be seen in a reference to what he calls his "theandric path" – an expression that introduces a concept which begins to form in this period and for which a few years later he would coin the term "cosmotheandric".

A year later, after having been offered a professorship in the United States, in a reply to a letter from Abhiṣiktānanda Panikkar makes a remark that is very typical of his quick-witted humour:

> You can use my name and anything else you want of mine. So, the passport: ... Father's name: RamuniPanikker (died 1954); Mother: Carmen Alemany; Marital status: (do you need to ask? – mystical marriage is not "civil" – therefore "single").
>
> (New York, August 7, 1965).

Mystical marriage is not recognised in secular society. It has to be practised personally and privately. Two years later he writes to Abhiṣiktānanda from Harvard:

> Here at Harvard I am a monk. my Tuesdays spent in silence, prayer and contemplation are purer here than in Varāṇasī. Today, as is very often the case, I have not moved, or even left my apartment (one room). I live in solitude.
>
> (March 14, 1967)

Panikkar begins to move more and more towards a type of monasticism that is practised in the heart of the world, and away from the radical and acosmic conception embraced by Abhiṣiktānanda. This is illustrated well in a note that Panikkar writes as a comment on a letter from Abhiṣiktānanda, dated December 5, 1969. In it he asks how might he respond to the contemporary world from within a contemplative vocation but at the same time being close to the world.

For his part, Abhiṣiktānanda is becoming radicalized towards the opposite extreme. On March 12, 1971 he writes:

> At least an attempt of theology must be made... or should the monk just keep quiet and simply "be"?... Here all these days free from all form... An *Oṁ* which extends (expands) in a communion that accompanies a minimum of formulas. *Oṁ*! That says it all, out of time and beyond, *sadasat* ... this *Oṁ* that awakens to the Self...

Abhiṣiktānanda increasingly refuses to attend meetings, which he considers useless. On October 6, 1973 he writes: «I do not believe in [the possibility of] developing a true monasticism here through the institutions. These are merely charismatic vocations.»

In these years, Panikkar was spending half the year in Santa Barbara (California) working as a university professor and the other half in Benares as visiting professor, living in his humble abode near the Ganges. These two models of life reached their culmination years later after he retired, in 1987, to the small village of Tavertet in the Pre-Pyrenees of Catalonia, where he endeavoured to develop a contemporary form of monasticism, integrating the contemplative dimension with human relationships and contact with nature—the cosmotheandric triad.

The Christian *advaita*

For both Panikkar and Abhiṣiktānanda, the two themes covered above (the Church and interreligious monasticism) converged in the mystical horizon of the two religions. In Hindū terms, this is the *advaita* experience. The difference lies in the fact that for Christianity what is a point of arrival, a high peak inaccessible to the majority, for Hinduism is a starting point common to all. The relationship of the One with the many, of the creator (Brahman) with the created (*ātman*) is experienced and coincides differently in the two religions. Christianity must deconstruct its traditional categories, not from the point of view of rationalism but of mysticism.

Although in their public writings both Panikkar and Abhiṣiktānanda present this deconstruction as evidence, it was neither easy nor immediate for either of them. The correspondence between them is all the more precious for the fact that it gives us an inkling into the extent to which they struggled and suffered over these convictions.

On February 14, 1966, when Panikkar was in Rome (in the throes of his own inner struggle prior to leaving Opus Dei, which occurred on June 21, 1966), he wrote:

> My life in Rome is unthinkable. I sleep 3 hours a day! But what is happening, what is continuing in me is also unbelievable: total emptiness, complete surrender, absolute freedom, the experience of a broken-down identity between both faith and non-faith, God and non-God.What more could one want? On a less profound level I try to base a Christian spirituality on *advaita*...

"Total emptiness", "full dispossession", etc. He finds himself in the midst of the *Dark Night*, when turning back is impossible but one is powerless to voluntarily move forward. This is a process in which one must let things go as they will, in complete trust and confidence. Several months later, now back in India, he writes to Abhiṣiktānanda:

> In recent times I have "suffered" – in the deepest sense – the unspeakable. *Advaita* on one side and *śūnyatā* on the other.
>
> (New Delhi, August 30, 1966)

Advaita is Hindū, and has to do with the union of *ātman* with *paramātman,* while *śūnyatā* is Buddhist, the experience of total emptiness; in both cases it implies the dissolution of the ego and the disappearance of the You, while the Christian way is constitutively relational. Panikkar's famous and much-quoted phrase «I started out as a Christian, I discovered myself as a Hindū and I returned asa Buddhist, without ever ceasing to be a Christian» must therefore be read in the light of this struggle. These confessions are essential in reaching the truth and fullness of such a spiritual adventure.

As for Abhiṣiktānanda, over the years he recorded his inner struggles in his diary. Only at the end of his life does he seem to have achieved a peaceful integration between his personal Christian perspective and that of the Hindū *Advaita*. In a letter to Panikkar he writes:

> All that is so-called "religious" consists of what is "superimposed", of a "man made" sacred intended to take the place of the truly Sacred, unperceived because of its translucidity
>
> (October 29, 1966).

Not giving in to any substitute for the Absolute requires great heroism. Both these men were alone, and not only as Christians. Abhiṣiktānanda, in particular, was very much aware that this struggle was not even understood by the Hindū world: «It is clear that our books [i.e. yours and mine (*Sagesse*)] are not meant for Hindūs» (May 18, 1966). Each was forced to make the journey on his own, and for this reason they identified with each other, though, having quite different personalities, they experienced this struggle differently. Abhiṣiktānanda's tone was consistently more radical and dramatic than Panikkar's. For example, in a letter he wrote from the Himalayas he tells Panikkar:

> I see no possibility of salvation for the Church (as far as secondary causes) except in an advaitic renewal. The traditional myth no longer comes from any direction (Hindū, Christian, Buddhist). Reason argues all its own conclusions.
>
> (November 18, 1966)

All these are mere glimpses from the bare peaks that each struggled to cross. Totally naked and exposed to the elements, they acknowledged each other, embraced, and each continued on his way. Reading their correspondence makes us want to read their respective diaries. They are complementary.

In concluding this prologue I must give the last word to Panikkar who, speaking to Abhiṣiktānanda in a posthumous letter written in 2005, says:

> I cannot write about you. I can only write to you. I was not able to assuage your suffering. I was unable to convince you because you felt I was making it too easy. Now you do not need my words; but we still profit from your strugglings.[2]

It is difficult to express in so few words the affection and intensity of a friendship that entered into *tempiternity* and of which, thanks to this publication, we are able to partake.

---

2 Posthumous Letter, Tavertet, February 7, 2005.

Acknowledgements

I am grateful to the Abhiṣiktānanda Centre for Interreligious Dialogue (Delhi Brotherhood Society) for giving me permission to publish Abhishiktananda's letters to Panikkar.

I would like also to thank the friends who have been with me in putting together this book, transcribing, translating and proofreading the letters, most of which are handwritten and not always easy to decipher.

A special thanks to Espedito D'Agostini and Maria Albanese and to Geraldine Clarkson, who translated the texts into English.

Lastly, a very special thank you to Javier Melloni, who encouraged me to publish this book and also enriched it with a valuable prologue.

MCP

Introductory Notes

Milena Carrara Pavan

The subtitle of this collection of correspondence, *The Gift of Friendship,* may seem a little unoriginal but actually it is the perfect title for a book that illustrates this great gift shared by the two authors, Henri Le Saux and Raimon Panikkar, as emerges both in their letters to each other and in the material that has come into my hands.

As the subject matter is correspondence, I have taken the liberty of writing these introductory notes in epistolary form, a choice, I am sure, would be appreciated by those to whom they are dedicated if they were still with us … and I like to believe that perhaps they are … who knows?, just in another form.

❖❖❖

Milan, April 9, 2023

Easter

Dear Raimon,

Do you remember when, to your great surprise (and mine also) I gave you the book *A Mass at the Source of the Ganges* by Henri Le Saux?

I had met you, almost by chance, in Assisi, having gone there with a friend who knew you through your books and wanted to take part in one of your retreats. All I wanted was to spend a few days in Assisi, "breathing in" the atmosphere of St. Francis and St. Clare, but I was struck by the intensity of your words and the peace they conveyed to me. I didn't understand them at the time, but I felt the depths from which they came.

When I heard that you would be leaving Milan a week later from the airport near my house, I decided to come and say goodbye and give you a small gift on behalf of all those who had listened to you, but the fact that I chose that particular book from my library was truly a strange coincidence ... Maybe because it was small, maybe because it was about India... I don't know.

I had read it a few years earlier and it had fascinated me so much that I eventually read all of Henri Le Saux's books, including his diaries, and it saddened me greatly that he was already dead because I would really have liked to know him and have him as my guide during those first steps of my own journey.

You were surprised and asked how I knew that the friend who accompanied Henri on his pilgrimage to the source of the Ganges and who celebrated Mass with him was you yourself, under the pseudonym of Sanat-Kumar, and I was even more surprised. I felt a shiver pass through me: it was as if Abhiṣiktānanda were telling me that he was gone but that I could rely on his friend.

There is no need to talk further here about how we continued together our pilgrimage, which would eventually lead us to the Kailāsa[1], the culmination of your all pilgrimages on earth, as you wrote in your diaries (September 23, 1994):[2]

> Mass at the foot of the Kailāsa was a powerful and real event – as well as an experience. It completed the Masses on Arunācala and in Gangotrī that I celebrated with Abhiṣikta.

---

1 The complete story of our pilgrimage together was later narrated in the book *A Pilgrimage to Kailāsa,* Raimon Panikkar – Milena Carrara Pavan, Motilal Banarsidass, Delhi 2018.

2 Raimon Panikkar, *The Water of the Drop. Fragments from the Diaries.* Delhi: ISPCK 2018.

You always wanted to celebrate the Eucharist in sacred places where the Spirit prepares us for the hour of full awareness, like when Jesus said to the Samaritan woman that the hour would soon come «when neither on this mountain nor in Jerusalem will you worship the Father. (...) But the hour is coming, and now is, when the true worshipers will worship the Father in spirit and truth, for such the Father seeks to worship him. God is spirit, and those who worship him must worship in spirit and truth (Jn 4:21-24).»[3] Then each of us will bring to the church[4] the treasures of truth and grace that the Spirit will build within us in its own time.

And at the foot of the Kailāsa, with me as mankind's representative, you celebrated «the cosmic sacrifice of the cross in the spirit of the *Vedas*, Melchisedeck and all the other "exchanges" between heaven and earth».[5]

This pilgrimage marked the beginning of a long spiritual relationship which led you to put your full trust in me.

In 2003, again to my great surprise, you handed me a suitcase full of your diaries and private correspondence, including the letters in this book, together with a touching note which said:

> ... I believe my "service" lies in my books, which are the crystallization of my life – although crystal is not flesh. I hope you will be able to find the incarnation—without falling prey to gossip.
>
> By entrusting you with these pages, I also entrust you with my life. You have full freedom in the Name of this Mystery that we still call Father, Son and Holy Spirit. May the Spirit enlighten you!

My dearest Raimon, I cannot say whether I have done justice to the trust you placed in me to publish and promote your thought with genuine commitment. The publication of your Opera Omnia has been completed, and also a first selection of your diaries, published under the title *The Water of the Drop.* Now, with this book, I would like to pay my last tribute to you and Abhiṣiktānanda, who have guided me and opened my mind and heart to the great mystery of life.

---

3 *Ibid.* Chapter 8.

4 The church understood as the symbol of the *sacramento mundi*, the mystery of the cosmos, as it was called by the first fathers.

5 See note 1.

I thank you from the bottom of my heart, dear friends, on behalf of all those who have loved you and through you have felt the gift of the divine Spirit, the foundation of true friendship.

Yours always,
Milena

❖❖❖

Milan, April 9, 2023

Dearest Odette,[6]

Many years have passed since we first met in Milan. You came to PIME[7] to present the beautiful film *Swamijī, an Inner Journey*, the story of the life of Henri Le Saux by French director Patrice Chagnard, to whom you had offered an enormous selection of precious material taken from the writings and diaries left to you by Le Saux, or Abhiṣiktānanda. The film also marked the stages of our long and beautiful friendship. You were several years older than me, you were alone and I offered to drive you to the station. The last train from Milan to Zurich, from where you would continue on to your home in Fraunfeld, was old and foul-smelling, perhaps one of the last post-war locomotives. As a refined lady you were uncomfortable at the prospect of the journey, so it was natural for me to invite you to spend the night at my house, certain that my husband would also be happy to meet you.

---

6 Odette Baumer Despeigne, Belgian-born, lived in Switzerland, spent 15 years in volunteer work (she saved the lives of many Jews fleeing Germany) before furthering her studies in theology and philosophy. She corresponded regularly with Henri Le Saux (receiving 75 letters) and was one of the last few people who were lucky enough to meet him after the great adventure of his Awakening, when he shone with inner light, as is borne out by the photos taken by her and her son Christoph at Indore, India, before his death.
She edited several of Abhiṣiktananda's books and together with Panikkar published the manuscript of his Diaries under the title of *La montée au fond du coeur*, Paris: OEIL, 1986.*La montée au fond du coeur. Le journal intime du moine chretien-sannyasi hindou* 1948-1973. Paris: OEIL, 1986. In English: *Ascent to the Depth of the Heart*, Delhi: ISPCK, 1998.

7 PIME: Pontifical Institute for Foreign Missions of Milan.

Some time later, I went with you to a conference held in Fez under the patronage of the King of Morocco, on the subject of spiritual films based on the three Abrahamic religions. Here you and Chagnard presented the film on Swamijī. It was a truly unique experience which ended in the desert with a large circle lit by the last rays of the setting sun on one side and the full moon rising on the other, while representatives of the three religions read excerpts from their respective scriptures: religious dialogue through images and more. When we parted I saw emotion in your eyes, as probably you did in mine.

Of your numerous presentations on Le Saux (held at some hundred monasteries throughout the world) I was present at the one you gave at the monastery of the Carmelite nuns in Haifa. Here, as always, you aroused great interest in the Benedictine monk who, though immersed in Hindū spirituality, nevertheless remained faithful to Christ as he journeyed towards the Source of the Father, where there are no more divisions but only the experience of Life.

Our relationship continued to deepen. In one of my visits to Frauenfeld you showed me the private correspondence you had exchanged with Le Saux and also the diaries of Marc, his disciple.

When your son Christoph informed me you were seriously ill, even though he advised me not to go and see you since you were unconscious most of the time, I rushed anyway to catch the train, carrying a bougainvillea branch hastily snatched from my garden. Not only did you recognize me but I had the joy of seeing you smile at me when I thanked you for your great and heartfelt dedication in spreading Le Saux's deep spiritual experience.

A few days later after my visit you passed away and Christoph phoned and told me that you had mentioned me in your will. You wanted me to join the editorial team with Raimon for the publication of Marc Chaduc – Svami Ajatananda's diary, recounting his interaction with Svami Abhiṣiktananda. This committee was eventually set up around Raimon in Spain in 2006 to carry out your last wishes.

I am grateful to you, dearest Odette, for your friendship and for your commitment. Please do not take it badly if I use one of your writings (unpublished, I believe) to narrate once again Abhiṣikta's life and teaching in your own words.

Your friend forever,
Milena

PS

Among your correspondence I found a letter to you from Raimon Panikkar, with whom you collaborated on the publication of the Henri Le Saux's diaries. I include it here as a seal of friendship between a group of exceptional friends, whose exceptionality lies simply in the fact that they allowed themselves to be urged on by the Spirit to reach the Source of Life.

❖❖❖

Tavertet, June 12, 1995

Odette!

Thank you for sharing with me. It is neither a question of subjectivity nor objectivity; it is mental. It is about pure revelation, the Me-You relationship reflected by the I-Thou relationship – since there is no *Ab-solutus*. We tend to panic if we believe it, because then there is a shift from me to you, from pole to pole. Reality lies in the relationship itself: *advaita*is the naked relationship in which there is not a being here (me) and another there (you). Being is a verb (therefore an Act and a Word), not a substance. We cannot understand reality; we can love it by becoming the Love "between" the Lover and the Beloved. Neither one nor two.

This is the experience that does not "touch" either the One or the Two. We could say it is the Trinity, which might be the cataphatic word for apophatic *advaita*. One *is*, every being *is* (including Being itself) to the extent that it*is* (Being is being), digging into *sat* [being] without falling into *asat* [non-being].

In moral terms: one *is*, to the extent that one is humble: being is ceasing to be without reaching non-being. These are all metaphors.

It is simpler than this. And the translation, the expression is when (everyday) life is (infinite = eternal) Life.

Thank you for your visit. I would have continued to write, but after the interruption silence remains – which is not understood by those who seek it…

In great friendship,

Raimon

I am sending you back all the papers[8] you copied with so much loving patience, without having duplicated them, of course.

8 Henri Le Saux' personal diaries were handwritten in a calligraphy that was not always easy to decipher and cost years of patient transcription.

Correspondence
(1957 – 1973)
Raimon Panikkar and Abhiṣiktananda

1957[1]

My most significant meeting was with Raymond Panikkar, who had come to Banaras to take part in a summer camp for students. We talked about theology on the road, in the sun, squashed together in the bus, in the restaurants, just as if we were in a room. We carried on our (very profound) discussions in Bombay under the same conditions. We will continue in Banaras in six weeks' time".

(from a letter written by Henri Le Saux to Joseph Lemarié on May 27, 1957.)[2]

Banaras,[3] March 18, 1957

Svāmi Abhiṣiktānanda,

Kulittalai

My dear Father,

Abbé Monchanin[4] writes to me that you will be coming here soon. I would

[1] From 1957 to 1959 the correspondence consists only of Panikkar's letters; those of Abhiṣiktānanda that are in our possession begin on 5 March, 1960.

[2] Fr. Joseph Lemarié, French Benedictine priest at the Abbey of Kergonan (France), with whom Henri le Saux carried on an intense correspondence (H. Le Saux, *Lettres d'un saṃnyāsi chrétien à Joseph Lemarié*, Paris: Cerf, 1999.)

[3] Banaras or Benares, originally called Varāṇasī, a holy city to Hindūs, seat of the most important and prestigious university of studies on Hinduism. From the '60s to the '70s Panikkar made his Indian home here, in a small house on the banks of the Ganges. For several years he worked as visiting professor at the university while serving as priest incardinated in this diocese.

[4] Père Jules Monchanin, in India Svāmī Paramarubyandam, founded together with Henri Le Saux the Christian *āśram* Śantivanam in Tamil Nadu, which was later under the spiritual guidance of Fr. Bede Griffiths; Monchanin was a promoter of the interreligions dialogue between Catholicism and Hinduism and innovator of Catholic missionary theology.

very much like to see you—and also I would be ready to accompany you on your pilgrimages (as a simple *śiṣya*[5]) for some time, if you would like.

I would be very grateful if you could let me know the approximate date of your arrival in Kashi, as I have to leave for a while to follow my summer programme (sounds very bourgeois, doesn't it? But I will not be going on holiday).

I read your wonderful article on "Vie Intellectuelle". I share your opinion completely!

Hoping to see you soon,

My best wishes in Christ,

Raymond Panikkar

❖❖❖

Banaras, Lanka,Viṣṇu Bhavan[6], April 11, 1957

My dear Father,

Thank you for your letter.

I was thinking of leaving for Almora after Easter, but my programme has changed slightly:

until 22 - here

April 22 - 28 - Catholic Center, Madras

May 3-10 - Deccan College, Poona - AICUF Conference[7]

May 10-15 - Banrasas

May 15 - June 15 - Himalayas - Almora, Ranikhet, Rishikesh, Dharwan, etc.

but I don't know my addresses yet.

---

[5] Disciple.

[6] Name of the *bhavan* (building where meetings were held) in Vārāṇasī.

[7] All India Catholic University Federation, movement of university students with the vision of a new and just society.

June 15-20 – Indian Philosophical Congress, Kashmir University, Srinagar

June 25 - Banaras, again.

I will be passing through Bombay between May 10 and 15, but I am not going to Pachmashi for Priests' Week.

I haven't been invited, but I think it would be interesting for you—for us—to go.

I greatly wish to see you and speak with you.

Unless we meet earlier in Banaras.

Regarding the Himalayas, I would leave by motorbike. It would be easy for me, perhaps, to come and see you, if it wouldn'tbe a bother. I understand that sometimes it can be.

My regards to Dr. Mehta.[8]

In Christ.

Raymond Panikkar

❖❖❖

Banaras, October 29, 1957

My dear Father,

I have prayed a lot for Fr. Monchanin, and also for you. I am convinced that the time has come to make your—our—dreams come true. We already have a victim, and death is always, in a Christian climate, the price to pay. Fr. Monchanin will help us better from heaven than on earth, if I dare say so. Don't you agree?

I think your report to the CBCI[9] is very important. It will give canonical *status* to all our efforts and also immediately solve your problem in Rome. You are simply a member of the CBCI, according to the order status of the Christian *saṃnyāsin*!

---

8 Dr. Dinshah Mehta (Parsi), founder of the Society of Servants of God.

9 CBCI: Catholic Bishops' Conference of India.

I will not be leaving for Europe until the end of the course, that is, in April or May. What should I do with your papers?

I think we should meet in Śāntivanam,[10] even for the sake of Śāntivanam itself, to show that the *āśram* is not dead, but quite the opposite. We could even consider the meeting as a sort of homage or tribute to Monchanin and publish "Mélanges Monchanin". What do you think?

Fr. Bede has just written to me that he is very happy about this meeting.

As for the date, I will be near Tambaram—Madras Christian College—from December 17th to 23rd. On the 28th the meeting of the seminary professors begins in Bangalore. We could fit it in between these two dates, or before, or, even better, after.

I have just finished the article—the *bhāṣya*[11]—on the Brahma Sūtras I, 1, 2, which neither Fr. Neuner[12] nor Fr. De Smet[13] in Poona liked. In part, perhaps they are right.

Please make it to Bangalore. I think it would be interesting. I fear that if we fail to begin applying some solutions, due to the difficult nature of the matter it will take on an even more conservative aspect.

I have just attended a "conference" of Protestant theologians in Nāgpur on the themes "Christian approach to Sarvodaya"[14] (Vinoba Bhave)[15] and "Theological basis for collaboration between Christians and non-Christians".

Extremely interesting. Protestant efforts cannot be ignored. I will tell you about it when we meet.

---

[10] Fr. Bede Griffiths (in India Svāmī Dayānanda), British-born priest and Benedictine monk, succeeded Henri Le Saux as spiritual director of Saccidānanda *āśram*, Śāntivanam, until his death (1993). Had a long and deep friendship with Panikkar. Wrote numerous books among which *The Golden Strig* (1954-1980), *Return to the Center* (1976), *River of Compassion* (1987-2001), *A New Vision of Reality* (1990), etc.

[11] Commentary.

[12] Fr. Josef Neuner, Austrian Jesuit priest, spiritual advisor to Mother Teresa and prominent theologian at the Second Vatican Council.

[13] Fr. Richard De Smet, Belgian Jesuit priest and missionary and Indologist.

[14] Sanskrit word used by Gandhi and later also by Vinoba Bhave, meaning "wellbeing of all".

[15] Indian philosopher and advocate of nonviolence and human rights. Ofter called *Acārya*, "teacher" (Sankr.), he is regarded as the spiritual successor of Gandhi.

I also met a Protestant "minister" who lives in an *āśram* near Bareilly and with Scrima[16] and others we will be holding a small group meeting to read, discuss etc. about Kraemer's famous book, on February 3-10, 1958.

I am currently reading Villain's book about Abbé Couturier.[17] It makes me tremble – and pray.

I am sending you a small article, which perhaps did not turn out very well.

In Nāgpur I did not talk with the Archbishop at great length, but he was very cordial. On my way back, by motorbike, I stopped at the temples of Khajuraho and had several "Nicodemus" conversations[18] with the clergy of Mathya Pradesh (diocese of Jabalpur). It is important to sow well.

Here, right now, I have work that would be overwhelming if I were to lose for a moment the spirit and reality of the contemplative life. Say a little prayer for me. When I left for Nagpur, I was physically exhausted. These fifteen days have been providential. As always!

My Hindi is not making progress. It is a pity—and humiliating.

I have not seen the Pachmahir brochure yet. Give my greetings to Fr. Dominique,[19] if you see him.

In silentio et speerit fortitudo nostra![20] Is. 30:15. This has upheld me for so many years!

In Christ,

Raymond Panikkar

PS. Did you get my postcard from Nāgpur?

❖❖❖

---

16 Fr. André Scrima, Romanian Orthodox monk, philosopher and theologian.

17 Villain, M. *L'Abbé Paul Coutourier*, Paris: Casterman, 1957.

18 Intimate conversations, with reference to the conversations between Jesus and Nicodemus as related in the Gospels.

19 Fr. Dominique van Rollenghen, Belgian Benedictine monk.

20 "In quietness and trust is our strength."

Banaras, November 15, 1957

My dear Father

Thank you for your letters. I wrote today to Fr. Bede to tell him I am writing to you to confirm that I will be arriving at Śāntivanam (from Madras) on the 23rd of December and leaving on the 27th (for Bangalore). This is certain. I must stress how important I feel it is that you will also be present in Bangalore. I believe that your presence alone will help us a lot to focus on the problem and not get lost in secondary issues.

If you feel you need an invitation, please write to Fr. Neuner in Poona, and of course [say] that I urged you to do so.

As to whom to invite for Christmas I leave it to you. You could write to ShāntiBhavan if you like. Maybe it would be good. And I take the liberty of suggesting Antoine.[21] As for the topic, we should at least choose one (rather than talking about everything as a subject). Importance should be placed on Liturgy, Contemplation and Friendship.

I think the idea of giving our support to CBCI[22] is excellent. I do not have a reference for the Calcutta publisher, but maybe you could tell him that I sent him a book and he will remember our conversation. He has a very good translator (who translated Renou, etc.) I am writing him a note today about it. Be assured that I'm praying for you, that you are not alone, and that this is the *climax* before the real fruit.

Cum osculo pacis. [with a kiss of peace]

Raymond Panikkar

❖❖❖

[21] Fr. Robert Antoine, Belgian Jesuit priest and missionary in India. Co-founder, with Pierre Fallon, of Shānti Bhavan, a dialogue centre in Calcutta.

[22] CBCI: Catholic Bishops' Conference of India.

Banaras, November 20, 1957

My dear Father,

[In reference to] my letter of the 15th.

You are well acquainted with Abbé Mercier[23] and André Scrima. They both would quite like to come to your house for Christmas. I did not invite them, I simply told them my plans.

What do you think? On one hand it would be nice, but on the other I think our intimacy takes on a completely different tone.

Send me a note, and with the excuse of space (that is, lack of space) I could very well arrange for them not to come. Fr. Bede and I are here. I don't think Fr. Antoine will be able to come. I don't know about Father Fallon.[24]

In my last letter I didn't have the chance to tell you how much I pray for you and that I'm looking for someone who will be able toefficientlyhelp you while you're here.

I will see Archbishop Malenfant[25] next week.

With all my love,

Raymond Panikkar

❖❖❖

---

23 Fr. Mercier, professor at the Christ Nagar missionary formation school in Vārāṇasī, today the Institute of Philosophy and Religion of the Indian Missionary Society.

24 Pierre Fallon, Belgian Jesuit priest and missionary in India. Co-founder, with Robert Antoine, of Shanti Bhavan, a dialogue centre in Calcutta.

25 Mons. Joseph Malenfant, Canadian-born prefect apostolic in Benares.

1958

Bangalore, January 2, 1958

My dear Father,

We will not leave you alone, even if no one comes – can come – during these days.

I have talked about you to Neuner, Fallon, etc. They thought Śāntivanam was dead, and that you had abandoned Monchanin.

I hope that now everything is clear and that one day we will meet with you as planned.

The conference is interesting, and important as a first contact.

Fr. Emmanuel[26] was a little unwell the day I went to see him, and I wasn't able to speak with him.

I am going to Malabar to see my family and will travel as far as Thiruvalla.

A good and holy year. After the death of '57, the resurrection of '58.

In union,

Raymond Panikkar

❖❖❖

Banaras, April 15, 1958

My dear Father,

I am sending you two copies of the "Christian Saṃnyāsin".

I will be leaving on Sunday for Delhi and on Wednesday—the day of Our Lady of Montserrat—for Tehran, Beirut, Athens, Rome.

If you have something to tell me these are my addresses: […]

---

[26] Fr. Emmanuel De Meester, of the Abbey of Saint-André-lès-Bruges. Together with Dominique van Rollenghen he rebuilt the community of Siluvaigiri, near Salem.

I hope to be back within two or three months (September at the latest) and plan to go to Śāntivanam later for our annual meeting.

If you need to come to Benares during my absence, my house is at your disposal. The curate of Benares will have the key.

I am happy about your meetings and I pray very much for all of your testimony. Please do the same for me. When the general picture isn't outwardly supernatural and life seems ordinary, it is very hard to raise the level and give a naked, moving testimony like yours. But when one succeeds, then contact with daily life is preserved. I would like to talk with you about this (I am writing to you at a 45° angle).

In action contemplatius! This is good; but so is *in contemplatione activus*! Have I talked to you about this? For me the Mother, Christ, Redemption greatly conditions our earthly life. Contemplation is not pure passivity, nor even pure love, down here. I believe there is always an element of action – contemplative, of course.

Pray for me.

In a few days I will send you the Magazine.

Best wishes,

Raymond Panikkar

❖❖❖

Barcelona, August 9, 1958

Mr. Svāmi Abhiṣikteshwarānanda[27]
Śāntivanam
Tannirpalli
Kulittalai
Tiruchirapalli Dt.
State of Madras

---

27 Henri Le Saux took the name Swāmi Abhiṣikteshwarānanda, meaning literally "the one who has tasted the bliss of the anointed Lord, (Christ)", which was later shortened to Abhishiktananda or, for those closest to him, Abhiṣiktā.

My dear Svāmi:

It has been a long time since I wrote to you. Don't think I haven't had you in my thoughts. I have been constantly thinking about the contemplative life in general, and in India in particular, and I think of you as a living symbol of this life. I am certain that despite all the difficulties we will be able to sow seeds and that the seeds will grow.

Fr. Bede Griffiths[28] has just written to me and tells me of a meeting in January 1959, or December 1958, after a meeting that will be held on the liturgical life in South India, I don't know where.

I am not sure yet, but most likely I will have to stay here in Spain for another two or three months; we'll see!

If you need my home in Benares I would be most glad to put it at your disposal.

It is better not to talk about the environment here, but it is still important to preach "*opportune importune*" [in season, out of season][29] and this will bear fruit at the most unexpected moment.

Forgive me if I am so brief today; I will write more at another time.

Please accept, my dear Svāmi, the expression of my whole soul. I ask you to pray that His Will be done, in me and in the project that my "people" are currently developing for India. It is not easy to make India's situation clearand take the necessary measures with the current crisis in the Church.

I feel I identify more and more with India and with you.

In Christ,

Raymond Panikkar

❖❖❖

---

[28] British-born priest and Benedictine monk Bede Griffiths was a close friend of both Panikkar and Abhishikananda.

[29] Cf. 2 Tim 4:2: Preach the word; be instant in season, out of season; reprove, rebuke, exhort with all long suffering and doctrine.

Villanueva, 13,

Madrid, October 7, 1958

My dear Father,

Father Griffiths wrote me a wonderful letter refuting the rumours that you described to me. He wonders whether it was you who wrote to me about this.

I still don't know the date of my departure. I hope it will be this month.

I wonder what kind of difficulties you heard I had to face. As far as I know, nothing out of the ordinary has happened.

I see, hear, and even suffer, because I have become accustomed to India and I feel the enormous difference there is with this Europe in crisis!

I really want to see you and talk with you. I believe we are on the right track, even though at times it is painful, even excruciating.

We pray a lot for you here. I am thinking of writing a review of your booklet for Kairos, a new Austrian journal of religious science. Is there something you would like me to focus on?

Father Duperray of the SAM,[30] in Paris, has just asked me for a piece on Monchanin. I am thinking of writing something similar to what I am sending here. I would like to ask if you could send me your corrections, suggestions, etc. Perhaps, once corrected (the French is awful, I know perfectly well), it might even help you with the lines you asked me for. I await your reply on this matter.

I am captivated by Meister Eckhart's German Sermons. Absolutely extraordinary.

Despite appearances, here in Europe there are wonderful strivings for a truly Christian and ecumenical rebirth.

As always, in true fraternal union.

Best wishes

In Christ

Raymond Panikkar

❖❖❖

[30] SAM: Société auxiliaire des missions.

1959

Banaras, January 20, 1959

My dear Svāmi,

Needless to say, I believe, my silence is only a token of my unity. I am increasingly convinced by your testimony. I will help you in every way I can.

As for the booklet, here are some addresses of German and Spanish magazines.[…]

After spending a night in Shembaganur[31] (I talked for half an hour with Sr. Teresa! Very good!) and another night in Kurisumala.[32] I went to Malabar and then to Bombay for the Students' Conference. I am here now trying to do in-depth work not only with myself, but also with others (for example, the small group of 7 students to which I belong).

Father Neumerwas here and Fr. De Smet is with me. Today and tomorrow he is lecturing at the university.

How did the Śāntivanam-trustee go?

In unity... with everything.

In Christ,

Raymond Panikkar

The group of friends of Śāntivanam must be kept alive at all costs!

❖❖❖

Bangkok, February 7, 1959

My dear Svāmi,

One hour before midnight, before I take the plane to Calcutta and complete my pilgrimage through Southeast Asia, I am again thinking of you and sending you these few lines.

---

31 The Jesuit formation house.

32 Kurisumalaāśram, Cistercian monastery of Syro-Malabarrite, founded by Mar Athanasios, bishop of Tiruvalla (Kerala).

Your booklet and your work are more well-known than you think. I have often had to talk about Śāntivanam. It remains a living symbol.

I don't know whether I told you that Fr. Griffiths wrote to me to propose that we hold our meeting at the end of January, but since you didn't seem very enthusiastic, I let the matter go. Fr. d'Hendecourt (Mysore), who has gone to Manila and with whom I made part of the journey, is truly a man of God who could very well belong to spiritual Śāntivanam.

The other day I read a report about a Benedictine monk who lives as a hermit somewhere in Europe. I thought of you.

I plan to stay in Calcutta perhaps forthe whole week and then I would like to rest in Banaras for a while (today, Sunday, God used me to preach four sermons (to the students, to the Brothers of St. Gabriel, to the Sisters of St. Paul of Chartres and to the Ursulines).

The situation of the Church throughout Southeast Asia is very similar to ours. This trip has been extremely interesting for me. It has also helped me understand the importance of our contemplative "mission".

I also spent a few days at the OSB Monastery of Kep (Cambodia), the *Pierre-qui-Vire* foundation.[33]

In Domino,

Raymond Panikkar

❖❖❖

Banaras, February 9, 1959

My dear Svāmi,

I hope you are well and that your silence can only be interpreted as communion in silence.

I believe you have received my letter of January 20th.

---

[33] Benedictine monastery of Kep, Cambodia, founded by the monks of Abbaye Sainte-Marie de la Pierre-qui-Vire in 1952.

Two copies of the book on Abbot M.[34] have just arrived. Thank you very much. It has made a very good impression on me. And I hope it will bear fruit.

Please send copies to: […]

I am sending Rs. 21 with M.D. Please tell me if it is enough.

It is still cold here. I am working a fair amount, not to say a lot: contemplation, study, apostolate.

You are always welcome here.

In actione contemplativus, and also *in contemplatione activus.*

In the friendship of the Lord.

Raymond Panikkar

❖❖❖

Banaras, April 8, 1959

My dear Svāmi,

Our letters crossed, as always, in fact (it must be a kind of telepathy).

I have already written to you about my plans: to go to the Himalayas and to Badrinath (and Kedārnāth) around the beginning of May (Badrinath opens its doors on May 12th).

I had originally planned to stay here to work, but in this heat it makes no sense. I got sick again. So I have decided I willtake a break and indulge in pure contemplation and Hinduism.

I will leave towards the end of the month. I realize that you need rest and *darṣana.*[35]Another thing: the new magazine "Kairos", of which I am "adviser", would like to review *Hermits of Saccidānanda*, plus the Monchanin Memorial. Do you know who could write it? I know you are thinking, "You yourself!" Perhaps, but apart from me who could write 2 or 3 "good" pages?

[34] "Le Père Monchanin", La Vie Spirituelle, 98 (1958).

[35] Beholding of a sage or saint.

It's urgent. Drop me a line with your suggestion if you have one. India has to be "conquered"– once more! – through Europe.

I hope we will have the chance to get together this summer. What do you think about coming to Badrinath?

Yours always,

Raymond Panikkar

❖❖❖

Banaras, April 13, 1959

My dear Father,

Received your letter. I am very sorry for the robbery.[36] Hope you will recover some of the things. The Ornaments were the best I saw in India.

This is just a word to tell you of a possible change in my programme. I am still hesitating and have to write to the Archibishop for permission, but I think I'll accept the proposition. In such a case my Himalayan journey would be by the end of May.

From May 8th up to 23rd there is at Bangalore a Study Conference for Christian University Teachers (Protestants) and they want me to give a course of lectures on St. Thomas Aquinas, plus some on Hinduism. Though it upsets a little my plans I think I have to accept such an opportunity.

So if I have the ecclesiastical permission I'll go there and come back here so that I'll be at Rishikesh by the end of May, or say round the 25th.

At least for one month I would like to make the Himalayan experience. Please let me know your definite plans. You need a permit for Badrinath but it is easy to obtain it. You can speak with Murray Rogers[37] as he made

[36] Refers to the burglary in the chapel of Śantivanam on April 6th, in which various ornaments, chalices and other objects were stolen. It was a lesson on unattachment and a reminder of the ideal of poverty and insecurity, traits of the Hindū *saṃnyāsin*, as Abhiṣiktānanda later wrote to his sister Marie-Thérèse, a nun of the Abbey of Saint-Michel di Kergonan, with whom he kept up an intense correspondence.

[37] Fr. Murray Rogers, Protestant priest, together with his wife Mary and a friend, Heather Sandeman, founded an ecumenical *aśram* in Karelly, near Bareilly (Uttar Pradesh),

already enquires in Delhi recently. My address up to 5th May, here; and afterwards c/o Archbishop's House, Bangalore.

I have many things to talk over with you. I hope you have already answered my previous letter. Scrima is leaving round the 20th and remembers you. The day after tomorrow I go to preach a retreat to the students from here some 40 miles from here.

Regarding Mass conveniences I hope to rely on you, for some Sundays. Do you know the places where there are chapels?

Excuse me for this letter so without substance. The heat, the interruptions, etc.

If Murry Rogers comes to you inform him of my plans for Badrinath about the end of May.

In real union with you,

Raymond Panikkar

❖❖❖

New Delhi, August 6, 1959

My dear Svāmi,

Peace!

I have just received your letter from Agra. I talked with the Archbishop for over an hour and in a very clear and open way. He listens, and well.

Now that you've spoken to Murray about the prayer meeting, I'd like to know your opinion and also if you think I should ask the bishop for his permission, suggestions, etc.

Christānanda[38] just wrote to me about secular institutions. As I recall, his idea was that his boys were not quite ready for a secular institution. It is true?

---

the Jyotiniketan āśram, which was often visited by Abhiṣiktānanda.

38 Svāmi Sadhu J. NelsonChristananda, Hindu Christian teacher and founder of several Evangelical schools in India.

My ear is better but it hasn't completely healed yet.

My arrivalin Delhi is very problematic. For this entire school year I prefer to be free as I already have too many commitments. I am leaving on Monday for Banaras. Will you have the chance to see the bishop about the problem of the Mass in Jyotinikatan?

Almost every day I walk for around two hours to get to and from the convent of the Mother of God. I have never spoken with the nuns but I have celebrated Mass and preached on Sundays.

I won't be able to stay in Bareilly this time. I have to finish my book before the 25th because afterwards I will be leaving for Mysore.

God lovingly uses us for the true conversion of our brothers.

We also must convert every day.

Always,

Raymond Panikkar

❖❖❖

Banaras, September 25, 1959

Om & Pax,

Thank you for your letter, which reached me a little while ago.

I havebeen spending all my time here with the students and also finishing my book,which is now more or less done. My health has not been very good.

In October I will have a retreat with the students, then maybe I will go to Kuneong and towards the end of the month to Kareli. On November 4th, 5th and 6th I will have three lectures in Delhi at the Cambridge Brotherhood.[39] Will we meet again in Kareli or Delhi?

Take care of yourself. I wrote to you in Ahmora. I have no doubt that your pilgrimage was moving: if possible you should write something about it.

---

39 The Cambridge Brotherhood, which later became the Delhi Brotherhood, belongs to the Church of North India, a union of six previously separate traditions.

And "*in medium montium pertransibunt aquae*"[40]! And despite all the obstacles, the living waters of Christ always open a way, even if they are surrounded by high mountains.

My regards to Venugopal[41]. I wrote to Murray a long time ago and have had no reply. Now I will explain.

In *agape*,

Raymond Panikkar

❖❖❖

New Delhi, November 19, 1959

My dear Svāmi,

The prayer school in Kareli was magnificent. The work of the Spirit is amazing. I pushed hard on the spiritual life and the response was very positive even though at the beginning I had the impression that I was speaking above their heads and even their hearts. The members of Jyotiniketan got the most out of it.

The conferences at the Cambridge Brotherhood[42] also went very well. Only "their" regular audience was there. I think I managed to express the problem fairly clearly.

After a week of visits, visas, etc., and when I already had a ticket to Banaras, I let myself be persuaded to have my tonsils operated on: my health was not good and I didn't know what to do. Now here I am unable to speak and in great pain. If I can, I will leave Banaras on Sunday. I saw Vivek[43] and Marie-Thérèse but only "on a visit".

---

40 "In the midst of the mountains the waters will pass".

41 Âri C. T. Venugopal, with whom Abhiṣiktānanda often stayed in Delhi.

42 Cambridge Brotherhood', which later became 'Delhi Brotherhood', belongs to the 'Church of North India', a union of six previously separate traditions.

43 Vivek Datta, an Indian scholar o philosophy, and his wife Marie Thérèse retired to live as hermits on a mountaintop, in an area which was later to become the National Park of Binsar.

The celebrations of the "Consecration" of Bishops: as if we were already the triumphant Church.

I have not fully understood Fr. Francis Mahieu's[44] plans. Fr. Bede has just written to me about India.

And what about you, what's new? I am glad you have rediscovered the charm of Śāntivanam (I am becoming more and more incapable of "active" life). Rest assured that we will support you!

In December I will have to go to Manila.

In the unity and peace in the Lord,

Raymond Panikkar

If you give me Christa's name and address I will send him my article on Melchizedek in German.

❖❖❖

Banaras, November 30, 1959

My dear Father,

Thank you for your letter. I am feeling better, but I'm not "completely" healed yet. Next Sunday I will leave for Calcutta and from there on the 9th for Manila, Rangoon, Bangkok, Saigon and Hong Kong. If you know of anyone from our "Spiritual Monastery" that I can contact, write to me in Calcutta. My address until 10 January will be:

Pax Romana Secretariat

Manila

Towards the end of January I will arrive in Madras. I had thought that on that date we could meet for our contemplative conference at Śāntivanam; but I see you are not very inclined to do so (anyway, if you like you can write to me at the Catholic Center—Armenian Street, Madras, 1, around 20 January).

---

44 Fr. Francis Mahieu, Belgian Cistercian monk who came to Śantivanam in 1955.

I think continually about the Magazine (or Notebooks) on spirituality, but I cannot be its "manager". Father Mahieu, I believe, has had an idea, but he should convert it into something universal and not exclusively Cistercian or Malankaresc.

Here I have spent an intense week of contemplation and activity, of love and suffering, truly wonderful.

The Manila Conference is not Protestant but another Pax Romana Catholic conference, and I will be there as chaplain of the Indian delegation and to take part in a UNESCO Symposium.

I received Venugopal in Delhi but I have the impression that he is not comfortable with me.

Advent, Christmas, Epiphany, all together before seeing each other! (I am happy about your news of Carmel).

In true union,

Raymond Panikkar

❖❖❖

Bangkok, December 17, 1959

Pax!

Thank you for your few lines which I received in Rangoon, as I only flew over Calcutta (I had to change all my plans at the last moment due to the incompetence of the travel agency).

I spent 3 days in Rangoon and 3 days in Bangkok. It is Himalayan Buddhism in all its strength and vitality. This is an important experience and one that helps me to know Hinduism better from the other side.

The change of plans means that I will not go through Madras but I will stop in Calcutta on my way back, which makes my visit to Śantivanam impossible for the time being (in spite of my own wishes). So we won't be able to hold our collective meeting. If by any chance I am able change my programme (though I don't think so) I will gladly come and see you.

If you leave SHV [Śāntivanam] in January or early February, please let me know (until 10/1 in Manila, at the address I gave you).

They are not familiar with your book here. Buddhism poses a similar problem. We will talk about the Magazine at a later time. I am also thinking about some "Notebooks" regarding "South-East Asia".

The Jesuits in Bangkok work well. The problems here, while seemingly different, are actually the same, and we could help each other a lot. But first and foremost is contemplation.

I have once again been an instrument of the Lord, and He used me fully.

Yours in the spirit of Jesus,

Raymond Panikkar

1960

Varāṇasī, February 25, 1960

My dear Svāmi,

Thank you for your letters! This is how I see the situation:

1 - On one hand, an ecumenical meeting with Murray and his—and our—friends.

2 - On the other hand, a meeting with individual Catholics like our previous meetings.

3 - Or do you think we could combine them?

4 - Or could we have the Catholics come a few days before and continue later with the others?

(It grieves me to make these distinctions, but it's just for the sake of clarity).

Apart from this, there is the question of the internal organization (plus the external one, obviously, for which we must at all costs find someone – wouldn't Stephen [disciple of Bede Griffiths] be willing if Fr. Bede asked him?). We need a very fresh theme and a very sound agenda. What do you think about the topic of "Christian āśrams, theory and practice"? (Though we should go into detail).

As for the people, I would suggest Murray, Cole,[45] Bede, Alexis, Britto,[46] Zeitler,[47] d'Hendecourt, Payant[48] (a Holy Cross from Chittagong is very interested in the āśrams, according to d'Hendecourt) and, if women may be admitted, Hermine, Christa, Lore Termehr (Madras), Francaux (Calcutta) and Siauve.[49] I forgot Dominique,sorry, and anyone else Murray may have in mind (I doubt that Devānandan[50] should be included).

For my part, it is not absolutely certain that I will be able to come as I will probably have to go to Europe this summer, but if I decide I really want to I can try to delay my trip, which is still hypothetical.

Sorry this letter is so blunt. I pray for you and I want very much to see you. (Did I tell you that I visited the Benedictines at Kep (Cambodia), of the La Pierre-qui-Vire Abbey?)

I hope the operation was not too painful and that you are already feeling better. Of course you cannot—and should not—take care of the material organization, but we must find someone. As soon as you write to me, I will answer you and write to Fr. Bede and whoever you wish. D'Hendecourt is with me now as he is on his way to Allahabad for a Priests' Conference (I am too bogged down with work to go). We must also think about the goal (specific, official, etc.) of our next meeting.

In Domino,

Raymond Panikkar

❖❖❖

---

45 John Cole, American Presbyterian missionary.

46 Fr. John Britto Chethimatham, Indian priest, philosopher and theologian.

47 Fr. Engelbert Zeitler SVD, member of the Society of the Divine Word (SocietasVerbiDivini), an organisation for training missionaries.

48 Fr. Philippe Payant, Canadian-born priest of the Holy Cross and founder/director of an āśram in the south of India.

49 Suzanne Siauve, French Indologist.

50 Paul D. Devanandan, Indian Protestant theologian, ecumenist and leading pioneer in inter-religious dialogues in India.

Pondi,[51] *March 5, 1960*[52]

My dear Raymond,

Your letter of the 25th only arrived today, twice as long as the letters from Paris!

Let me sum up our discussion in order:

The ecumenical meeting must be different from the meeting of Catholic theologians. For the ecumenical meeting Murray will extend the invitations as he wishes, within the limits I have directly specified to him. For this meeting I would very much like you to attend, especially if Murray invites Protestant friends who are to some degree representative.

If you do come we can also invite Fr Bede to take part. If not, I wonder if he would come anyway even though I will receive him on my own; it would be a little different, but also interesting.

With Murray, Cole, etc. ... the external organization will be very simple. Both of them are a great help in case of need, and also make the others feel at home.

Murray and J. Cole will be at SHV [Śantivanam] from Saturday April 30th to the following Saturday. I suggested that he invite the others for Monday May 2nd. Murray has written to contact possible attendees. I await the answers here. Then we'll see what to do.

If there are still places I would also invite Christa and Hermine.

The other meeting wasn't able to be arranged primarily due to lack of space and also because the atmosphere must first be prepared.

Your invitation list is excellent: Alexis, Britto, Zeittler, Gayarit, d'Handecourt. I personally know Payant very well. He came to visit us at SHV and also in Tiruvannamalai in '54.

But straight away it becomes difficult to organize. These priests will all want to say their private mass. How do you think they will get along?

Stephen as an assistant is out of the question. I have no wish to see him set foot again in Śantivanam; Stephen has no practical sense to help with the

[51] Pondichéry

[52] Unfortunately Abhiṣikta's previous letters to Panikkar have been lost; this is therefore the first on record. All his letters are signed in Sanskrit characters.

actual organizing - I have had too much experience of this. If the matter becomes clearer I could try to enlist the help of one or two seminarians.

(If places are still available – on the same question – we could invite 2 or 3 of the ladies mentioned.)

The two meetings cannot be consecutive. Initially I thought they might but it would be too much. We would have to have a break of at least a few days. In any case, we couldn't do it much before mid-May, as there is no time left between Easter and the meeting with Murray.

It could only be March 17/18 and then I would take a break until Easter. I will be absent in Bangalore and also in Trivandrum on Holy Week and Easter Week. So I would only just have time to prepare for April 30th.

If these two meetings are held this year, we could consider extending them further and also joining them together and preparing Śantivanam accordingly.

Let us keep the ecumenical meeting informal. Basically private: the Protestant friends of a Catholic svāmi coming to spend a few days of meditation with him.

The theme of the āṣram: good, but focusing on the aspect of prayer and contemplative prayer in āṣramic life. This is really what Murray and John Cole want.

For the other meeting I could accommodate eight people in single rooms and maybe two double rooms.

If you think this is feasible, let's get to work as soon as possible beginning May 12th.

I will immediately look for 1 or 2 seminarians who can be ready to help by then.

From a medical point of view, everything went well. However, I am still in bed for a few more days and will not leave Pondi until around March 14th-17th. If you write back to me in Pondi, please send it to the Archdiocese of Pondichéry.

Abhiṣiktānanda [in Sanskrit characters]

❖❖❖

Varāṇasi, March 17, 1960

My dear friend,

I spent all day yesterday with Murray, who has come to visit me here. He is an excellent man and we talked about many things. We have also decided on a second retreat in November, if I am in India. I think Jyotiniketan could become a good point of reference in India. He told me about his concern for Hermine and I think he is right and that she should not be invited. She must first consolidate her vocation, whatever it may be.

I had to go to the Priests' Conference at Allahabad last week. It was very interesting. Despite everything (and this is no small matter) there is still hope for this Church of India. I spoke there with Zeitler, Antoine and d'Hendecourt. All three are very interested in the Śāntivanam meeting, although the first is still not sure whether he can attend as he has to go to Malabar for this shameful recruitment, but he asks to be kept informed. The second would like to participate but doesn't yet know if he will be able to and since I did not know what you think about him or Fr. Fallon I didn't say too much. The third is ready.

Well, this time I am the problem. I have to go back to Europe as soon as possible. This means that I cannot come and consequently everything will fall to you once again, unless you write to d'Hendecourt, who will be in Pondicherry next week for a retreat, and ask him to take care of it or to come and see you to arrange the meeting. I'm sorry I cannot attend, but rest assured that I will be with you and will be praying for you. I believe the meeting must take place at all costs. I have asked Fr. Bede what he thinks of C.A. Abraham to see whether we should invite him too.

A possible theme on the idea of the Christian *āśram* could be contemplative prayer in relation to the apostolate and also to active life.

And how are you? Take care of yourself! I would like to come and see you and talk about many things, but I have to leave right away. Let me know if you have any errands to be done in Europe, because this time I hope to be able to "walk" a bit.

Everything is according to providence. I am rereading the whole of Saint John of the Cross, half an hour every day. It is much more "Indian" than is generally thought, because it is much more ontological than psychological.

If you would like me to take care of the invitations or some other service, please let me know.

In anticipation of Easter,

In Domino,

Raymond Panikkar

❖❖❖

Śantivanam, 28 March, 1960

My dear Raymond,

In answer to your letter of March 16th.

I will reply on a separate sheet regarding this nun. She wants to spend a long period in true solitude; this is the only reason she is not receiving her mail. The fact that she seeks inspiration from non-Christians – and she is not the only one – simply shows that Christian leaders are keeping the profound light of Christianity hidden (Jn 14, for example [...] under a bushel and that Christians who feel the call of the Spirit deep down are forced to go elsewhere to seek substitutes.

[...]

Now let us talk about you. The Easter meeting is impossible. Everyone we've contacted so far is busy in April and May. But the meeting with Tarcisius will be fruitful and act as an infusion of blood to the central arteries of the Capuchins.

Cuttat says he will only participate in the meetings if they are chaired by the right person. [...]

I can't think of anyone other than you who can do it. A few difficult financial matters. Cuttat would pay the bill, and would also help with the journey, if needed. Personally I would not have the means to sustain these expenses. And this applies to many others (including Murray, Lazarus,[53] *Britto – who needs help if he is to stay free of his superiors, etc.). The memory I have of Cuttat in Nagpur is too unpleasant to wish to begin again, except perhaps in a small group.*

My schedule is always flexible. It also depends on the publishers. I'll keep you posted... So the programme for America is decided. Where? If it will be in Brazil, just in case I'll give you the address of some friends of Âantivanam who translated The Hermits into Portuguese: Monastery of San Benedetto, Rio de Janeiro – or the nuns of Belo Horizonte.

Till next time, in Domino.

Abhiṣiktānanda

Send me at least a postcard to tell me when you're leaving and when you'll be back.

❖❖❖

Banaras, March 29, 1960

My dear Father,

I have just received your letter. I have already written to Fr. Bede telling him that for the moment there will be no meeting and that I will also be unable come at the end of April.

I am truly sorry not to have seen you. But there's no way I can back out now. I assure you that during my trip to Europe Śāntivanam will be in my heart and on my lips.

At the moment, it seems that the Lord is asking us for more than our presence in Śāntivanam.

We all send our thanks and are indebted to you for being there.

---

53 Fr Lazarus Moore, English-born Orthodox priest, regarded as one of the great missionaries and scholars of the 20th Century.

I am preaching a retreat in these days to a young local priest. Miss Vaudeville[54] is also here right now. The *bhikkhu*[55] is making progress, pray for him.

I have sent you my article on Iśvara and Christ. I agree with you about what SD, SVD, etc. tell me.

C.A. Abraham is a young Jacobite priest (married) and now a convert.

Do you know that Otto Müller (Salzburg)[56] will soon be publishing *Les Hermites du Saccidānanda* in German? I am glad. Sachit Dhar[57] has got married—to his cousin. He is at St. Xavier's in Hazaribagh.[58]

Wishing you a good Easter resurrection.

Always,

Raymond Panikkar

❖❖❖

Rome, RUI[59] Foundation

June 24, 1960

My dear friend,

I didn't want to write to you immediately so that I could be more objective, but I am afraid my first impression has not changed. We dream of the invisible Church—which we used to call the soul of the Church—but now the Church is clearly visible, and the invisible—which we sometimes dream is visible –continues to be invisible.

The *kenōsis* of the Church is part of the *kenōsis* of the Saviour.

---

54 Charlotte Vaudeville, French Indologist.
55 Ordained Buddhist monk.
56 Otto-Müller-Verlag, publisher in Salzburg, Austria.
57 Former Marxist Bengali and frequent visitor.
58 Private Catholic primary and secondary school.
59 Residenza Universitaria Internazionale (International University Residence) of the Opus Dei.

You ask me to influence or access the Preparatory Commission of the Council! I can only do this in the same way as you: by example and prayer. And I begin to fear that if I were to gain access through other means, the former would suffer. They say there is a very strong reactionary wind right now, but perhaps it is just a reaction. I continue to believe that the Church has always been like this: one soul and one body, those who are too spiritual and those who are too carnal, incarnational types and transcendent types. We must not get discouraged but pierce through the superficiality of everything, including the Church.

I don't know anything for certain, because I too am in my Śāntivanam: this student residence with 70 students from 25 different nationalities, at least for the next course: Africans, Asians, non-Christians, everything. Pray for me that I will be able to discover in each soul the temple of the Spirit that inhabits it, and to help it discover itself.

(Cont.)
July 2, 1960
(the Visitation)

I assure you it won't be the first time I've been tempted to bury myself in the forest of Śāntivanam, but it should not be an escape. The Lord has his ways and his plans which must be respected and followed. At this moment I am more hidden than you—in anonymity, in the world (the best refuge) and in Rome itself. Despite my efforts at adaptation—internal, of course, because externally it is total—I become increasingly aware that I am as maladjusted as always, without, however, disdaining or deeming worthless the other ways and while remaining faithful to all the canonical requirements.

Abbé Duperray[60] has just sent me the collection of testimonies on Abbé Monchanin. I spoke to a father of the Cistercians of Boquen, who seems very refined. I have just been invited for a "Monks' Week" in Spain, but for the time being I'm not moving from here.

---

60 Fr. Édouard Duperray, close friend of Fr. Jules Monchanin.

Nayṣkarmya![61] We renounce the fruits and at the same time: "*Clama, ne cesses!*"[62]

I agree with you that there should be some sort of French Mission in India. We will also learn that the Alwaye [today Aluva] Seminary already exists, the "greatest" in Asia...

Don't think I am pessimistic, but there is a set pace, and we cannot rush into things.

In the union of the Lord,

In faith always,

Raymond Panikkar

1961

Rome, RUI Foundation

June 6, 1961

My dear friend,

I have so much to tell you that I have chosen silence. After all, the Roman forest is so much denser than the deserts near the Kavery [river]!

My work is interesting and hopefully profound and perhaps not entirely useless. I work a little intellectually, in contemplation (but I must say that I am writing and, in fact, little by little I think I will publish many things that I have written in India). I am also accessible to people, especially the students of whom I am chaplain (two large residences with more than 300 tenants, plus their friends, and almost 75 different nationalities). I also have the opportunity to introduce many ideas into people's heads and hearts.

There are also confessions and retreats. And yet, as you can imagine, sometimes I have to resist the temptation to pick up my suitcase (or better, without a suitcase) and flee to India. But that would be running

61 Realization through renunciation of action.

62 Isa.58:1: "Cry aloud, spare not…!"

away. Pray for me, and also that I do not let myself be pervaded by this "civilized" spirit that reigns here,without, however,becoming a mere misfit or a man of reaction.

And while we're on the subject of myself, I haven't yet told you that the Protestant students who gather in Bangalore after the WCC assembly[63] in New Delhi in November/December have invited me to give a lecture. I would be happy to go back to India even for a short time, but I don't think it will be easy unless the Apostolic Nuncio, for example, writes to the ecclesiastical authorities that my participation is considered important—and this also for the New Delhi assembly. To that effect I have written to Bangalore, but I don't think it would be appropriate to take any steps myself. It is always better to be passive in the arms of God.

I saw John Cole here. He is an extraordinary man. I know he wanted to visit you. I am also very happy for Murray.

Father Zeitler wrote to me about Almora, but unfortunately too briefly, like you yourself. I understand that a full account is being drawn up. Would you send me one? Did you receive my letter in English that I wrote to you from Cuttat's[64] on the subject of *advaita* contemplation?

I have been asked to give my opinion about the "Medical College" in Bangalore. I'm afraid my words can only be negative, because the important thing is not only that we should not do this thing, but that we should do other things[65] – or allow them to be done.

Did you know that Fanchette[66] has made a very positive evolution towards monasticism? (that is, by detaching himself from the priesthood). We should talk about all this!

Last but not least, your Atmaram [Abhiṣiktānanda's disciple]. Tell him that I am praying for him. Let me know how he is doing. I give thanks to God with you. I have the same fear that an anxious mother has when a loved one is away. But we live in hope, don't we?

---

63 World Council of Churches.

64 Jacques-Albert Cuttat, former Swiss ambassador to India, today ambassador to Greece.

65 Cf. Mt 23:23.

66 Philippe Fanchette, seminarist in Rome.

In September there will be a Monks' Week in Montserrat. I have been asked to take part, but I cannot go. If I still find the time, I think I will send something in writing. Perhaps an account of "our" meeting in Almora would be useful?

I have nothing to report to you about the Council and Roman politics. I know that at least they are working.

Let me know about your plans.

In the joy and peace of the Lord and the union of the Spirit,

Raymond Panikkar

❖❖❖

Rome, RUI

September 1, 1961

My dear Svāmi,

I have just received your letter. Thank you. I feared for your *śiṣya,* I felt his initial enthusiasm and then his silence was suspicious. I sensed failure. Praise God!

May I confirm to you that you can always count on me? That my prayers are always with you, that you are never alone?

Perhaps the Lord wants us to work here in Rome as well. I try to be faithful—which is not easy when faithfulness to Christ and the Church involves so many complications, additions and forms… *viveka*[67] is more needed than ever.

I still don't know whether it will be possible for me to come to Bangalore. His will be done! But just in case, do please keep me informed about our *guha.*[68]

I am probably responsible for the fact that the people at Logos wrote to you.

---

67 *Viveka*: intuitive discernment.

68 Cave.

I completely agree with your opinion about Devānandam.[69] We need to help him to know how to stay in line.

I have not seen Philippe Fanchette at all this summer.

I am happy about the success of Kurisumala and agree with you.

What is Fr. Bede doing? Because he was much more open to Hinduism.

I am working a lot, that is, praying, contemplating, loving, studying and trying to help others.

So far I am holding firm, despite my life (even ascetic) being very hard.

My regards to Mary and to Murray and to John Cole.

Raymond Panikkar

❖❖❖

Jyotiniketan, October 9, 1961

My dear Raymond,

A ticket from Jyotiniketan, where I have been for a few days, walking towards the mountain. I found everyone here. John Cole told me again about his meeting with Leiain Rome and also about his meeting with Philippe F. It seems that they profoundly "recognised" each other. It is no wonder, in any case, that the Lord uses non-Catholics to bring Catholics together. It was like in New York. John spoke about Śantivanam to a Catholic audience. This is what is actually being done, it seems to me, to bring Christians back to visible unity, much more than pedantic conferences. The ecumenical problem takes on a completely different aspect when seen from a community life with fervent Christians like those here. Ronald Rose has also been here for a month and will stay for a few more days. It is often a matter of guessing where he is concerned. I stopped at Poona and saw G. Deleury[70] *for a few days.*

[69] Paul Devānandam, Indian Protestant theologian, ecumenist and one of the leading pioneers in inter-religious dialogue in India.

[70] Fr. Guy Deleury, French Jesuit priest, co-founder of an institute for inter-religious

*What has been decided regarding your return to the Indies? Write to Murray and he will let me know. Here is my programme: from around 15/10 to 15/11in Uttarkāshi. From 22/11 to 3/12 in Delhi, c/o Venu (B-3 Wellesley Rd.) with Murray. Then here for the post-assembly meeting. On around 12/15 I will go back down to the South, but probably via Indore. Towards the middle of January Ilsa Friedberg will be in Śantivanam. If all goes well I will come back up again in the spring and stop in the Himalayas. Here is my temporary address in Utt.: Abh. Gyansu, Uttarkāshi (Dt & P.O.), Uttarkand Div. U.P. Post takes 4 to 5 days to arrive from Delhi. We are preparing the December meeting which promises to be very interesting. A letter has arrived from the Moscow Patriarchate, but in Russian. We are waiting for the translation to find out whether the answer is yes or no... Murray is preaching everywhere the primacy of the interior life. How needful it would be for this to be repeated endlessly. The day Christians learn to live at the level of the "heart" (*hṛd*), the union between "churches" will become something other than the organizational compromises that allow each to maintain their own opinion. Is not Rome also much more a "court" and a "secretariat" than a heart that ceaselessly pumps "blood" into the arteries? Who is Prof. Pieper?*[71] *Forgive me, I am ignorant in philosophy, especially modern.*

When will you come to India? Fr. Bede now wishes to stay in the Indies. He is still reading and writing about Hinduism, but I cannot understand how he could get so carried away with "Syrian" [monasticism]. *The idea of trying to revive the Syrian-Indian Church through Syrian monasticism is excellent, but the Malayali character is truly hopeless and I find them less and less fit to be the "true" apostles of India that their situation ordains them to be... As far as India is concerned it is a deviation, and one which risks losing sight of the authentic character of the Indian contemplative vocation. However, since Christian India responds so little to this call (unfortunately!), what would be needed are centers like those that are found almost everywhere here. Have I have already told you about the collapse of the "Benedictine Sarvodaya āśram"? According to the latest reports, St. (not named) was given the honors of the New Leader*

dialogue in Poona (Pune).

71 Prof. Josef Pieper, German Catholic philosopher, important figure in the revival of interest in Thomas Aquinas in 20th-century philosophy.

"bogus-religious"[72] *Benedictine Catholic and Protestant mendicant", for his Christian* sarvodaya[73]...

In the joy of the Lord always.

Abhiṣiktānanda

❖❖❖

Rome, RUI

November 12, 1961

My dear Abhiṣiktājī,[74]

Your last letter is dated October from Jyotinekatan.

I can tell you that at the moment I am not coming to India and I don't even know if I will return one day. In any case, it seems that my place is here in Rome indefinitely. Give my greetings to Murray, Cuttat and all our friends from Delhi or in Delhi.

Fortunately, India is not a geographical category and I can continue to experience India and strive to integrate its wisdom into the Mystical Body. I have been working little since I am involved in the direct apostolate – and this is right since I am a priest.

I knew nothing about the "Benedictine Sarvodaya āśram" and so I did not quite understand your allusions. Dom Bede hasn't told me anything.

Obedience is a vow and it is good that it is, otherwise, in criticizing others we risk falling prey to the most refined activism, but activism nevertheless. I live and that's all! I try to live His Presence, to be His Presence and not to think about anything else.

I pray for the W.C. assembly and for "my" S.C.M.[75] conference in Bangalore. If you can send me news, especially of the former, it is always interesting,

---

72 "Holy fool."

73 "Universal uplift" or "progress of all."

74 The suffix *jī* added onto a name or honorific title, such as Abhiṣiktā or Svāmī, indicates respect and devotion towards the person.

75 Student Christian Movement.

since although I live neither by geography nor history (I don't even have time to read the newspapers or watch television—obviously) I am stillin time and in space.

Do you remember my article on "Hinduism and Christianity"[76] with a long study on "God and the World according to the *Brahma-sūtra*, I, 1"? It ended up as a doctoral thesis at the Lateran last year. I would like to publish it, but at the moment I don't have the time. Everything will come.

What are your plans? *Hermits* will be published in German very soon. The translation was not without errors and had to be proofread.

I am with you to the Himalayas and always on your pilgrimages.

Do you think your "Christian *Saṃnyasin*" could be published in Montserrat's[77] "Studia Monastica"?

Raymond Panikkar

1962

Taizé[78], May 23, 1962

My dear Svāmi, and friend,

My silence has continued for a very long time. Did I never tell you that the Roman jungle is thicker than those of the Himalayas and the [river] Kavery?

The school year, the second after my arrival, passed in an immense work of spiritual direction (liturgy, sacraments, sermons, etc.) and almost every sacred morning contemplation and intellectual work (so that by the end of the year I might be able to publish some decent books).

---

76 ters.

77 Publicacions de l'Abadia de Montserrat, publishing house in Barcelona, Spain.

78 International ecumenical Christian monastic community founded in 1940 by Roger Schultz, better known as Frère Roger. The community is situated in the village of Taizé, Burgundy, France.

It is hard, unrewarding work but that does not mean that it is not good and important (we are not dealing with sublime and charismatic souls but with the people of God in the mass of the world).

Nevertheless, God uses me for the unity of the university apostolate in Rome, making sure that the various groups get to know each other and collaborate. We have also introduced the reading of the *Gītā* and prayers from the *Gītā* in a paraliturgy at the university, as the first inspiration of the Cosmic Testament, and in the Ethiopian seminaries we play and sing (with corporal accompaniment, of course).

I have half a dozen theses on India on my shoulders.

For the first time in 12 years I went to Paris for a meeting organized by "Informations Catholiques Internationales"[79] on atheism (my simplified thesis): "Christianity, a source of atheism for all". I visited Fr. Lemarié, who is very good, sympathetic and western. He gave me your "Pelerinages" to read, which I have not yet read. I am sorry that you have never talked about it to me (or about your other text on the *guha*) but I think I will like it. (To those who would compare you to Monchanin I say that they will have to wait until you are dead). I believe your path is now very clear, if arduous and difficult: testimony, solitude, love and the experience of the total renunciation of direct fruits (*naiṣkarmya).* It is, however, not very different from my own. I think that if the Lord wants something else from me, he will have me do it. I am at his disposal.

On my journey to Rome I will spend a day in Taizé. It is a fine effort. Sister Lila (Orthodox nun) and Mitchel were there. The latter showed me the photos of Almora. How did it go?

Murray Rogers spent two days in Rome and I now learn that Fr. Dominique is in Burges.

I promise to write more often.

In *agape,*

Raymond Panikkar

❖❖❖

[79] ICI, Informations Catholiques Internationales, Catholic journal published in Paris.

Milan, July 6, 1962

My dear Svāmi and friend,

Thank you for your letter, and allow me this personal, intimate and *confidential* explanation.

I fully understand your "indignation" about my absence from India.

This is my situation after more than two long years of life in Rome: obedience keeps me here and I am working immensely from a sacramental point of view and that of spiritual direction and apostolate – but always in a down-to-earth way, of course. I manage, however, I believe, to find a life of contemplation and silence (and also, to some extent, mornings of study and intellectual work).

I think two things: in the actual temporal order, I see no reason for disdain and my trust, my faith in the Lord in his Church is total and I am happy to be able to imitate Christ, obeying to the point of death on the Cross. I trust in Christ. If He wants me to be elsewhere or in India at another time, it is up to Him in whom I trust.

Secondly, in the contemplative order outside of time: I am here (to me now India is neither a geographical nor practically even a historical category).

Here I preach total submission, absolute indifference, salvation which is already there; if I believe in Unity, in God, in *advaita*; if I love and burn and am consumed, then why would I move, why would I want to leave my western jungle, why isolate myself and seek a "mission", an action, an activity, even a testimony?

I would ask you, rather, to pray for me so that "I" can be faithful, so that I can resist the temptation of wanting to "show" myself (Jn 7:4-5), so I can resist the (almost mortal) influence of a "microdoxical" and dualist spirituality, so I may truly die and He may resurrect! Help me to *be,* to realize (I would say to become) Being or, better still, Him.

Let us establish a true community that transcends time and space.

Why would you wish me to leave Indian passivity – and stop doing the "little" thing that demands every moment of me? In *vyavahārika*[80] it makes me suffer, but in *pāramārthika*[81] what does it matter? That requires the realization of the *gurū*. Well, being a teacher to others carries a special charisma, but being a simple *śiṣya* of the Teacher, that we can do. And who can say whether it is also true that it is not good for a prophet to perish outside Jerusalem (Rome)?[82]

I assure you that my peace (arduous) and my joy (crucified) is total. For this very reason I speak and do not keep silent. Who knows what the Lord wants—if you have a word to say to me, that is all I could wish for.

I know very well that obedience is also active and that I must always have the courage to make decisions, but I don't forget that my cry to obedience has always been "*abscondita cum Cristo in Deo*"[83], and that my existence has always been founded on the words of Isaiah: "*In silentio et in spe fortitudo vostro*".[84]

I entreat you with all my heart: *clama, necesses*! I assure you that I listen to you.

Raymond Panikkar

❖❖❖

Rome - RUI, August 24, 1962

St. Barthelemy, Apostle of India

My Dear Father and Friend,

My western pilgrimage continues – but maybe I am a little closer to the Sources. I am certain that the Lord guides me and that I do not have to do anything for my itinerary to change. If He so wishes, He will do it.

---

80 *Vyavaharika:* Empirical reality.

81 *Pāramārthika:* Absolute, spiritual reality.

82 Cf. Lk 13:33.

83 «Hidden with Christ in God» (Colossians 3:3).

84 Isaiah 30:15: «In quietness and trust is your strength.»

I have read your manuscript and, as I wrote to Fr. Lemarié, I believeveas a testimony it is almost unique in its kind and should certainly be published.

I had someone less involved and less initiated than me read it. Basically he agrees, but he pointed out to me that the style is at times somewhat heavy and difficult to digest because the text is too dense or presupposes a very deep knowledge of India. An effort should be made to revise it a little and make it clearer in some passages. But I assure you it's worth it. I find you more here than in the *Hermits*; and I remember well when you described your experiences to me.

I spent a day with Murray and his whole family in Switzerland. They are charming. I wish Murray could have a little deeper and more theological contact with Catholicism.

You will certainly have had news about Philippe Fanchette. I pray for him.

I forgot to tell you that the books I borrowed from you are here with me. I can send them to you if you like; I would just like to hold onto Paul Muy's book a little longer if you don't need it.

How I would like to see you and talk to you about so many things and reassure you that you are not alone, that your adventure is a part of our common destiny, that Śāntivanam already exists, that everything is being done according to His Plan and that it is not *for* the future – horizontal – that we act but *in* the present, including historical, where we are.

Have you received my article on pluralism in Hinduism? I would like to know what you think.

I hope its North-South dichotomy will soon be eliminated.

As always, in brotherly friendship,

Raymond Panikkar

❖❖❖

Rome, November 8, 1962

My dear Svāmi,

Thank you for your letter, which I have just received. And here I am dropping everything to send you a word of *koinonia,* of brotherhood and also of consolation, if you wish. Please stand strong and stay put. Yesterday I had lunch with Sr. Suave, who was on her way to India, and Fr. Daniélou[85], etc. He works hard and I think he is doing very well for the Council. But I cannot help but "feel" that there is yet another step we must take, much more profound. I am in God's hands, and I hope and believe that if I remain faithful to Him, He will do the rest. If He wants me in India I will come, like the real "miracle" of the first time. In Allahabad a "Catholic Information Center" has been built and, according to Fr. Extros, the Bishop would like me to look after it. It's not up to me, of course, and the idea itself doesn't seem to me to be very exceptional (a kind of "hostel" for scholars or retreat in the same "compound"). The "impression" of the Indian Fathers at the Council is not the best, nor anywhere, as you can imagine. The Council itself is something. We realize now what we had come to and although we cannot do everything this time, it will be an initial shock, and quite a positive one, I think.

Fanchette told me about your letter. I will have to see him again one of these days and help him make a decision. I will also try to see Mons. Mendonça.[86] I am expecting Fr. Dominique by the end of the month. There is a dimension in which man cannot do anything, don't you think? And we must keep to it. This is how the Śāntivanam of the spirit already exists. I can assure you that these two and a half years in Rome have confirmed many things to me and have given me, I believe, a freedom of spirit which makes me feel—not just know—that I am free even in the most "cramped" or closed structures.

I no longer have your manuscript, so I cannot talk to you about it in detail. I still insist on the importance of its publication, now or at a later

[85] Fr. Jean Daniélou, French Jesuit theologian and cardinal, who was a member of the Académie Française and, together with Yves Congar and Henri de Lubac, one of the leading figures of the Nouvelle théologie.

[86] Mons. James Mendonça, Bishop of Tiruccirāpalli.

date. Perhaps Cuttat could also take an interest in it. Fr. Britto sent me his circular letter, which is not bad, I thought. On the contrary, I really liked it. I believe we are making steady progress, even though we are behind (but that seems right to me). Well, I must finish now so I can post this letter, which I am writing practically on borrowed time. I am sending you another pamphlet: "Hinduism and Christianity". You already know it, at least in part.

Yours always,

Raymond Panikkar

According to Father Mercier, the Jesuits in India want me. Fr. Extros himself believed that this was the reason for my return here.

Usque tandem?[87]

This gives me the ability to forgive and try to put into practise the overabundance of good to suffocate the evil.

In Christ,

Raymond Panikkar

❖❖❖

Rome, December 4, 1962

Advent

Here, my dear Father, is a letter that will certainly please you.

Heaven and earth will pass away, but His Words will not! His Word is permanent and so are we when we are the Silence from which His Word emerges. All other structures are temporary. The true Śāntivanam already exists. All else passes away. Fr. Dominique will tell you in person.

Unless the grain of wheat dies…but the seeds are scattered everywhere. My hope, however, does not look to the *future* but flourishes in the *present*, real and true.

Sincerely

Raymond Panikkar

---

87 «How much longer?»

I delayed sending this letter because the good Fr. Bruno[88] has received a negative answer from his Father Abbot. This is one more difficulty, but the Lord is great. I will see him tomorrow. We will write to you.

❖❖❖

Śantivanam, 8 December, 1962

My dear Raimon,

At midday I received a note in Latin from Fr Bruno, a Cist. [Cistercian] of your acquaintance. He had already sent me a short note six months ago. This time he announces to me decisively that he has asked Archbishop Mendonça for permission to come and join me in Śantivanam. It is a bit rushed. I don't know him and I have had terrible experiences with the Cistercians. I still have one in America who bombards me with letters, even when I don't answer him, he's half "sick" and has been trying, mainly unconsciously, to escape from his monastic life rather than dreaming of coming here for the past ten years. Fr Mahieu, whose qualities I am the first to recognize, has proved to be seriously lacking in frankness and by coming to stay with us (presumably) when he had another intention in mind he did us a great wrong.

A monk of St. Wandrille[89] (keep this to yourself) who would have come if he had been granted a visa has now become involved, together with others of his monastery, with a certain Indonesian esotericism. Thank goodness he didn't come here. There were still others on the list of SV postulants. With regard to Philippe Fanchette it is a different matter. I have been corresponding with him for a long time. I have talked about him with many friends of SV and no one has a negative opinion. All this to tell you that I remain terribly cautious (plus the experiences here with Stephen, Mathiew and the so-called Atmaram) and I have no desire to embark on new adventures.

---

88 Fr. Bruno Barnhart, monk of New Camaldoli Hermitage in California and author of various religious works.

89 The Abbey of St. Wandrille, a Benedictine monastery in the commune of Rives-en-Seine, France.

The current political situation (China) will not make the government any more disposed to allowing foreigners in and that will simplify the matter. In any case, tell me what you think about Fr. Bruno, who has met you once or twice. You know SV well enough and you know me well also. Isolation and disappointments have not softened my character. Bruno is 32 years old, he says, and I am 52. The 15-year difference between Fr. Monchanin and myself was already a problem. My long-standing relations with Philippe made me see the problem differently in his case and yet I was not without doubts about his coming. The Cistercians are perhaps less "moulded" than the Trappists, who are very much so, more than the Jesuits. However, if in coming here he forgets he is OSB or OCR or whatever, there's no need to worry.

If we do not have the evangelical freedom of the "progressive leaders" of the Council, Liénard, Frings, etc. compared to the clergy (who will never understand anything in SV) it is useless to come. And I am not talking about the essential: full Indian life, acceptance that God speaks in India, the spirituality of "O pantônepekeiha" that Philippe understood so well. It would be better in that case for him to join his brother at St. Bernard in Kurisumalai. I will reply kindly to Fr. Bruno but without encouraging him. If however you regard him as a possibility for SV, tell me, and we'll see later.

I plan to go north after the Epiphany. I don't know what the situation will be like in Ut. At midday today I received a letter in Roman Urdu.[90] It is so unclear that I cannot tell whether or not it contains any restrictions. In any case, until the Chinese business is settled – and according to Nehru it might take years – the situation 70 miles from the border will by no means be peaceful. Here the Forest Department is trying to seize all the land between the road and the river. We have our documents in order, but...?

The vote of November 21st was encouraging, and also the appointment of the co-presidents of the Replanning Commission! That was well worth three months of long, academic debates. The Curia will now have to deal with the bishops who are in direct contact with "life". However, I am sorry that the speeches preceding the vote were so pragmatic and that they did

[90] Roman Urdu is the name given to the Urdu language written in Latin script or Roman script.

not fully discuss the problem of the Scripture and the Church, regarding which the real solution lies neither with the Prot [Protestants], who make of the Church a religion of the Book (something God never intended), nor with the De Fontibus[91] that I studied 35 years ago!

I think I have answered your last letter – Philippe wrote to me about his bishop's decision. In his previous letter he spoke about his plans for next June with such confidence that I thought the matter with his superior was now settled. I appeal, of course, to the ministry of solitude, no longer in words or writing but in re et veritate.

If Europeans come, one should absolutely go north; the local clergy cannot bear the lessons of the European monks.

In the Lord's hands. Answer me as soon as possible also regarding Bruno. If I still had any illusions I would say that his name is predestined. When you see him again, if he really is devadatta[92] for SV, and if my answer has surprised him, please sort it out.

Write to me at SV. I will tell you later where to send your letters, certainly c/o J. Stuart in Delhi (the Kareli hotel is not well-known).

In Spiritu

Abhishiktananda (in Sanskrit)

1963

Gargano, June 2, 1963
Pentecost
11:00 am

My dear brother and friend,

The day is grey, rainy and with a *"ruah"* wind that does not know where it comes from or where it is going

---

[91] Refers to a heated debate conducted at the Second Vatican Council regarding the content of the document *De Fontibus Revelationis* (On the Sources of the Revelation).

[92] *devaddata*: "granted by the Gods".

The Pope is dying, or perhaps he is already dead. It is a lovely day—the day of the birth of the Church—for the "*natalis dies*"[93] of a vicar of Christ such as John XXIII. Yesterday evening until 10.30 I was in St. Peter's Square, which was full of people praying, waiting and hoping. Once again the testimony of death is more powerful than that of life! "*Qui per mortem tuam mundum vivificasti*"[94].

Since Friday I have been in a retreat house in the "Castelli Romani", 30 km from Rome, leading a retreat for a small group of people, all already well placed in the world. In the little free time I have I have been reading your *Christian Experience of Saccidānanda.*[95] I have read up to the 14th chapter (and tomorrow or Tuesday I will send the manuscript to Father Lemarié – with a good recommendation from me).

I don't need to say how much I agree. I would go even further with regard to the "rediscovery of oneself"—but, in my opinion, as long as time lasts and the pilgrimage continues. If "no one can see God and live" and if "we will see God as He is", it means that the old man, the "creature", the contingent, the temporal, etc. will die seeing God – isn't this true?

Philippe is getting on very well, and making great progress. In a very discreet way the Lord used me to bring him to Himself through the regal path of total surrender.

There is now another case I would like to tell you about. Enrique Aguilar,[96] a thirty-year-old monk from Montserrat, who has served as a priest for 5 years, has requested and been granted the possibility to be lacizedfor two years (until the summer of 1964) because, after discovering Indian "monism" (especially Rāmaṇā Mahāṛṣi[97]), he has not been able to reconcile this supreme truth with "*ad usum*" theology and the current Christian way. He lived, in any case, as a monk with his parents in Barcelona. He came to see me this last Holy Week and the "miracle" happened. From monist

93 *Dies natalis*, lit. "the day of the birth".

94 Has by thy death given life to the world.

95 *Saccidānanda*: compounded Sanskrit word describing the subjective experience of Brahman (Ultimate Reality): *sat*, existence, *cit*, consciousness, and *ānanda,* bliss.

96 Enrique Aguilar Matas, monk and scholar of cultural anthropology and history of religions.

97 Rāmana Mahārṣī, great Hindū saint who lived for many years in a cave in the hills of Aruṇāchala, Tamil Nadu. He had a great impact and influence on Abhiṣīktananda.

he has become "*advaita*" and sees that this is not incompatible with the true Christian faith. So, with the permission and also the "mission" of his abbot, he will come, albeit still as a layman, to India to live the *Advaita* and Christian monastic experience, at least for a while, and then return to Montserrat to decide what to do in compliance with the full canon law.

Well, my dear father, I find myself now*, minutis minuendis*, of course, in the position of Paul when he wrote to Philemon. Would you care to offer him hospitality, both Hindū, Christian and also Benedictine? Do you feel you could guide him, direct him, advise him and, let's say, spiritually take him under your wingso he can find his way? It is with this hope that I advised him to come to India and it is thanks to my advice that his monastery and his parents are willing to help him.

I can assure you that, besides the fact that you would not be risking anything since for the moment it is not a question of considering him a "member" of Śāntivanam, it will be a joy for you to meet him, and who knows whether the Lord might use him to cast another grain of *advaita* in western monasticism. You could always send him to Kengeri and Kurisumala for a while, but I truly believe he should start with Śāntivanam. Philippe knows him and agrees completely with me. Thank you.

I have been here in Rome for three years—and if the Lord does not clearly show me his will, I will stay here for many more.

I assure you that it is not easy for me and that there are times when I "dream" of returning to India, of hiding in Banaras or the Himalayas.

Outwardly everything is fine and, apart from sleeping very little, I manage to conduct a contemplative and prayer life with 4 or 5 hours of religious meditation, 4 or 5 of study and 8-10 of apostolate and ministry.

But I feel an uneasiness, which perhaps comes from the actual environment, both specific and general (Rome, the West) in which I find myself. Believe me, I seriously wonder whether the Lord wants more from me; but how would an *advaitin* take the initiative?

Would he ask himself if it is important? If it matters where he is? I appeal "*ad Cesarem*"!

Despite my capacity to adapt, however much I try to westernize myself, to take a "cautious", dualistic, legal view of things, I cannot do it—and of course (although one can even accept success in certain circles) I am beginning to "stand out".

So today I am confiding in you. And despite (and, who knows, perhaps also thanks to) all this, the Lord makes use of me for his action for souls, for his apostolate, and he also lets me live in the beyond, on the far shore (because from the point of view of an intellectual, engaged as I am in the ministry and studying privately, so to speak, I cannot think of great things in, shall we say, an academic context).

Emitte Spiritum tuum et creabuntur et renovabis faciem terrae![98] (between the pages of this letter I have just prayed over this Psalm).

I am sorry if this letter is so long, so "personal" and full of me, instead of speaking to you, as I would have liked, about Him and also about you.

Hallelujah!

Raymond Panikkar

❖❖❖

Rome, June 26, 1963

My dear Svāmi,

As "providence" would have it, your letter, which arrived in Rome on Friday 21st, reached my hands only yesterday, Tuesday, after Philippe and Enrique had already left!

I know things have come to a head but I think it is for the best. Moreover, P.F. [Philippe Fanchette] had written to you and I am amazed that on 17/6 you still did not know about him and his plans to come with E. [Enrique]. He has a three-month tourist visa. Neither his parents nor "Montserrat" have wanted to take advantage of the opportunity of P.'s company. I am sure that you too will not regret that circumstances have been precipitated.

98 Ps. 103:30: «Thou shalt send thy Spirit and they shal be created; and thou shalt renew the face of the earth!»

I told him to trust you, and to wait, if possible, for two months before turning to you, and to ask you if for the third month he may visit whichever āśrams you deem appropriate. Obviously, he wants to stay longer and study languages, etc., but I think everything will work out smoothly. He is sincere and meek. I thought it would be good to inform Mendonça (and only him) of his situation, which is, after all, very normal. Of course, you have the final say in it all. I have no wish to impose anything on you.

P. [Philippe], remarkable and charming. He has made wonderful progress. I completely agree with you, and it was based on this that I spoke to P. and to Bruno about receiving his "initiation" from you (providing you see fit, of course), and then going around on their own.

Doesn't the new A. of St. A. grant permission to P.D.?

As for me, I agree with you. I am just waiting for a sign. Pray that I will be able to recognize it!

I know M. Kalap well. Very intelligent, refined, critical, Parsi[99], potential founder, a "beguine"[100], regrettably, but we would lose nothing by establishing relations with her, quite the contrary. I believe in the possibility of a positive symbiosis.

Toto corde

Raymond Panikkar

PS. My *namaskāra* to Cuttat, Venugopal[101] and all the friends in Delhi and elsewhere. It would be nice if I could come in December, but I am not counting on it. I'm glad to know Klostermeyer[102] is well.

---

99 Member of an ethno-religious group of the Indian subcontinent adhering to Zoroastrianism.

100 The Beguines were Christian lay religious orders whose members lived like nuns but did not take formal religious vows.

101 Śri C. T. Venugopal, with whom Abhiṣiktānanda often stayed in Delhi.

102 Klaus Klostermaier, German Catholic priest and scholar of Hinduism, Indian history and culture.

To Paul Anand and Marianna I send all my sympathy.

I hope everything is going well with your book.

❖❖❖

Castle of Urium
Lake Como, Italy
July 10, 1963

My dear friend,

Here is my situation (I will avoid saying my "thought" or "opinion" so as not to give the impression that it is a "theory".

I entrust myself to providence, if you wish, or to *advaita*, we might say. I do not believe in voluntary decisions or trials of strength. I believe, on the contrary, that true freedom is obedience (to God through consciousness, of course) and that true obedience is freedom (both together!).

Humanly speaking, I feel that I am not in my place—but what could my place be? And anyway, is it so important?

If we transcend both time and space, if we concern ourselves not so much with doing (whatever it is) but rather with being, what does it matter that we "fill" our time in one way or another?

What I ask is to always maintain this virile passivity, this active meekness so that I may always be free, willing and therefore ready, even to come to India, if the Lord wishes.

To penetrate the mystery of time and live already in eternity—this is what is essential.

In the end, I find I am unable to express what I had to say to you.

Louis d'Hendecrourt will be returning from India this month, but I don't think I will be able to see him.

Anyway, you know very well how united I feel with you and how I admire you as a brother. I greatly value your opinion and advice.

Raymond Panikkar

❖❖❖

Rome, September 28, 1963

My dear Abhiṣiktā,

Allow me to put everything in this letter. You can read everything I write. You will see that the Śāntivanam of the Spirit is also touching other rivers. Let us hope so! The two girls that Phil knows very well are writing to you to ask if it's possible for them to stay for a while, not too far from Śāntivanam. Marina V.,[103] the Italian, has obtained a two-year scholarship. Bettina[104] is accompanying her and after a month or two will return because she still has to finish her studies. The third, who seems to me the most mature, will have to wait another two years. Have you ever heard of a certain Mother Veronique, a former Poor Clare from Rabat?

I am at peace, but I feel the inner tension in Rome is increasing. I obey and die. At least one tries to preach by example. It is up to the Lord to change his plans if he so wishes! But Malenfant has decided to put up a fight in order to snatch me away and take me to India. We will have to meet one of these days. I haven't seen any bishop yet. Have you heard of this Secretariat for relations with non-Christian religions? It seems to me a very important thing.

I hear that Raymond[105] of Allahabad has published an article on Monchanin.

I don't know how Śāntivanam will continue. Is Anand[106] not coming? I would like to know your opinion about E. A. [Enrique Aguilar], not just in relation to Śāntivanam, but in general, and about his work in India. I hope Philippe can come back soon. Is Fr. Dominique never given permission?

---

103 Marina Vesci, Italian Indologist.

104 Bettina Bäumer, Austrian Indologist.

105 Mons. Leonard Joseph Raymond, Bishop of Allahabad (later Archbishop of Nagpur).

106 Anand Kumar, young postulant of Abhiṣiktānanda from Tamil Nadu.

This letter has been interrupted a hundred times, forgive me.

On Monday I'll try to write to Enrique, if I find the time.

Sincerely,

Raymond Panikkar

❖❖❖

Rome, October 15, 1963
St. Teresa of Avila

My dear brother,

I have just returned from Milan (where I attended a Priests' Week for the priests of Opus Dei) and your letter was waiting for me.

Be assured that I support you—and understand you (including with regard to everything that concerns Monchanin and you—do you remember what the Curé of Ars made St. Philomena "do"? ...).

I don't know what will become of me. I am reluctant to confide in you by letter, but you see, my "death" is total: neither India, nor true Theology, nor Philosophy, nor Culture, nor Friendship, nor support – immersed, yes, in the "ministry" and with a hidden dimension of solitude and contemplation. I can pray: *in manus tuas commendo spiritum meum*![107]

I haven't seen either Mal or Extrass or anyone else again. I will in any case try to find a moment to see them. Nevertheless, the theological "problems" of the Council are totally different from them.

M. and B. [Marina and Bettina] have left, I think the day before yesterday, and they will write to you—and they will also explain the rest in person. I really want them to receive from you if not a true *dikṣā*[108] at least more than just a *darśana*.[109] They have nothing to do with Opus Dei!

---

107 «*Into thy hands I commend my spirit*!»
108 Initiation.
109 Beholding of a sage or saint.

I didn't understand exactly what Enrique wanted from me for Mahadevam[110] or Murti.[111] Tell him that I will gladly do what he wishes. That he must write to me in detail. Also, I completely agree with you regarding your opinion of him. Only that we must hope for a true "conversion" (I am including a letter for him).

(Cont.)

October 17, 1963

The Council continues. We are at a standstill -on a juridical level, in any case (which is also necessary), but the forum is open. Nothing is known about the Secretariat for non-Christian religions, but the idea is already official. Mons. Raymond (Allahabad) spoke about it in the Osservatore Romano.[112]

Mercier has just sent me his speech at the Bombay Durga Pūjā[113] (Interfaith Conference). Not bad, but so classic that it will only heighten the misunderstandings.

My regards to Śāntivanam.

Raymond Panikkar

❖❖❖

Milan, November 26, 1963

My dear brother,

I have received your letter of the 21st and I am replying immediately.

First of all, if B. [Bettina] wants she can stay longer, as long as it is good for you and you think it's the right thing. R.[114] wrote to me from Paris that she would like to spend the Christmas holidays with B. She is free from 20/12 to January 3rd. But nothing is necessary in this world. I am thinking

110 T. M. P. Mahadevan, renowned contemporary Indian philosopher.
111 T. R. V. Murti, Indian philosopher and professor at the University of Varāṇasī.
112 The Holy See newspaper.
113 Offering, ceremony, rite.
114 Roselyne Lombard.

of going to Germany (near Karlsruhe, I think, from January the 3rd to the 5th to give a lecture at the Evangelishe Akademie) and then from the 7th to the 14th I think I'll be in Rome for Castelli's[115] meeting.

It might be interesting for B. to be there. But I think she needs to feel free.

I wouldn't for anything in the world want to bind people to me. Moreover, I cannot. However, for her studies I don't think it is necessary for her to change direction. I am thinking of accepting the "lecturing post" anyway. Here in Milan there is a young lady acquaintance of M. and B.: Caterina Conio,[116] Via degli Olivetani, 3, who told me that she had already invited B. to her home when she passes through Milan and which she now confirms.

So B. could also come to Milan for a few days. For the rest we will see.[117]

I want very much to know how it went. I assure you that I felt their weight on my shoulders. But I am very happy about your news and reception. Through Caterina Conio the "inas"[118] can write to me. To conclude about B.: she can come back whenever she wants, but I would like to know if possible. I would also ask you to write to R. so she can make arrangements with her.

I would like to know also if M. has received a copy of a letter sent to her at Sr. Candida's in Bangalore.

The good Raymond did not have time to speak at the Council on this occasion. He did, however, hand in a written text. I am very happy about the news regarding Enrique.

I hear—as I feared—that the atmosphere in Rome is bad. This is the natural reaction. I would like to know the address of the "inas" after you.

---

115 Refers to the "Colloqui Castelli", international meetings on the philosophy of religion, held at the home of Enrico Castelli, philosopher and historian of Italian philosophy. Panikkar was a frequent participant and wrote many articles for the Colloqui.

116 Caterina Conio (Nuccia), Italian Indologist, founded in Milan the "Henri Le Saux" interreligious center.

117 Marina Vesci, Bettina Bömer, Roselyne Lombard and Caterina Conio were students whom Panikkar supervised in their studies on Hindū culture and spirituality.

118 Short for "signorinas", young ladies.

I just wrote a short thing in German about the apophaticism of being in Buddhism.

I am writing at full speed and I must stop now if the letter is to go out today.

Talk soon,

Raymond Panikkar

❖❖❖

1964

Rome, January 27, 1964

Dear Svāmijī,

Thank you for your letter of the 21st.

Here is my plan:

1 - We can tell anyone (I'll leave it to you) that I'm coming back to India.[119]

2 - For the moment I would not like to have E. [Enrique] with me.

3 - I must first find my way and afterwards see about my integration.

4 –This is why I think it's important that we see each other. I could also go to Uttarkāshi with you, and return to Banaras (headquarters for the time being) for Easter.

5 – I will leave here (hopefully) on February 7th. I am waiting for permission to make a stop at Mount Athos, because I believe the experience could be important for India.

6 - In this case, I will be in Bombay at Mercier's by around February 20th and there I will await your news. We could meet at the beginning of the

[119] In January Abhiṣiktānanda learned that his friend Raymond, after an interval of four years, would soon be returning to India. Panikkar had recently defended a doctoral thesis, which was later to be published with the title of *The Unknown Christ of Hinduism*, about which Abhiṣiktananda said «Panikkar's courage far surpasses my own in *Guhantara*» (a work that describes his first experience on Aruṇācala, which had been banned by the Paris censor and harshly criticized.)

month in Delhi (didn't you receive my letter of the 15th?).

If you have time to send me a word here before the 7th that would be even better – or, to gain one day, a copy to Mons. Gad in Athens (pending your arrival). Thank you.

7 - Your manuscript has arrived and is with me—I will pass it on to B.

In the joy of seeing you again,

Raymond Panikkar

❖❖❖

Rome, February 4, 1964

My dear Svāmijī,

I have just returned from the last exercise of the University entrance exams (public lecture) – *Deo gratias*! – and I find your letter dated 31/1.

I will be arriving in Bombay, God willing, on Wednesday 26th February – after that I have no plans.

From April 2nd to 7th Murray has invited me to Jyotiniketan and I would like to go. What I propose would be to meet up as soon as possible in Delhi and go together (if you think it's a good idea) to Uttarkāshi – but I would like to spend Easter – March 28th—with a Christian community, perhaps in Varāṇasī. But we will see, since I don't want to be limited or assume anything. If it suits you, I can be in Delhi whenever you want.

Here there is a general sense of desolation and it really must be said that *avaita* does not mean not loving people.

So I will wait to hear what you decide at Mercier's, who will pass on the news to me.

M. has written to me that he wants to see me. I won't be going down just yet…maybe I will tell him to come to Bombay if he can.

I will tell you about Athos, if permission arrives in time.

In Christ,

Raymond Panikkar

❖❖❖

St. Catherine's Home
Andheri, February 29, 1964

My dear Svāmijī,

I am writing to you from the By-Poona train, since the two suitcases that the good FFM had offered to take by ship from Naples to Bombay, despite all admonitions are now in Poona, en route from Madras.

I find it interesting to be able to see the Cardinal. This will keep me here at least until the 4th or 5th. Then I will have to see the Archbishop of Bhopal (and I don't know whether I will have to stop there on my way to Delhi). On the other hand, I don't want to delay our retreat at Uttarkāshi. I am willing to do what you tell me (either to give up seeing the Cardinal or Bhopal or even to meet up after Easter from April 2nd to 7th at Jyotiniketan, or I could come and see you (as a civilian, of course) in Uttarkāshi around mid-March.

Unless there is a very special, urgent reason (to see each other immediately) or for purposes of discretion (in Uttarkāshi), I would say the last option (which would allow me to come to Delhi and then on to the UK without having to rush) is the best. What do you think? Send me an unsigned telegram here at the Archdiocese of Bombay (on 4/3) with your suggestion and I will follow it. Then you can leave a note, address, etc. with Cuttat in Delhi, with the rest. I still feel lost and disoriented.

Raymond Panikkar

❖❖❖

Najipur, April 15, 1964

My Dear Brother and Svāmi,

You will undoubtedly be wanting news of our meeting in Jyotiniketan: according to everyone it was "a great success, unlike Nagpur". I cannot compare them. There were 16 of us, but 13 were active participants (5 Catholics: Cuttat, Kalapan, [...] and myself) and the atmosphere was good. I prefer to give you my detailed impressions in person (when?), but in general the meeting was a revelation for the Protestants and although we are not yet dealing with true mysticism, or even *advaita*, it still counts for something that we are considering the Upaniśads as sacred scriptures.

The letter you sent to Bombay reached me in Banaras and here I have received your letter of 4/3 that you sent to Bhopal. Thank you.

In Banaras I would have the possibility of a chair in comparative religions, but I am very afraid of the "politics".

I don't have a house yet. I would like to get a small *sunyapit* near the Ganges and not far from the University, but it isn't easy. I could then have one room as a library and another as a chapel. A real *āśram*, if you will, but without calling it such.

I see my theandric journey a little more clearly (a synthesis between action and contemplation, spirit and body, Hinduism and Christianity, etc.).

Here the conference of priests has been very instructive for me (better here than in Allahabad) as it made me understand once more where we are – or better, where one is. Distant, distant, still very distant. The Institute has a project (...) for the study of religions. I see clearly that I should collaborate but absolutely not be in charge. My place is solitude and the Hind¥ world.

The heat is good (45°!) Tell me freely if you think I should come (either to stay a while or for a pilgrimage). In any case, I would still like to accompany you to the South when you go.

Sincerely,

Raymond Panikkar

Vārāṇasī, April 29, 1964

My dear brother

On the 15th I had written to you from Nagpur, but by the 21st, the date of your letter, you still had not received mine.

So, if you want me to, I will come. Write to me immediately with detailed instructions (you are a teacher) and what I should bring for you and for me. I could stay with you for a few weeks and, as I said, spend some time in total silence – and also in solitude.

So far I have neither a house nor a job (the latter will come, at least as a researcher of a new "Philosophical Centre" directed by Murti[120] – the chair still remains to be seen). The house is a problem.

I will leave here around the 13th-17th but I would like to stay a few days in Rishikesh and Hardwar, after which I would come to you, with the whole month of June free. In August I think I will go to Pondicherry. We could therefore go on a small tour of the *āśrams* together, taking advantage of your move southward (all depending on the interview, etc., for the chair of Comparative Religions—which I think I have explained to you).

With regard to the pilgrimage to Gangotrī[121] or elsewhere I leave everything up to you.

My vocation is gently taking shape. I must respect the rhythms and let the Lord take care of it. This is the theandric vocation about which I have written a lot over the past several years. As for the rest, *os a os et cor ad cor loquimur.*[122]

As always, in the tempiternal Easter,

Raymond Panikkar

❖❖❖

---

120 T. R. V. Murti, Indian professor, philosopher, writer and translator.

121 On May 19 Panikkar arrived from Vārāṇasī to spend three weeks with Abhiṣiktānanda in the Himalayas. In the first week of June they followed the pilgrim route to Gangotrī, and one day climbed up to the point where the stream issues from the glacier, so that they could celebrate the Mass at the very source of the sacred river.

122 «Let us speak mouth to mouth and heart to heart.»

Gyansu, June 11, 1964
8 in the evening.

My dear Raymond,

... I have just received a letter from Śrī Poonja[123]*, which I am copying on the back of a telegram. Is not this the real advaita? And as for ours, whatever we do, is it not a qualified, viśiṣṭa advaita*[124]*? – and the advaita is lost as soon as there is qualification. There is a world of difference between being fascinating by one's own "mental constructions" and having the genuine experience. It is good to feel yourself recalled to the real thing. How dramatic it is to be there between the two camps, misunderstood and rejected by both alike. And yet this painful struggle is necessary, so that one day the two arms of the Cross may be reunited by those who will have been strong enough to bring them together against all opposition, in their body, their soul, their lacerated heart.*

...

Abhiṣiktānanda

❖❖❖

Almora, June 18, 1964

My dear brother,[125]

Finally, (after two days at Mlle Boner's[126]) I have settled in Bimar for my retreat. There is no one in the hotel (so to speak) (it was in fact closed), so my solitude is total – and I believe that the retreat is going well.

In Almora I have met a *sādhu,*[127] born in Switzerland, in India for the past

---

123 Śrī Poonja, born Hariwansh Lal Poonja, ofter called Harilal ("issuing from Providence") by Abhiṣiktānanda.

124 Qualified *advaita* that maintains a degree of duality between the soul and God, as in the teaching of Ramānuja.

125 From this date onwards Panikkar uses the informal "tu" instead of the formal "vous" when addressing his friend/brother Abhiṣikta.

126 Alice Boner (1889–1981) was a Swiss painter and sculptor, art historian, and an Indologist. She lived in a house in Delhi, near the river Ganges.

127 Monk, ascetic in India.

dozen years, still quite young, named Gianānanda. Made a good impression on me. His outward detachment, at least here, is total (he has only what he carries with him). His most permanent residence is in Hardwar.

For the whole of this month my address will beat Mlle Boner's (the mail doesn't arrive here), then Vārāṇasī. I have given in my documents. We'll see.

The days pass in the name of what I call the theandric vocation, which is not that of renunciation but of the assumption of the whole for the purpose of redeeming and transforming it—not naturally, through the technique of action, but through the path of theandric spirituality (again) which includes that of the Spirit.

I think about you, your testimony, your path, your "cosmicity" (so Christian, so charitable) in your acosmism…

I know nothing about my future. Everything depends on the interview, which will decide about the teaching post; but I am doing everything according to the plan to go to Pondicherry in August.

In the mornings until 1 pm absolute (inner) silence and yoga. In the afternoons prayer, meditation, spiritual reading.

I hope you have received the papers from the Liturgical Commission.

I embrace you fraternally,

Raymond

❖❖❖

Gangotrī, June 24, 1964

... The note on the "a-Christianity" of the Psalms is written. I will type it out and tidy it up when I get back to Uttarkāshi. This is what we should talk about in the South or in Benares. Now that the question is open it has become extremely serious. And so few of the psalms are unaffected. A bombshell article could come out of my essay. Is the Psalter a Christian prayer? If any periodiocal were sufficiently bold! The Psalter is terribly

Judaic and bogs down the Christian unconscious at a pre-Christian, non-evangelical level.

...

Abhiṣiktānanda

❖❖❖

Vārāṇasī, July 21, 1964

My dear Mahātmajī,

I see that the p 7.1 of my article is missing. If you still have it, could you send it to me?

(Cont.)
July 23, 1964

I have just now received your letter of 13/7. Thank you. I have no news (teaching post and house). I am forced to live in pure verticality.

You are a sensible, cosmic, orderly man (and I admire you and therefore you can live acosmically (with an eye to "Last year at Marienbad"—important!). Well, first of all let us make a programme.

1- If I am "free" I will go to Pondicherry (August 14th to 21st) and we could then meet earlier and "do" Aruṇācala,[128] etc.

2- If I don't go now I don't know if I will have a chance before the Bombay Congress. So it would be good to stop off at Banaras once you are in Bareilly (I have written to Murray asking him to give you a manuscript).

3- I have just finished correcting my article and making all the alterations (if I say thank you I would feel it is almost an insult, and if I don't, bad manners...); I am not very satisfied with it, but if I don't finish it now it will just end up inflating the archive of unpublished works. There are three possibilities, which I would put in this order of priority:

---

[128] Sacred hill in Tamil Nadu (Southern India) where numerous ascetics have lived, including the great saint Rāmaṇā Mahāṛṣi.

a) preface to your book

b) article for "Christus", which has asked me to collaborate (if it is not too long)

c) developing it into a book (which can always be done later),

I will send it to you tomorrow and I hope you'll have the time, the inclination and the kindness to edit it (I doubt it will be necessary to add notes—because then it would become almost twice the size)

4- If I haven't found the time for your two articles (Secretariat and Baumer) I still hope to this week.

5- I wonder if you could ask Venugopal if there is any way to approach Sampurnanand (governor of Rajasthan) or some other member for a "little thing": my Mandir[129] (near Dasarwamethghat), which previously belonged to the Maharaja of Jaipas, has been put up for rent (500 rupees for the whole thing). I would like 2 rooms and I wrote to the "Property Officer of Rajastan-Kathra-Allahabad" but they told me that without a "recommendation" it is not possible to rent only a part of the building (before someone lived there without paying – but I am willing to pay). It would be best, if Venu could write to someone, to just refer to me as Dr. Panikker, prof. etc. (without mentioning the Church!)

6- If I go to Pondy, do I have to write to the bishop? Who is he and what is he like?

Jai Ganga Ki Ma![130]

Raymond

❖❖❖

[129] Hindū temple dedicated to a divinity.

[130] "Hail to Mother Ganga" (in India the river Ganges is often referred to as Ganga, the personification in the form of the goddess of purification and forgiveness).

Varāṇasī, July 28, 1964

"A Mass at the Source of the Ganges."

Impressive and excellent! I totally agree. It absolutely must be published. I do not think it's indiscreet, either for Christians or for Hindūs.

Where could it be published? It is very long for a large illustrated book (but why?). Unfortunately almost all the photos are mounted on top of each other (because the apparatus fell). However, there are some that could be useful. I will have them developed now. In any case, your article is a document!

The dialogue is very good.

As changes I would suggest:

p. 12, 4, line 6: instead of "ascribe to the Church the incomparable mystery" write: "ascribe to the Church these incomparable treasures" (to avoid any possible risk of being accused by theologians of an improper use of the concept of "mystery".

p. 13, 2, line 3, add: "tionelle", being as it is the apex and perfection of the Christian life.

line 22, replace "habitable" with"full of the joy of the Creator".

line 23, replace "social" with historical.

"25, add "is no longer" to"mainly".

"31, replace "ce ne sont plus" exclusively "cessa-!"

p.13, last line: add "these are also disciples".

As you can see, these are small things.

In short, I think it is worth polishing up. I don't know whether the narration on Kedārnāth will make the article too long. A second reading will also tell you whether it would be best to get rid of or shorten some of the passages to avoid repetitions of the concept (which are not bad for the reader, but do make the article longer. It all depends on its destination). For Italy I could think about it.

We will need to continue our pilgrimage next year and resume our dialogue…

Do you plan to giveit your own name or anonymous or a false name?

I embrace you fraternally,

Raymond

❖❖❖

Apostolic Prefecture of Banaras
Banaras, August 22, 1964

My dear Svāmijī,

This letter will welcome you to Śāntivanam, which does not belong exclusively to you since it is in a way the living symbol of this community of the Spirit, which He has taken charge of "guiding" ...

This letter is also to thank you for having travelled hundreds of extra km to come as far as Varāṇasī. Of course, everything is fragmentary and imperfect, but I do believe we have taken a step forward, even after Uttarkāshi.

I was particularly happy with our conversations during the midday meals, even though I was very tired—I don't know exactly why.

Advaita and Trinity! You seek the Trinity in *advaita*; I seek *advaita* in the Trinity. The starting point for a Frenchman is *advaita*; that of an Indian is the Trinity, but it is for this reason that one finds oneself at the very center of the Cross!

As soon as Mme Boner answers I will try to "settle" (a bad word), and if the problem of my teaching post permits, I will dedicate myself to my book on Indian Spirituality, especially the great *mahāvākyāni*[131] (beginning with *tatvamasi*[132]). It is not a matter of speculation but crystallized experience.

[131] The great Vedic sayings in which the Vedantic doctrine is condensed.
[132] "That thou art".

We have to both help and correct ourselves at the same time. Even life (I am not saying work) is ecclesial. It is within us – in the *antaryāmin*[133] – that the great conversion must be made.

At St. Mary's everyone knew about your arrival and Fr. Ivan[134] spokc very well of you, and of your cosmic nature. The Ganges is lowering and the heat is rising.

I am beginning to think it wouldn't be a bad thing if you went to Bombay. It will be necessary to bear witness of this kind – at least for the Europeans to come.

Yours,

Raymond

❖❖❖

Vārāṇasī, September 2, 1964

My dear brother,

Did you know that "waking sleep"[135] is an expression from W. Hilton's *The Scale of Perfection* II, 11, where he also speaks about *kaivalya*: "oneness of the soul"? It is all a description of the eye of spirit.

I am staying with Fr. Ivan once again, as Mme Boner asked me to leave her house at the end of August (as a result of my letter asking her for the ground floor).

Then again, you were the one who gave me (and I believe you are right) scruples about acquiring my *mandir*. So I am still homeless! Maybe I will be able to have the room next to Mme Boner (no running water or toilet), but she's not sure.

133 "The one who controls from within."

134 Fr. Ivan Illich, Austrian Catholic priest, theologian and philosopher.

135 "'I sleep, but my heart is awake' (Song of Solomon 5:2)... I cannot be awake to Jesus, except I sleep to the world." W. Hilton, *The Scale of Perfection*, p.284.

Incidentally, I don't think I will get the teaching post. Mme Basu is far too clever at manouvering. Tomorrow she will give a lecture at the University on […]

Yours,

Raymond

❖❖❖

Vārāṇasī, September 11, 1964

I have read Enrique's letter. Very good. Do you see the miracle?

I am enclosing a letter from J. Laurencin,[136] and ask you please return it to me and see if you can "invent" something in French about Nagpur which he could then have translated. I wasn't there, so it is not up to me. If you cannot, what could we do? I think it is interesting that, little by little, our meetings are becoming a kind of myth.

I wrote to you this morning: Mahadevan[137] is the third member of the commission of 24. I am sending you a copy of my article *Technochronie,*[138] which has just arrived.

In spiritu, quo scientiam habet vocis![139]

Yours,

Raymond

❖❖❖

[136] Teacher of French.

[137] T.M.P. Mahadevan, Indian writer, Advaita scholar and professor of philosophy.

[138] "Tecnica e tempo: la tecnocronia" ("Technology and time: technochrony"), in Il nuovo Osservatore, Rome 1965, which is in part found in the Introduction of Vol. XII, *Space, Time and Science,* Opera Omnia, Orbis Books, Maryknoll, New York 2022.

[139] "In the Spirit, by which all spoken things are understood".

Śantivanam, 15 September, 1964

My dear Raymond,

Have you become the raja[140]*of the Man Mandir*[141]*? If so, my humblest pranam*[142]*! And above all, don't invite Mr. Cuttat at night, he might play the same game through the windows, which are even more dangerous than those of the Swiss embassy in Colombo.*

By the same post I sent you parts 2 and 3 of your article. In several points I failed to grasp what you meant. It's not so much the French that is difficult as the composition that is too broad. And yet many of the ideas expressed deserve to be comprehended and meditated on, and others at least to be discussed, since they give us much to think about.

The young Swiss man arrived on Sunday and stayed for a few hours, too little, as he seemed very pleasant.

Yesterday I had the surprise of receiving a letter from Mercier asking me to give a lecture to the French-speaking group! Very unexpected. I decided from the beginning to be completely "acosmic", as monks should be, and not to go to the Bombay "show" unless very important meetings were to be held on the sidelines. I don't think it would be useful to accept Mercier's invitation. In fact, he has combined into one meeting (of perhaps 2 hours) a talk (with discussion) by Deleury, another one (idem) by Ceyrac, and one by myself, plus a "community" Mass in French! He is ruining things. Deleury and Cyrac will be more than enough.

The day before yesterday I celebrated Mass in Tamil. My "parishioners" attended with great enthusiasm, and would like me to celebrate more often in Tamil. But it's a problem without a book and with the awful habit of imitating Tamil in Lilliputian script and poor lighting. I set up a portable altar in front of the stone altar, facing the people. I am exceeding the permission officially granted ... but the bishop is in Rome. I also introduced into the litany of the Offertory (that too) the prayers for the Pope and the

140 Indian honorific title originally reserved for kings of autonomous countries and subsequently extended to important dignitaries and also gurus.

141 Hindū little temple in Vārāṇasī at *Hanumanghat*, on the Ganges, above which Panikkar was later to find a place to live.

142 Obsequious greeting, usually addressed to a gurū or important person.

Council taken from the prayer composed by John XXIII.

I don't receive the "Examiner",[143] *but I have no doubt what it's about. Do you know that after some years diocesan priests have to pay a levy of FOUR MASS DOLLARS for the medical school in Bangalore. They celebrate masses and the dollars go to the medical school!*

I would be very happy to get in touch with the "divine" B.[144] *I saw in the magazine Spir. a CR of the book consecrated to this hermit of Florence. The CR says the book is useful but lacks originality.*

I would have enough room to receive those participating in the retreat on condition that they bring something to sleep on and help a little with the housework. The solitude and peace of SV are truly unique.

I told you about Bruno's letter to the bishop. Fr. Dominique fears that he is a little too "acosmic" and that he does not tend to lean on others. Or that I, much less, have any vocation as prior or treasurer, or cellar master, as the monks say. He has not written to me and I have told the bishop very clearly that I would never accept a European here except by direct agreement between him and me before embarking for India. I don't want a European monastery here.

So finally, in eight days' time you will have your professorship. This is one of those cases in which total spiritual indifference is called for. If the Lord finds it useful (what anthropomorphism!) for you have it, the steps you have taken so far will have been enough. It is his business. If you don't get it (which is more likely) it will be easy for you to make use of yourself. Sort out your writings to begin with and make it so they are not reserved for certain specialists but can also enlighten the Church of India.

As soon as you can, therefore, organize your schedule for December. There will be three weeks between the two congresses. Wouldn't it be better to hold the meeting here in the Christmas period, before Madras?

If you are at the Man Mandir say hello to the nice [...], and if you are in Bung. 45, please express again my admiration to Fr. Ivon for his organ! The Jesuits of the 16th Century were interested in telescopes and astrolabes,

143 Catholic weekly news magazine.

144 Reference to Fr. Divo Barsotti, Italian priest, writer and founder of the "Community of the Sons and Daughters of God."

and brought them to the courts of Peking and Fatehpur Sikri. Isn't the Holy Church always ahead of science???

In Domino.

Abhiṣiktānanda

❖❖❖

Śantivanam, 3 October, 1964

My dear Raymond,

I received your letter last night. I will send the article immediately, but I am very afraid that it will not arrive by the 15th. It will take at least 2 or 3 days. It will have to be improved a little and it takes a week from here to Paris. Send a copy also to Fesquet. You could also send him a copy of your text and tell him that a corrected copy will arrive in a week at the latest. I know Fesquet, I met him in Delhi in 1961, an ex-novice who has been changed by the war. Very nice but extremely ignorant about India. They are terrible about style and are so ignorant of India in France that one does not know how to feed them any solid food. I am still busy with my book Experience,[145] *working on the notes received from the editor.*

I have not opened the file on Gangotrī for months, since I am busy with these other manuscripts. I'll try to get into it again. Give me your exact addresses of the courses along your journey, so I can send it to you. [...]

So, let's organize everything for the week of Christmas. It is absolutely vital for at least Marina to come – I will write to Lili today, because otherwise it would be impossible to receive her at Śantivanam. Last year I had Enrique and my cook's family here. This year I am alone. So tell Marina.

Organize your schedule. I told you where you can meet Poonja if you wish. Will you have time for Tiruvannamalai? [...] I have to go there for 2 or 3 days. I could wait for you, otherwise I'll be going this month. I'm afraid that if you'll only be in Bombay on December 15th *you won't have*

---

145 *Saccidananda: A Christian Approach to Advatic Experiences,* originally published in French in 1965.

time to do everything, including the trip to Kerala.[146] *You can either go to Kerala first and then come to Tamil Nadu – or do what you have to do in Tamil Nadu and then go to Kerala between Tiruvannamai and SV. Kulitalai is on the Cochin Tiruchi railway line (direct trains). Or else, if you are not in too much of a hurry, you can go from Pondy or Madras to Tiruvannamai, which is very easy to reach from either place.*

The cause of this post-viral fatigue? We have to be a little realistic. How do you deal with food in Hanumanghat? Just the way I live pushes me to my limits. And I take all the necessary precautions. What about you? But I also know that "fatigue" is created much more on a psychic than a physiological level. It's not at all comfortable to be sitting on two chairs at the same time. Psychically also, integration (or the process of individuation, in Jungian terms) has to have been fully completed... But it is this terrible tension itself that is fruitful for oneself and for the world. Wasn't this tension also in Christ? "Non mea voluntas, sed tua" – the tension that is essential for being.

In Domino

Abhishiktananda

For Śantivanam don't just settle for 2 or 3 days. We know from experience how long it takes to cultivate truly fruitful conversations ...

❖❖❖

Śantivanam, 10 October, 1964

My dear Raymond,

Our last letters crossed. I've been constantly waiting for news of your professorship and the Man Mandir. How did the interview go? Results? What are your plans for after the Congress? Has Nuccia arrived?

I'm very busy finalizing the book that will be published by Centurion. They have sent me the model of the style they want: analytical, short sentences, words common to everyone. You would find it even more difficult than me to satisfy them!

---

146 Panikkar wanted to visit his father's family, which was originally from Kerala .

Fr. Mercier has not yet decided about the Congress. I don't think I will go either.

I received a note from K. Klosh in Bombay. I had also heard from John Cole, who had arrived in Vrindavan around that time. I'm afraid four monks were too much for Vrindavan! We need to be discreet.

This short letter is just to find out what's happening with you.

Have the photos of Gangotrī been developed?

I sent Dr. Castelli a letter by air mail as well as a parcel by ordinary mail with the book Eremites in English for Cardinal Marella. I haven't received anything from Divo Barsotti yet.

Abhishiktananda

❖❖❖

New Delhi, 16 October, 1964

My dear friend,

The expression is too common and therefore it has become inflated, but wouldn't friendship be compatible with acosmism?

For me being is love and therefore true life, friendship. And I assure you that at times one finds oneself without friends.

I came to Delhi for a seminar of the CSU (AICUF)[147]of North India (in all 25) and I talked to them about the "Christian student in a changing world". Fr. Ceyrac[148] also came. There would be an immense work to be done; but the Church is not so concerned with the "problem"... The internuncio, a very nice person, told Ceyrac and me that we should "convince" the hierarchy of the importance of the intellectual apostolate...

I think you know Svāmi Chinmayanda (who is a disciple, I believe, of Tapovānanda[149](?) of Uttarkāshi...). A svāmi who dresses in silk *kavi* [robes], with a gold watch, a car and a plane ... Well, he was

147 CSU: Catholic Student Union; AICUF: All India Catholic University Federation.

148 Fr. Pierre Ceyrac, Jesuit priest.

149 Svām Tapovan Maharaj.

with Ranghanathānanda and Mahādeva (plus Murti and Devaraj of the BHU[150]), the experts of the Chair of Comparative Religions. Intolerance and fanaticism (visible and frightening) together with petty politics have again resulted in the chair being declared deserted and Mme Basu, who is already a lecturer, being asked to lecture on the subject for two years. …

So the matter is settled. On one hand, I am glad. I will stay in Varāṇasī as *sādhaka,*[151] since serious intellectual work is not possible under these conditions. This pleases me. On the other hand (and here in Delhi right now I feel this before the state and the Church) I remain a somewhat special figure, without *status* ("what do you do, Panikkar?" is the constant question) and also without a great deal of social or ecclesial justification. But if this is the Will of God…

At last, I have found two rooms and I can settle down. Around 7/11 I will hold a retreat in Jyotiniketan, then in Bombay and then in the South. What have you decided for Bombay?

In peace,

Raymond

❖❖❖

Vārāṇasī, October 28, 1964

My dear Svāmi,

Fesquet[152] has asked me for a 7-page article on autochthonous religious India (?) by November 15th for "Le Monde".

My first reaction was negative, but today I decided to write something. Here is my question (in all simplicity—from your part also). Would you be willing to rewrite or correct it so that my manuscript is "French"?

Since there isn't much time for the post I am asking you now, because if you (for reasons of your own) cannot do it I could ask Mercier or try

150 Banaras Hindū University.

151 *Sādhaka*: he who devotes himself with every effort to his chosen path.

152 Henri Fesquet, religious columnist for Le Monde.

to write in English… Could you answer me right away? If you can't do it, please don't worry. If you can, I would send you the article and you would then send it directly to Le Monde.

I leave here on the 15th to hold the retreat in Jyotiniketan. Then to Bombay until 15/12. Then, if all goes well, to Śāntivanam.

Have you had time to rewrite *The Pilgrimage to Gangotrī*? I would like to have a copy – also so I can show it around.

I am tired beyond all strength, but "*in nomine tuo laxabo rete*".[153]

Raymond

❖❖❖

Varāṇasī, November 5, 1964

My dear Svāmijī,

You have not replied to my letter of the 28th, but I cannot do without your advice.

1- Do you want to read, correct and adjust the article "India and the Church" – if you think it might be publishable in a newspaper like Le Monde? If it fails to pass your censorship or if it requires a substantial amount of changes, I will drop the matter and we'll talk about it when we see each other. If, on the other hand, it seems passable, it should be sent directly to M. Henri Fesquet, Albergo Nazionale, Montecitorio, Rome (with a copy for me).

2- After writing the letter to Mons. M. [Mendonça] (copy enclosed) I added that he should not do anything about it, since he is leaving Naples on the 15th.

3- With the same courier or the next I will also send you a second introductory article which also needs to be corrected, etc. I would prefer a pseudonym for this, and maintain strict anonymity.

---

[153] Lk 5:5: "But Simon answered and said to Him, "Master, we have toiled all night and caught nothing; nevertheless at Your word I will let down the net."

4- Please send this second article to M. Veronese with the enclosed letter, if you think it's appropriate.

5- *Il va sans dire* that I leave it up to you in both cases. I have hesitated a lot about writing these two articles, but I finally decided to do it because I think one needs to take advantage of such opportunities.

6- The big problem is time. Fesquet wants the articles by November 15th. I think you could send "India and the Church" first.

I am leaving on the 16th for Jyotiniketan and from there on the 22nd for Bombay (at Mercier's). My two-roomed house here is always open for you (remember what we talked about). I saw very clearly the other day what my role is here in India. I am very glad I didn't get the teaching post (although from an "objective" point of view it is deplorable).

If from December19th to 26th we are to be with you – with Uma, Nuccia,[154] Maria (and maybe a fourth)—and I will be free to leave Bombay from the 15th onwards, could we not consider holding the Mass on Aruṇāchala during that time? Let us see later on.

Thank you, and of course if you can't take on this thankless job, please, it doesn't matter. It will be the sign that decides for me.

Raymond

❖❖❖

Śantivanam, 10 November, 1964

My dear Raymond,

Your message arrived this afternoon. Immediately after dinner I had a big dose of Nescafé and sat in front of the typewriter. I have just finished the long article, the short one I will do tomorrow. Time was running out and I wasn't able to edit it, but I think it's okay. I followed the advice of my "repeater" for the book (the editor of Centurion, Paris, who regularly sends me my "corrected copies") and simplified the sentences as much as I could. Even though it is for a Le Monde newspaper the readers are

[154] Caterina Conio.

exclusively Hindū and Christian doctors of science. I did not understand the word procédure on p. 11. In French it has very specific connotations which are strictly legal. Whatever seemed too difficult to express in different words I have left almost as it is. On the whole it is very good, and your French is much better than that of Uttarkāshi!

I am also very happy with the letter. I find it difficult to understand Sanatkumaralemany.[155] *I am putting simply Sanat Kumar, which is excellent. I will send it then to Mr. Veronese. If I weren't afraid of overdoing it I would have also sent it to Inf. Cath. Int. [Informations Catholiques Internationales] and our friends in New York. I think it would be good for you to send it yourself. Addresses: [...]. Remind them about the excellent letter published in early October on the Congress and offer them your text. In New York send it in French from me to Mrs. A. Stokes [...]. They are the friends I told you about. Send it in French and write in French. This lady is a Breton, the widow of an American... it will be worthwhile.*

I understand that nothing should be sent to Msgr. Malefant.

So tomorrow morning I'll send you by air mail

1- for Fesquet the article + my personal letter

2 - for Veronese welcome greetings with your letter

3 - for you 2 copies of the article and 2 copies of the letter. I will add one of the two examples you sent me. Why two copies?

Today I received a note from Seuil basically saying they are interested in my book on Nagpur. I will send them a message asking their impressions and opinions before the final draft

I am sending this note to Vārāṇasī but the package with a duplicate of the note to Jyoti. I am afraid it's too late for Banaras.

If you leave Bombay on the 15th and plan to be here on the 19th, we cannot consider Arunachala. It takes 2 days from Bombay to Tamil Nadu.

---

155 Refers to the name Panikkar was to adopt for the book *At the Source of the Ganges,* later shortened to Sanat Kumar.

It's better if you come via Madras. Above all, I should be here before our guests arrive. I don't have a cellar master father.[156] *It is impossible for me to leave Śantivanam after December 15th. We will talk again about the Arunachala project once you are here. (Of course you can come via Bangalore if you have to make a stop there. From Bangalore to here it takes one night. From Madras further south there are excellent express-buses (3 per day to Tiruchi) .*

Has Nuccia arrived? So it will be Christian commentary of the Mandukya under the palms of Śantivanam! A fine challenge!

Until next time.

In Domino.

Abhiṣiktānanda

1965

Rome, Hotel Astor
January 8, 1965

My dear Svāmi,

I left on Monday night from Delhi; arrived here Tuesday morning (dead) with no time to stop in Athens to see Cuttat.

On Wednesday, the Epiphany, I opened the Colloquium with my talk – which didn't go badly, but it wasn't sensational either. Besides, it was not understood at all. I had to speak in French…

Castelli wants me here at all costs and is pushing me to leave the O.D.[157] He has also talked about it with the Pope, whom I should see one of these days…

I spoke to Bettina, who has really evolved positively.

---

[156] Term used ironically to mean that he had no father to help him.

[157] Opus Dei. Catholic religious institution founded by Josemaria Escrivà in 1928 at the end of the Spanish civil war, and to which Panikkar belonged for many years until he left and became a priest incardinated to the diocese of Varāṇas°.

Well, here I am right now in a hotel with the other conference participants, like a fish out of water.

A lot of problems, under pressure, forced to make decisions and with a course to teach, a round table to attend (they paid my travel expenses) and a thousand people to see, not to talk about me but about their problems…

I'll keep you posted – who else do I have?

Raymond

❖❖❖

Ernakulam
January 11, 1965

All departures are painful, but the other day was heartbreaking for me. And I wish I knew why. Maybe even "heartbreak" is good.

Thank you for everything.

If you go to Aruṇāchala don't forget that the function of the SanatKumar[158]who has accompanied you is not writing, nor theology, but action, sacred action. You are not called to say, or to discuss, or to write, but to do, to perform within the living fabric of the Mystical Body of Christa delicate and difficult operation: that of opening up the vital communication between Hinduism and Christianity, so that new blood and also new chromosomes might bring new life to the Body of the Lord. This is a sacred action which culminates in Christ's sacrifice, but which is prepared at every moment, and reaped and offered at the appropriate time. But there, I can't explain myself as I should –yes, my function was theology.

[158] Sanatkumara: Mythical religious figure often referred to as he who imparts the science of self-realization.

(Cont.)

Kottayam, January 16, 1965

I stopped off at Kurisumala and then went on to Sabarimala, the sacred mountain of Ayyappan. Apocalyptic and fantastic. There were maybe three bags assembled for the Theophany of Light at the top of the hill. More impressive than the Himalayas in a certain way. True enthusiasm!

How I would like to write a theological book, *Indian Pilgrimages*, but I am a dreamer! I have to live, which means to suffer, and to write only if circumstances allow (and are not unfavorable).

A good conversation with Bede – more about Christian theology than Hinduism.

In the joy of the Lord, very fraternally,

Raymond

❖❖❖

Varāṇasī – Hanumanghat, March 9, 1965

My dear Abhiṣiktājī,

I will write to you in a few days. Finally I am beginning to have a more "regular" lifestyle – that is, "*chez moi*", and almost without moving. Good!

Concilium, the magazine in 7 languages)[159] has asked me who could be the correspondent in India for the news section – to give a theological background, of course.

They suggest I do it, but I am not very well informed, I would need someone else.

An S.J.?[160] Who? Britto?

I have to give them an answer immediately.

---

[159] International journal of Catholic theology.

[160] S. J.: Society of Jesus, or Jesuits.

If you feel inspired, please write to me.

My home awaits you,

Raymond

❖❖❖

Śantivanam, 13 March, 1965

My dear Raymond,

We haven't written to each other for a long time. How are things? I am particularly busy with the latest revision of my two books and am dependent on the letters and wishes of the publishers, which means that I cannot make any plans for this summer. I hope to be able to leave for the North at the beginning of May, but I am very afraid it won't be possible.

For 8 days I have had here with me the young Capuchin you met in Rome and Bombay, Tarcisius. He is really very likeable and open. He is remarkably happy in Śantivanam.

Unfortunately, he still knows too little and has never been open to a life of prayer that is neither sentimental nor rational. There would be much to do with him and, through him, with many others. It is the first time a local priest stays with me for some time and appreciates Śantivanam.

Now he would like us to hold a small meeting here after Easter with a few priests who are especially interested in training in seminaries and houses of religious formation. This would also pave the way for a seminar, for example on moral theology within the framework of Indian ethics and true Indian sociology. All this of course in a strictly private context, but the subjects must first be studied privately in order to prepare for the future and to present the ideas to the officials in charge, if necessary. I recently came back from Shembaganur, where the dean has an excellent training programme, for example.

Tarcisius suggests that this first discreet meeting could be held in the context of Śantivanam. Despite the difficulties, I believe he is right. It would be for around 6 to 8 participants, the most that the āṣram can hold.

Of course he would like you to come. I didn't dare promise him anything, since I don't know all your plans... What do you think? I would like it to be in the last week of April.

Tarcisius would be the ideal companion for the trip up to Gangotrī and this would do him enormous good. Unfortunately from here it is too expensive, otherwise he would easily get permission. Who could have hoped that he would be granted permission to stay here for 2 or 3 weeks?

For this meeting I would think of inviting: Britto and Alexis (from Bangalore); someone from Shebal, the dean, if possible; a Frenchman from Tiruchi-Manly, an OP from Nagpur whom I met in January 1964, very nice and open; perhaps an MEFS from Nagour (Carvalho), another Capuchin, and someone from Kurisumalai.

Let me know your reaction soon so I can decide before the 25th of this month.

In Domino

Abhisiktananda

❖❖❖

Varāṇasī, March 16, 1965

My dear Abhiṣiktājī,

I have just received your letter of the 13th and I hope you have received mine of the 9th.

I am very glad about what you tell me about Tarcis and completely agree with you.

I read a nice review of your German booklet together with mine and two others!

I think the idea of the meeting at SV[161] is very good. I advise you to go. Unfortunately I cannot take part because in April and May I think I will be in South America on an official government trip. However, please keep

[161] Śāntivanam.

this to yourself because you know what the world is like, even the clerical world. I think I will be back towards the end of May; and therefore ready to go to the Himalayas. A svāmi from here (Ānandāmayi *āśram*) would like to take me to Nepal on a pilgrimage, but I don't think he can wait for me now.

Bede writes to tell me that the Archbishop of Nagpur (*sic)* is very interested in continuing the meetings (with Cuttat, to give a name) and asks me if I would like to be the organiser. He wants to consult you too, of course, but fears you will find too many Jesuits there. I will encourage him but tell him that I won't be able to organize the meeting. After you (and even in a way even more so, since I don't even have someone to send to the post office) I am the loneliest of all and with the least means. On the other hand, it is worth it and if we want the Church to not stop here in India we must continue. What to do? The proposed meeting in Nagpur would be in August.

I am sending you a personal letter, and ask you send it back to me with your impressions and write to him directly if you think it's appropriate. *Messis quidem pauca, operari autem multi.*[162]

Nuccia is fine, but maybe we don't need to influence her. She is and wants to be European, but everything helps.

Sister Nelly[163] is here, but since she is no longer mother superior she hasn't spoken with me.

The Colloquium in Rome for next year will be: "Myth and Faith"!!! They absolutely want me to go and they have even talked about it with the Pope. *Me autem minui.*[164]

The real heat is about to begin. Our ecumenical meetings are continuing. Malenfant is a little like before. We celebrate our liturgy "crouched down" throughout the first part and I also try to encourage talking. A book for

---

162 The harvest is very small, but the workers are many.

163 Nelly Shanta (formerly Gariglio), a French nurse who left the Confraternity of the Little Sisters of Jesus to become a Buddhist nun; she was a faithful collaborator of Panikkar in India.

164 I am humbled.

intentions and intercessions, etc. I hope the epistle is read by a Protestant pastor and commented on.

Raymond

❖❖❖

Vārāṇasī, March 24, 1965

Dear Svāmi,

Thank you for your letter on "Concilium". It is not a question of giving news but of providing the *background* for the news. Good.

Here is the drawback of writing without a copy and by hand: I don't remember what we did with your essay "The secretariat for religions and the existing *kairos* of the Church"!

I was thinking of sending it to Concilium with your name, or anonymously, but I would need to know that it hasn't been sent elsewhere.

I sent your essay on the psalms to Dossetti[165]—with no reply. (Do you know the book by C.S. Lewis, *Reflections on the Psalms*? It attempts to answer your questions).

Tell me, then, if you think I can send you the article to Concilium.

No news for the moment. I am beginning to settle down into solitude. As soon as you know your plans for the summer, write to me. The Little Sisters have asked me whether I would like to go to Binsar to work (and celebrate Mass for them). Another pilgrimage, done well and without hurry, would perhaps be appropriate and good.

I will be free for the month of June and maybe also July.

You will have received my last letter of the 16th.

[165] Giuseppe Dossetti, former Italian politician who became a Catholic priest and monk. He was a trusted expert consultant of Cardinal Giacomo Lercaro and had a great influence at the Vatican II Council.

In osculo pacis.[166]

Raymond

❖❖❖

Vārāṇasī, April 4, 1965

My dear Abhiṣiktā,

Thank you for your letter of the 28th. How can I disagree with you – both concerning the monastic and contemplative life, and concerning "theological" meetings? Yet (and I am referring to the latter) the good is the enemy of the best. Asmouldering wick should not be lengthened.

I agree about chairing [the meetings] (and privately and personally finding the means to bear your expenses) but I cannot organize them. We are still a long way off. I have been told that everyone is in agreement about our seminar in Bombay.

I will leave here on Wednesday and on Saturday (probably) from Delhi to Rio de Janerio, via Moscow and London. If you have any other address to give me (write to me in Delhi) and a copy to Mercedes Panikker[167]…: … or c/o the Indian Embassy in Buenos Aires. I think I will be back here by July at the latest. Let me know your plans for a possible pilgrimage. The Little Sistershave asked me to celebrate Mass this summer at Vivek's in Binsar and to work quietly up there. I might go there in July if we arrange something together.

Have you received my *The Unknown Christ*?

In Domino,

Raymond

❖❖❖

[166] In the kiss of peace.

[167] Panikkar's sister.

Rome, Excelsior Hotel,
April 29, 1965

My dear Abhiṣiktā,

You have been in my thoughts and also on my lips very often.

I concelebrated (more than 80 people) on the night and day of Easter in Montserrat, with also Fr. Anselm (Enrique). I spoke at length with him and also with Don Estanislau, the hermit—a simple, openminded and wonderful soul (now my mother's *gurū* and the curator of her metaphysical anxieties). In Montserrat there is strong tension among the "younger" and more pastoral. The abbot confided in me deeply and would also like me to occasionally go and hold a retreat with them.

But the days do not pass without me realizing more and more that my place is in Varāṇasī.

The wealth and excess that overflow from the rich West (because there are poor people here too) is suffocating and one drowns in it.

Don Timoteu, secretary of the Episcopal Commission for the Liturgy, an excellent person, and French monk Don Domingos Sandriy of a foundation in Curitiba, an open minded and exceptional man who is seeking a monastic path for the West – which? And how?

My journey is twofold: cultural – huge ecclesial success at the university (profound conversations even with the Dominicans –but superficial with the SJs [Jesuits], since they have the pontifical Catholic universities and are busy with teaching and administration.

I want to come back soon, but I need one more month until July.

With all my heart,

Raymond

❖❖❖

Santiago, Chile, June 1, 1965

My dear Svāmi,

Received your two letters of Easter Tuesday and May 3rd. Thank you.

I want to return to Vārāṇasī soon but at the same time I know I must take advantage of this opportunity, do my duty, sow seeds and return as late as possible. I don't think I will be back, therefore, before the end of August, probably.

I am delighted about your booklet and the preface. I also understand you want to retire to Uttarkāshi. My regards to Jyotiniketan and everywhere.

My journey is exceptional and the angle from which I am able to consider things is unique (mostly secular); I am discovering another America—anti-Christian—and also an India-oriented one – theosophical, esoteric, etc.

……

... A church which makes a feeble but touching effort to pray. Ideas put forward: the 19th Century and the Vatican Council II together. A serious social effort in Chile. A West dismayed by excess and surplus. My theories on morality are confirmed: when one believes it is his duty to ask why, there are no longer any satisfactory answers.

The danger of evasion – for me at least – is strong, but if we drop the dichotomy "*amare caelestia et terrena despire*"[168] what is left? We are then invaded by the *terrena.* It is all very well to say (and I try to do it in any case) that I have renounced everything, even renouncement…

These days I am seeing the abyss of a bare life, a pure life for nothing, for doing nothing, without wanting to justify it through deeds (even good deeds). I have understood the Jesuits—like most: one holds oneself, maintains oneself because one functions, carries on, believes one is doing something and has a mission. When one is left without doing, without action, without having, when one has nothing to do with one's life but live it –*abyssus abyssum invocat*![169] – then the Spirit appears.

168 "Love heavenly things and despise earthly things."

169 "Deep calleth unto deep", Ps. 42:7.

I wish I could let it!

Very little is understood of anything I say in my lectures – which are, by the way, tremendously successful.

Veni sancte Spiritus! Et hoc quod continent omnia, scientiam habet vocis.[170]

Raymond

❖❖❖

Bogota, Corpus Christi, June 17, 1965

My dear Svāmi,

How I long to come home! And not because my life here is not interesting, pleasant, intense, fruitful and also comfortable (who could say the same, since I sleep on the floor in the luxurious rooms of the best hotels?)

(Cont.)
June 18

But because my *karman* pushes me to another kind of life: that of the bare experience of life and existence. It is easy to justify oneself – or to consider oneself – not for the good one does, for the "mission" one accomplishes. Then action or a form of living seeks to justify being, in place of being, pure "being" that flourishes in action or a given form of living. Is that clear?

(Cont.)
Sunday, June 20

I'm afraid not!

I didn't intend to write after this Latin American experience, but sometimes I feel the desire to.

The myth of development. True development.

170 "Come Holy Spirit! And that which containeth all things hath knowledge of the voice." Cf. Wisdom 1:7.

Pitiful underdevelopment: when one attempts to imitate, admire and realize that which is wrong. Here in Panama the impression is wretched. We truly must go back to a cosmic vision, otherwise the situation of humanity is desperate—and it has always been.

So our mission—we, the aristocrats of the Spirit, the *elite* of spirituality, oligarchs of true religion ...—what becomes of it?

I am writing to you a little at a time. Not just from day to day, but moment to moment. I have already given 45 lectures.

I hold on, I pray for you. There is nothing better than dying and disappearing. I have had some excellent experiences of anonymity.

I think about you a lot – and now that I have practically no ties on this earth you remain constant firm.

In Love,

Raymond

❖❖❖

Mexico, July 13, 1965

My dear Svāmi,

Let me know your plans and your movements, although it is possible that we won't see each other, since I probably will not be back until the end of September (it all depends on whether I have the money, time, etc. to wait for the conference on the History of Religions in Los Angeles).

I think about you a lot! It is an important experience, that of living solely for the sake of living, but not of doing nothing—without a mission, without work, with nothing ahead of you to draw you towards the mirage of the future. It is not even contemplation, but emptiness.

I met Fr. Lemercier OSB,[171] who wants psychoanalysis for all his monks. He does not want celibacy or monasticism to be justified as a mission to be fulfilled *for* others.

---

[171] Fr. Gregorio Lemercier, Belgian-born Benedictine prior of a monastery in Mexico.

I have sown some ideas that I believe are very important, but there is always an even deeper dimension. I see a difference between the individual and the person: the part of limitations destroys the former and frees the latter. The essence of the person is not the drop (surface tension), but the water. We will have to talk about all this.

Ah, if you only knew what the Church is like here! Truly poor (in every sense!)

Raymond

❖❖❖

Mount Saviour OSB, Elmira

August 7, 1965

My dear,

Thank you for your letter of 29/7 to New York, which I am replying straight away to tell you that you can use my name and anything else you want of mine.

So, the passport: ...

Father's name: Ramuni Panikker (died 1954)

Mother: Carmen Alemany

Marital status: (do you need to ask? – mystical marriage is not "civil" – therefore "single").

Home address: Bungalow 45, Varāṇasī. Work address: Department of Philosophy, BHU, Varāṇasī.

I came up here, to the monastery of Fr. Minard[172] after speaking with Mme Stokes[173] (by phone), to hold a kind of retreat (instead of in the Himalayas and Uttarkāshi!), since I have decided to take part in the conference on the

[172] Fr. Peter Minard, French Benedictine monk.

[173] Anne-Marie Stokes, French-born, living in New York, one of Abhiṣiktananda's correspondents. Worked with Dorothy Day and the Catholic Worker Movement, and also with the UN.

History of Religions near Los Angeles, from September 7th to 12th—and after that to go to Japan. So don't count on me returning until the end of October.

I'm sorry and it's hard for me, but I think it's worth it (literally). I need to have this American experience—which is not same as the European. I'm counting on you to help me complete it. It is wonderful when the Communion of Saints becomes a true Fraternity of Friendship.

You are reading *Informations* D.C., etc. and I don't even read the newspaper.

Mme Stokes is very nice. I met an American priest—professor at a university here, more syncretist than neo-Hindūism, but without wanting to be. Understandable reaction.

I can't say anything about this monastery yet.

"*Adoptionem filiorum perfecta*"[174] said yesterday's liturgy. I understand what this means: it is not I (who "receive" the grace (of sonship), but exactly the opposite: I *am* insofar as I am adopted (as a son) since there is only one generation: that of the Word....

Raymond

(Cont.)
Claremont, California
August 16, 1965

Your liturgical "adaptations" interest me a lot. Could we try to use the Viṣṇu Bhavan (Vārāṇasī) as a second step after Uttarkāshi?

The obsession with "morality" and the "subconscious" is always with me. This is why we have to "give up" learning and knowledge. The (rational) demythologization exasperates everything.

You still have not mentioned my English book.

If I try to justify my life, for what I have to do, it's easy: action which justifies and sustains being; but if I want to sustain myself without doing anything, with no mission, with no "neighbor" in pure being, then emptiness – *śunya* – is the only fullness. Is work (I am in America) a

174 "Full adoption to sonship."

type of alienation? (a substitute – *Essatz* – for worship as sacred action, without doubt).

My retreat (today is the first day) consists in going to the heart, a good concelebration (with brown bread) and staying in my room, practically "doing" nothing.

I would like to tell you many more things.

Talk soon,

Raymond

❖❖❖

Mount Saviour
Sainte Claire, 12 August, 1965

My dear Swamijī,

This is a letter of conscience, since no one is a judge of himself and it will help me to be humble, obedient and ecclesial. As for the subject, you will understand that it is difficult for me to talk about it with you, even though you will agree that I don't have many people I can consult and confide in.

The prior events are clear: 25 years of Opus Dei and now without *saμnyasa*, family, diocese; without even an external mission to draw encouragement from and make "work", but in the experience of being and nothingness.

In short, my friendship with (…) has for both of us turned into true love, not only human, but also natural. And six months of being apart has only made this clearer.

To explain myself better: I have just read Bishop Roberts' Introduction to "Contraception and Holiness"[175] which, among many other things, shows me once again the Manichaeism and latent dualism (in the form of a variously puritanical moralism) of almost all Christian ethics. I have just studied here once again the problem of the theological justification

[175] Bishop Thomas, unconventional English Jesuit priest and former Archbishop of Bombay.

of celibacy and find, with the exception of the eschatological argument, all the other justifications very weak, not to say erroneous.

To all this we can perhaps (I don't know) add the classic temptations against chastity.

In a nutshell, my problem of conscience is the following: to what extent can I cultivate a friendship that is true love? To what extent can the "spiritual" part be justified and must the "corporal" part be rejected? Isn't this Pharisaism? Or the paganism of courtly or romantic love?

If to all this you add my experiences with Hinduism and my thoughts on Âaktism, you can well understand my perplexity.

In addition, she feels passionate love and the fragility of innocence (as perhaps I do also).

Possibilities:

- End it all! I ask her to leave Vārāṇasī. But I cannot see that this would be fair to her, or good for me, or moral in itself. It seems to me that it would just give rise to the "moralism" that I criticize.
- Accept it all! I fear that in the long run this would lead to the loss of virginity. Can I run that risk?
- Distinguish the spiritual part from the corporal? This seems to me to be Manichaeism, pharisaic, artificial and dishonest.
- Avoid the issue, be cautious, keep the brakes on, try to deny reality, to emphasize the aspect of working together, of spiritual direction or apostolic activity.

But isn't all this to do with the prudence of the flesh – in the sense of St. Paul? Is it not deceiving oneself, living a lie?

- Pray together, without fearing intimacy (even human intimacy?), be a unit, a kind of spiritual marriage, and wait for further, positive development – a new experience and a new state of consciousness awakened everywhere.

Isn't this pride, presumptuousness? Or even unfaithfulness to my priesthood?

You understand my position. It is concern about honesty, holiness, commitment to Christ, faithfulness to a mystical experience even if it brings me to present the problem so bluntly.

Almost the entire retreat is centered around this issue; I see it without obsession and with serenity and joy, but also with the conviction that a solution by means of evasion would be cowardly.

Perhaps it is fear and lack of courage or old taboos that are still at work in me. You understand that for me and for you - and for her too - I feel ashamed and humbled in writing to you. It is a good humiliation but also, I believe, it is the last link that was missing from our friendship: we immersed ourselves naked at the sources of Mā Gaṇgā; now you also see my naked and sinful soul - with the immense desire to immerse myself in soul also in the Gaṇgā which leads to the far shore of the *saµsāra*.

Could the *advaita* solution that leads to the indifference of a Rāmaṇa be acceptable?

I think you understand me. It is not, I believe, a question of a crisis of faith (I burn!), nor of the "*femme*", nor of attachment or selfishness (almost the opposite), but only of the bipolar human experience of the One Love.

I will stay here one more month and probably be in Japan for another month. I spoke to the monks here – with revolutionary success.

I embrace you and thank you,

Raymond

❖❖❖

New Delhi, December 31, 1965

Happy and holy New Year!

We should have known that we would barely have begun to talk, despite 20 days of living together.

I have the impression that you also have been going through some substantial spiritual and attitude-related changes.

Even your attachment to the Church, which is both cosmic and at the same time historical, I see has evolved remarkably in relation to contacts and possibilities of radiation.

I am beginning to suffer from being pressured to go to the West (and when one thinks of the time and energy that is wasted—the Form has not yet arrived, though it seems it has already been approved, so therefore I will leave on Monday the 3rd or Tuesday the 4th), my brother, an invitation from another American university, the language problem (I have to decide! but what?), etc.

And at the same time I still think that Vārāṇasī as a "headquarters" would not be bad. The Lord will guide me, as He has so far.

In any case, I would like to come back in March if possible.

We must at all costs continue the liturgy – Sanskrit, etc.

I hope to leave on Monday the 3rd.

Much love,

R

❖❖❖

1966

Śantivanam, January 7, 1966

[...] India has a message for the whole Church. Only on the further side of speculation will the Church rediscover the essential truths freed from myth. We should not create new myths, at least, not if we can help it. Myth will probably always remain underlying the expression of experience. But Man will make use of myth as its master, not allowing it to control him.

In an atmosphere like that of Banaras, I once again experience the itch to think, to do liturgy. Is that a temptation?

[...] It is from Sanskrit that the liturgy and the Christian theology of India should come to birth.

[...] Exhausted by the journey from Banaras and with a bad cold, I shall need some days to recover.

...

Abhishiktananda

❖❖❖

Pondicherry, 18 January 1966

[...] *Last month*[176] *I understood all too well how Benares should become the birthplace of an authentically Indian Church. This is why it is very important that the bishop of Benares is an "openminded" man.*

...

❖❖❖

[177]Rome, February 14, 1966

My dear Svāmi,

My life in Rome is unthinkable. I sleep 3 hours a day! But what is happening, what is continuing in me is also unbelievable: total emptiness, complete surrender, absolute freedom, the experience of a broken-down identity between both faith and non-faith, God and non-God.

What more could one want?

176 Panikkar spent a fortnight in Vārāṇasī in December 1965.

177 Back to Rome and to his priestly life within Opus Dei.

On a less profound level I try to base a Christian spirituality on *advaita*, in my countless sermons, conversations, dialogues, lectures, etc. You can imagine what happens among those who understand a little…

Here I am like a fish out of water – but the air is also beautiful. Am I an amphibian?

The Church is truly the continuation of the Incarnation – in every sense. I see how these men of the Church gave their lives for it, but a little (I am inclined towards psychoanalysis) like how one consecrates oneself to the family, a political party, a noble cause, a job, etc.; that is, the dynamism, the background, the life is always *for,* for others, the justification of *being*, of life as being what one does, for the "mission" one believes one has. What is left when one sees the folly or, shall we say, the spiritual narcissism or the activism of such a position? I do not criticize. I take note and question myself. Do you understand me?

I embrace you – yes, because there is also a body.

Raymond

❖❖❖

On the train from Bologna to Rome
February 21, 1966

My dear brother,

I've been told your third book has just come out.

Fr. Barsotti has it. Yesterday I preached the new retreat to the community.

This time I really gave myself fully—as always—but also intellectually.

However, I fear that only 25% of what I am saying is understood.

The theme of the day of meditation was *The Presence of God* – according to *advaita* spirituality, of course.

I don't know when Barsotti is thinking of coming to India.

Concelebrated with Cardinal Lercaro[178] a Mass to collect 80-90 million lire for famine in India.

He then wanted to go to India to bring the money to Cardinal Gracias.[179] He listened to me and decided not to – so it seems.

The left hand must not know what the right hand is doing.

I have sown right and left, *"opportune, importune"*, a whole theology of salvation – which I will tell you about. I wish to return as soon as possible.

I hug you,

Raymond

❖❖❖

Śantivanam, Palm Festival (Rameaux),
April 3, 1966

[…] *Easter Joy. But like Christmas, Easter is less a past and commemorated event than an eternal or, rather, timeless awakening. The narration of this awakening and its liturgical anamnesis can no longer have the charm of the past. Everything has doubtless now returned to the ecclesial plan of essential awakening. Nevertheless, nothing that is said or accomplished ever completely fulfills it,* akhaṇḍa *and* asparśa,[180] *according to the formula that seems to me to define this situation well.*

Abhisiktananda

…

❖❖❖

[178] Card. Giacomo Lercaro, at the time President of the Vatican II Concilium for the liturgical reform.

[179] Oswald Garcias, Indian cardinal and later Archbishop of Bombay.

[180] "Whole, unbroken, entire" and "free of contact (with the phenomenal world), free of support, absolute".

Vārāṇasī, April 7, 1966

Good Friday

Thank you for your letter of Palm Sunday!

You can count on my discretion for everything – besides, I know hardly anything.

Uma left last week and Nuccia leaves today.

Shanta[181] is still here, for at least 15 more days.

Bynki also, and is living with me.

I read your text for the rite. I will talk with about it.

I am not thinking of moving from here, if I can manage to bear—and why? – the awful heat.

I have to work. I saw Cuttat when I passed through Athens, he is all for India and for you right now.

What news of Bruno? Write to Vereno,[182] or for Vereno—it will do him good.

I have been reading your *Sagesse Hindū* every morning (I haven't seen the other one yet. We willl talk about it.

I embrace you in the joy of Easter.

In these days Easter is being celebrated at the Viṣṇu Bhavan.

Alleluia

Giorgio[183] and P. Valayatil and Bynki are all leaving in a few weeks.

Raymond

❖❖❖

[181] Nelly Shanta; see note 145.

[182] Fr. Matthias Vereno, German-Austrian theologian, priest and svāmi, and Panikkar's friend.

[183] Giorgio Bonazzoli, missionary of PIME spent many years in India and then in Papua.

Śantivanam, April 7, 1966

My dear Raymond,

I am reading Cuttat's article in "La Mystique et les mystiques". The more I read his article, the more I think it is dangerous, precisely because of all this. It is right on several points, almost right in many others, and so the falsity of the general view automatically misleads. There is not an iota of true epoké or dialogue. Everything is initially considered and then judged from a Christian/western point of view (osmosis of the two). As I had already told him, his general view is biased: it aims from the start at a desired conclusion. It is this that steers everything, instead of being a de facto conclusion. Contrasts are emphasised and described precisely in view of this. I was reading the page on the "saint". He defines the saint and holiness in such a way as to support his thesis. This is all the more serious as the elements of these definitions contain many accurate characteristics which prevent the western reader (more than happy to receive satisfaction and reassurance at so little cost) from seeing that the real problem has not been touched upon. He observes that the easterner is incapable of epoké. But obviously the westerner is capable of epoké because he stops at eidos, and this does not concern the real values of his life. It is a purely intellectual view. The photograph may be accurate, like that of a sleeping person or a dead person. But "life" is left out. The easterner has no use for an intellectual epoké. In these vital problems he refuses to limit himself to the eidos. I am not saying that he is wrong to not question whether there might also be something he can receive from the West (in fact he receives plenty existentially), but his attitude should not be judged from the point of view of western values. It is precisely this discomfort that I feel increasingly while reading what has prompted me write this letter without delay.

In Spiritu

Abhiṣiktānanda

❖❖❖

April 12, 1966

My dear Svāmi,

I received your Sanskrit text and your letter regarding Cuttat's contribution. I understand your point very well, but this is precisely what leads me to press you to write in an objective and dispassionate manner your objective criticism. I think it is important. There is no point in having personal quarrels provided we get on a scientific level. I think what you say about Lacombe[184] and Gardet[185] is completely right and we should avoid another mistake of this type. If you want, you could send the copy to me and I could make my comments on it. I must confess that except for his synoptic scheme I have not read the text. I will try to do it as soon as possible. You will well remember that Cuttat and myself began our friendship precisely because of my sharp criticism against his conception of Yoga and his rather biased comparison with Hesychasm.

I am still reading your book and I enjoy it.

Abraham has asked me several times if you are supposed to be in the South during the month of May. I told him to write directly to you. He is really a wonderful fellow. We are having interesting talks with Shanta. In spite of all, the will of God is being done.

With my best wishes

Yours

Raymond

Forgive me for this almost official letter. The heat is exhausting; the work slow. I would like to finish "*Silence of the Buddha*", but I don't know when yet.

---

[184] Olivier Lacombe, French philosopher and President of the Catholic Center of the French Intelligentsia.

[185] Louis Gardet, French Catholic priest and historian.

My time passes, at least half of it, giving my life for my friends.

Always,

Raymond

❖❖❖

Śantivanam, April 19, 1966

My dear Raymond,

It is hot here also and I really don't have the strength to work. Or rather, the work requires a concentration that is no longer within my capacity. I finished the article by C. [Cuttat]. Impression confirmed. The Indian experience is requested to seek integration there based on viewpoints that will be more favorable to the contrasts here. The images are often excellent but the overall impression seems to me to be terribly "steered". On the other hand, the more you read this book, the more you realize how C. has been influenced by Guénon[186]*. Much more than the Hinduism that we know through śruti and long personal contacts, it is the Hinduism of the neo-Gnostics, as he says, that C. has in mind. A Cartesianized experience, with which it is barely possible to identify. Although converted from Guénonism, C. still remains obsessed with it, and this explains many of his reactions. In the end, the very last pages point this out, and Augustine is his guide as a Christian. But Augustine, personalist par excellence, does not represent the full Christian experience. All this is very serious, especially since the style and the dialectic are brilliant. And it is experts like this who will influence the Marella Commission.*[187] *Writing a critique on this is very difficult because, as I said the other day, it is all almost true; it would have to be discussed page by page. The best answer, I believe, is what V. [Vereno] asked from me—my two old books, in which I have tried to make myself transparent to the experience of India. I don't see how I could do anything else.*

---

186 René Jean-Marie-Joseph Guénon, French philosopher.

187 Cardinal Paolo Marella was president of a commission for the preparation of the Second Vatican Council.

Oṁ

Abhiṣiktānanda

❖❖❖

April 25, 1966[188]

My dear Mahātmajī,

Thank you for your letter which I have just received. I am delighted that Dominique is coming in December. *Deo gracias.* I will tell Abraham you're expecting him. He is an excellent man. He will be the ecumenical link here at BHU. I haven't had time to read Cuttat yet, but I consider, for the same reasons you mention, that your critique is important. So go ahead. You might well speak of his Guénonism. I am just finishing your book, *Sagesse Hind¥.* Sensational! Nevertheless, we must talk about it. It will still irritate (not necessarily in the same way as my book, however) many Hind¥s. Fortunately it is in French. I believe that we must now overcome an embarrassing exclusivism. Your sentence on p. 257 (halfway down the page) is significant. I don't think it should be argued that there can be nothing new and good outside the Church, as a historical reality.

Here at 43 degrees I try to work but… Ceyrac[189] has invited me to Changanachery to lead the Camp, but I am resisting. My cousin is getting married in Kerala one of these days (big family celebration), but I won't be going.

(Cont.)
April 27, 1966

Another thing: is there not a certain contradiction between (p. 266) knowing by tradition the experience of Jesus and note 28, where you speak of personal experience? I would be for the latter. Moreover, I believe in a kind of ontic experience, that is, at an existential (but not necessarily concrete) level.

---

[188] Panikkar sometimes wrote his letters in stages, over a period of days or even weeks.

[189] Fr. Pierre Ceyrac, French Jesuit priest.

I think about you often. I am living a twofold experience: the Hind¥ one and the modern one. It is excruciating – but I live in joy and freedom.

It has been more than a month since Uma and Nuccia left. Giorgio will leave in a few days. The Jesuit has also gone, Bynki is leaving soon, the Little Sisters next week.

We have a Vedic *vajñā*[190] nearby! 100 cows [have been paid].

Always.

Raymond

❖❖❖

Vārāṇasī, May 2, 1966

Dear Abhiṣikta,

I have just finished your book. I say again: excellent! – despite the fact that the famous summary did not turn out well. For an English translation, in my opinion, it would be best to avoid certain irritating phases, *"piarum amicum indianorum."*[191]

(Cont.)
May 11, 1966

I can't understand how this letter has stayed here.

(Cont.)
May 21, 1966

I have received your letter dated 18/5. Thank you. I agree with you. I was not criticizing you.

Finally, at the end of the month I will be leaving for a fortnight for the meeting of the Academic Council of the Ecumenical Institute of Jerusalem (best keep this to yourself).

---

190 Hindū ritual performed in front of a sacred fire.

191 Dear friend of Indians.

Here with 44° I am working constantly on *The Silence of the Buddha* and I am "passing" through the overwhelming and terrifying experience of atheism. It is formidable – in an etymological sense!

Everyone has left except Bynki – here, like me, he finds your liturgical text better for *pūjā*[192] than for *jajñå.*

Once again there are rumors of an *episcopatum,* but I am convinced that it will not come and now I am determined to refuse.

Any news from Fr. Bruno? So are you writing for *Religions and Society* – or not?

And what about Vereno?

I understand you very well—yet you talk about raising awareness in the Church, but it must also be immunized.

In the faith of the Spirit that blows strongly,

Yours,

Raymond

Abraham has written me a wonderful letter. Give him my sincere greetings.

❖❖❖

May 18, 1966
Eve of the Ascension

My dear Raymond,

It is clear that our books (i.e. yours and mine) are not intended for Hindūs. Our immediate role, whether or not we have sought it, is to sensitize Christian thought to the riches that await here, and to prepare Christians for dialogue. We have to be among Hindūs, physically and spiritually, so as to gather the honey for the Church and pass it on, while awaiting the hour when Christians as a whole will be capable of gathering it for themselves.

---

192 Worship ritual performed by Hindūs, Buddhists and Jains.

... For my book I had 8 months of correspondence with my publisher: style, technical terms, ideas, everything was combed through page by page. Often the footnotes are simply replies and justifications for sentences I refused to change. More than once I became discouraged and on the verge of giving up, but as it is the book has had a good response...

... Śantivanam is really difficult to keep going. And in order for Fr. Dominique to be installed there, it is absolutely essential to find him a companion; for if the upkeep of buildings etc. is hard enough – even unbearable – for me, what will it be for him?

Abhiṣiktānanda

❖❖❖

Vārāṇasī, June 28, 1966

Dear Svāmi,

Thank you for your book *La rencontre* which has just arrived. I will read it right away.

We have not written to each other for a long time.

Griffiths writes to me that he is very impressed by your books, which he considers to be the most profound work on the subject.

Sister Marie Louise[193] has written to me about her plan to ask you to bring together at Âāntivanam all those who are interested in this "Hind¥-contemplative" approach.

I went to the meeting of the Academic Council of the Ecumenical Institute of Jerusalem in Zurich. I stopped off in Rome and I am no longer part of the Opus Dei – butsooner or later I will be welcome, or accepted,as a priest in this diocese of Varāṇasī. *I would rather you keep this news to yourself.* I will tell you all about it when I see you.

I am working intensely on the *Silence of the Buddha*; but it is more than a year now that this silence – the ontic Silence of God – has been working

[193] Sister Marie Louise Cutinha, of the Franciscan Sisters of Mary in Bangalore, who later founded Ananda Āśram near Śāntivanam.

in me. It is so bright, but as soon as one talks about it, it vanishes…

The rains have begun. University starts next week.

In the union below and above everything,

Raymond

❖❖❖

Vārāṇasī, June 30, 1966

My Svāmi and brother,

With a fever of 39° I have just finished reading the work I already knew but not in book form. It is all good. Naturally, I would have liked a more in-depth theological and scientific study, but it is not the character of the book, which is therefore easy to read. I think it does enormous good. As you can see (despite those such as Fr. Lambert O.C.D.,[194] etc.), there is no turning back. One position has been decisively gained. Now it is time for the next one. I congratulate you. The fact that the book is easy to read is a brilliant idea.

Here is where I stand:

1- God is neither a substance nor the Other. I cannot summarize my *Silence of the Buddha* for you, but, well: prayer, dialogue, contemplation.

2- Must we insist on preserving our creatureliness, our contingency? It would be terrible to never be (God). Here on earth, "*in regno dissimilitudinis*"[195], fine, but to seek still to preserve "the human condition" in God? I have come a long way on this point. I'll talk to you about it.

3- Even though in Zurich I opposed in the name of India—at least to Culman, Cogar and many others who regard the *Heilsgeschicht*, salvation history, as the essence of the Christian message, I have to acknowledge that all of Christianity is found precisely in this. The Christian faith is specifically a historical faith. Now the problem is to see whether there may be a deeper dimension of faith which is not historical, and therefore

[194] Father Lambert of the Order of the Discalced Carmelites. See also note 317.

[195] "In the realm of dissimilitude", St. Augustine, *The City of God.*

not specifically Christian. But are the two experiences compatible? Am I being clear? I don't think so.

I'll leave you in peace. Did I tell you that Poonja came to see me and that we truly "connected"? If you have his address let me know, because I would like him to be invited to the meeting that the Quakers are organizing next year.

I haven't left the house for three days, I hope my fever breaks. Too much effort, emotions and trials.

In the nothingness of everything,

Raymond

I wrote you this letter on impulse, prompted, also by impulse, to ask you for a favor. If you are too busy, PLEASE don't worry but just send me the manuscript back. I'll find someone who can put it into good French for me. As you can see, it regards correcting the review enclosed herein. Thank you.

❖❖❖

Yercaud, July 5, 1966

Dearest Raymond,

[...] My book "Sagesse" has brought me several moving testimonies from contemplatives (Christians), who for the first time in their life have recognized their own experience in the experience of the Self which I described in the first chapters. At noon today I received another shattering letter on this subject. Even John of the Cross, said the writer, had not been able to explain so clearly the interior stripping and the passage from the "self" to the "Self" (words used spontaneously by this person, despite the shock given to his rational mind). How clearly it spells out the universal – and so, Christian, Catholic – value of the advaitin *experience. What is needed above all is to invite Christians to make this experience their own. Otherwise the theological conclusions that we draw for this experience will continue to seem to them unthinkable or blasphemous. It is therefore only in a deepening of contemplative awareness in the Church*

that there lies any hope of the ecumenical and "pan-ecumenical" passing beyond that we need. That can never happen at today's ordinary level of awareness. Until then there is only the loneliness of the prophet (have you read sometimes Moïse by Vigny?[196]) and the impossibility of being at one's ease anywhere except with those few people who have an intuition of this "trans-cendent" level – like travelling faster than sound, or escaping from the earth's gravity, to use physical metaphors.

In Domine

Abhiṣiktānanda

❖❖❖

July 15, 1966

[...] You cannot be torn apart in the depth of your soul, as we are by this double summons (from advaitin India on one side, and from Revelation on the other), and by this double opposition (from India and the Church, in their ritualism, their formalism and their intellectualism), without being lacerated even physically.

... Yet another letter from Europe strengthens my conviction that the advaitin experience underlies all true mysticism, Christian included. All these letters in short say this: "Your book has taught me nothing new, but for the first time in my life I have understood what was happening in my soul". That consoles one for many things, doesn't it? It is just one more proof that we are not heading in the wrong direction.

[...]

Abhiṣiktānanda

❖❖❖

196 Alfred de Vigni, 19th Century French poet and novelist, renowned for his works of historical content. The poem *Moïse* speaks of the loneliness of Moses.

Varāṇasī, August 23, 1966

My dear Svāmijī,

This is what happens when you want to write a nice long letter: you never write it!

Since my return I still haven't fully recovered. I constantly have a fever, but I am living an enormously intensive life.

Here is my programme:

I will leave on Sunday for New Delhi, where I will stay until 1/9. Then I will go to Jerusalem for the Ecumenical Institute and continue my pilgrimage until November, when I think I will comeback here. Buenos Aires, UNESCO (Government Representative in India), Cambridge (Teape Lectures:I am preparing my *mahāvyākhyānām bhāṣyam.*[197] How I would like to comment on them to you! I refer to 5: *Ekam advitīyam,*[198] the first one.

An entire book should come out of it, which I would like to show you later. I have finished *The Silence of the Buddha* but I am letting it sit until I get back, maybe in November.

Uma is back and Nuccia also; Shanti has left and Enrique Aguillar has written to me that he wants to come again to do in Buddhist spirituality what you do in Hindū *saṃnyāsa.*[199] Have you heard from Bruno?

Until the 1st: c/o 13 Prithviraj, New Delhi

Until the 7th: c/o St. George College, Jerusalemme (Jordan) POP

Until 16/9: c/o Roux, 127, Barcelona (Sarrià) and this will be my permanent address for the rest of the time.

If you want any errands run in Europe…

[197] Comment on the great Vedic sayings in which the Vedanta doctrine is condensed.

[198] "One only without a second", *Chandogya-upaniṣad* VI, 2, 1.

[199] Total surrender, one of the four stages of life.

I hope this letter finds you still in Śāntivanam. I will be with you on your pilgrimage to Uttarkāshi. Congratulations for your book on the Ganges. I have sent it to Hans Urs von Balthasar,[200] to Monsignore here, to the Viṣṇu Bhavan, etc.

In the hope that I will see you again before the end of the year. Always in true union,

Raymond

Vereno tells me that you told him you had given me *Mysticism and Mystics* to review. I haven't received anything and I knew nothing about it, but if you like…

❖❖❖

New Delhi, August 30, 1966

My dear Abhiṣiktā,

I am back in Delhi, leaving for Jerusalem. It costs me a lot to move and I would like to be alone, quiet, working and living in Vārāṇasī. But … I think, for example, that my presence at the Academic Council of the Ecumenical Institute of Jerusalem is important, since I believe I can be the tool that ensures this new initiative does not fall prey to "Christian provincialism".

You are right with your comments and advice. In recent times I have "suffered" – in the deepest sense – the unspeakable. *Advaita* on one side and *śūnyatā*[201] on the other.

I will be speaking a lot about mysticism in Cambridge. You know, also, that Murti does not reject my interpretation of *tat tvam asi.*[202] He simply finds it superfluous since, in his opinion, it would not add anything to

[200] Hans Urs von Balthasar, Swiss Catholic priest, considered an important Catholic theologian of the 20th Century.

[201] Void, emptiness, nothingness, structural condition of reality and all things; represents the ultimate reality in Buddhism.

[202] "Thou art that", expression of the relationship between the individual and the Absolute.

the traditional interpretation. He has to say this, of course, since this also touches on the Trinitarian mystery.

In November I will have to teach a course here on "The Being of God and the God of Being" – one of the problems of my book on the Buddha. I see that I see – and not only one, but the enormous difficulty is integrating all of this into life, daily life and Christian life.

I am tempted to withdraw into mysticism. Here in Delhi I have so many people to meet and I don't see anyone. Renouncing Renunciation is hard.

All the best,

Raymond

(Cont.)
August 31, 1966

I have received your letter of the 24th. Thank you.

I am sad to hear about your bad experience in Varāṇasī. Forgive me.

So, in principle, to Jyotinikatan. We will see because I have to teach a course at BHU in November-December.

❖❖❖

Mar del Plata, Buenos Aires

September 22, 1966

My dear Svāmijī,

I know you wrote to me in Barcelona, but I had already left. I think I will spend the next week on retreat in Montserrat and then I will receive your letter.

The Jerusalem Institute is doing well and the Lord uses me to broaden horizons and open up new perspectives. Here it is the UNESCO for Oriental Studies in Latin America and here also the Lord is making full use of me. Because He wants me to take part in so many things; I who would like to be quiet in "my" temple in Hannumanghat![203]

These are wonderful experiences. My health is better. The "post-conciliar" world is in a profound crisis and the "clergy" are very "disoriented".

I am aware of your choice and I accompany you. I would like you too to accompany me on my pilgrimages. Today I escaped to write a little and pray in my room. What a life is ours!

A beautiful conversation in Beirut with the Dominicans.

God willing I'll be back around November.

In Madrid, a friend of mine - a secular priest - would like to know a Taizé-style monastic way and also an interconfessional one. Intercommunion is at the door …

In your Uttarkashi retreat, please think of those who are hidden in the experiences of active life.

Forever yours

Raymond

❖❖❖

Westminster, October 16, 1966

My dear Abhiṣiktā,

.. Can the place be important? Murray came looking for me and we spent a day together. I think about you so much! I have a great desire to escape to the Himalayas, but I still have to wait until November before I can come to Varāṇasī.

Here I am staying with M. Warren;[204] I believe that hospitality implies more than accepting a room, so today, Sunday, I attended the service in

[203] The *ghāt* on the Ganges where Panikkar was living in a building above a temple.

[204] Max Warren, general secretary of the Church Missionary Society (CMS) and British missionary statesman.

Westminster Abbey and also received Communion. It has come to this.

I embrace you in friendship and in Christ,

Raymond

❖❖❖

Uttarkāṣī, October 29, 1966

Dearest Raymond,

... We are approaching a real nuclear explosion in the sphere of religion. The "countdown" was started by Pope John. A chain reaction will spread from Rome to the ends of the earth. All that is so-called "religious" consists of what is "superimposed",[205] *of a "man made" sacred intended to take the place of the truly Sacred, unperceived because of its translucidity (cf. The Ten Picture of Zen).*[206] *Oxygen flasks inside a sealed cave, ignoring the fact that the air,* vāyu, *is everywhere. You have that terrible phrase on p. 63* [of the *Unknown Christ*] *that Christianity is "provisional", only of this world. True, but then ...? It only has the consistence of* māyā*??*

We have to prepare the world for inevitable disintegration; to make the divine, sat [Reality], *felt in its immanence and transcendence, in its translucidity.* Apertis oculis attonitis auribus, vacate et videte.[207] *Otherwise this explosion will be a disaster. Too soon. Atomic power in the hands of Neanderthal man, as Grousset said, I think.*

How "different" and "clear" everything looks from the mountain top! How petty men's thoughts and deeds appear! It is more than ever the hour of the Upaniṣads. *Both world and Church need them.*

---

[205] In Indian thought all conceptualization about God or the Self is a 'superimposition' (*adhyaropa*) upon the ultimate Reality, which is beyond all concepts.

[206] The "Ten Oxherding Pictures" of the Zen tradition, a series of short poems and drawings illustrating the stages of the path to enlightenment and the return to society to bring wisdom and compassion.

[207] "*Apertis oculis attonitis auribus*" (eyes open, ears attentive): from the *Rule of St. Benedict,* verse 9 of the Prologue; "*vacate e videte*" (be empty, and see): from Ps.45:11: "Be empty, and see that I am God."

It is through Vedānta that the atheist will re-discover the mystery of God and discover the ecclesial puruṣā.[208]

In the joy of the Light,

Abhiṣiktānanda

❖❖❖

Varāṇasī, November 14, 1966

Svāmijī,

Thank you for your two letters. I hope I will have a chance to speak about the first.

From December 8th to 12th there is the conference on Indian philosophy, but I don't think I will go. I won't even go to Jyotinikatan for now.

You are therefore always welcome to come here for 2 or 3 days, as you wish.

Raymond

❖❖❖

Gyansu, November 18, 1966

Raymond,

As I have already written, I see no possibility of salvation for the Church (as far as secondary causes) except in an advaitic renewal. The traditional myth no longer comes from any direction (Hindū, Christian, Buddhist). Reason argues all its own conclusions. The only possible foothold is the experience of depth, aside from all symbols, myths and concepts. The Council has chosen to adapt to the modern, "coller au monde" *mentality. But its modernization is still too superficial, remaining in the* antarikṣa[209] *of pity, of thought and again of the myth that one is trying in vain to revive.*

---

[208] Universal Man.

[209] Intermediate space between heaven and earth.

The urgency of India's mission is not to superficially convert some poor local populations to a "mythical" and external Christianity, but to allow the Church to rediscover the advaitic *dimension that is deep inside it. This is why there is absolutely no hope for the Church of India as it is. The most advanced of the hierarchy, who are already far ahead of the main bulk of the troops, are hundreds of leagues behind us. Among them are a few scattered friends who, for better or worse, follow us more out of affection than out of any deep conviction. Which of them has accepted this twofold and non-dual belonging which alone allows true osmosis?...*

... These are a few reflections, too concise, but which arise here with special clarity and strength in this emptiness and inner freedom that come with solitude and silence.

In deep friendship

Abhiṣiktānanda

❖❖❖

Cont. of November 21, 1966

I have just this moment received your letter of the 18th.

Please tell me your Kareli dates, as exact as possible, as I understand you have given up Calcutta and therefore Vārāṇasī.

I was thinking about going to spend a day or two with Murray—unfortunately every day I am busy (and I have a course to teach at the university, it seems). [...]

In the One

Raymond

1967

Delhi, January 3, 1967

Dear Abhiṣiktajī,

Difficult to write even a couple of lines from Vārāṇasī! Anselm, Josep, Prajåpati, Harvard. The Cercle Saint-Jean-Baptiste in Paris wants me to talk about incarnation and Hinduism. It is Père Daniélou,[210] and it would not be good if I stop in Paris and refuse to talk.... So, another change. (Incidentally, why can't Charlotte Vaudeville open her mouth without slandering me whenever she gets the chance?).

I spoke for two days about contemplation with Murray, Mary and Heather. Apart from personal issues we talked about a possible new direction for Jyotiniketan:

1- Union, so to speak, with Śāntivanam, i.e. "inter-confessional", giving also morc space to solitary prayer, etc. and to meetings and hospitality, without harming the "solitary".

2- Greater openness towards Hinduism and Islam.

3- Possibility of relocating

4- A few small details regarding schedule, etc.

I wouldn't mind talking about it with you to see if the proposals might be merged together. Murray is going to Ceylon in February, I am not. Could you not come by Âanivanam? Since everything is still concerned with more personal problems we would have to be very discreet, that is, even if you write to him, don't tell him that I am the one who is "pushing" now. As you mentioned on the bus to Delhi, maybe it would be enough to write and invite him. I am convinced that changes need to be made at Jyotiniketan and that now we have the chance to do it.

---

[210] Jean Daniélou, French cardinal and Jesuit.

I could do it for us!

Until the 17th I will be at the address below, and afterwards: Center for the Study of World Religions, Harvard University, Cambridge, Mass., USA.

This morning I am following the silence of Tuesday until 3 pm, when I have a meeting with Gita Ram and then with Ramachandra,[211] etc.

The Cambridge Brotherhood tells me that here in Delhi nothing is being organized with the Roman Catholic churches for Unity Week – What is going on?

According to Prajāpati I speak of "original guilt" and not "original sin".

Would you like something for Paris? Is it possible to send a Gangotrī to Ramachandra?

Poonja of course did not come to Vārāṇasī (until the 30th).

Everyone says Christmas this year at the Viṣṇu Bhavan was better than last year.

Give my greetings to Fr. Dominique.

In the joy of Epiphany,

Raymond

❖❖❖

Śantivanam, January 6, 1967

[...] my rhythm of life gets slower with age.[212]

... And here especially I feel lost for having so many things to take care of...

... What we need here[213] *is a return to the Christian monastic sources starting*

211 Vinoth Ramachandra, Sri Lankan theologian, today Secretary for Dialogue & Social Engagement of the IFES (International Fellowship of Evangelical Students).

212 The effort of putting the āśram in order after four months of absence weighed heavily on Panikkar, but he had to prepare for the visit of the French ambassador and his wife and for the arrival of Fr. Dominique soon afterwards.

213 Referring to India in general, and here specifically to Jyotiniketan, where in those days they were seeking a new formula and where Abhiṣiktânanda declared "neither

from the traditional saµnyāsa. *The evolution of Christian monasticism must begin here. Otherwise it will have to stop.*

[…]

Abhiṣiktānanda

❖❖❖

Barcelona, January 25, 1967

For 15 days my mother has been dying in a clinic here. Does one have the right to artificially preserve life? She would like to be left to die, but the family and the doctors are against it.

The mystery of pain. I would have many things to say, but I would not want to be like those writers who take advantage of such an experience to indulge in "interesting" and "profound" reflections.

Life is cruel.

[…]

Always in the One – who IS not!

Raymond

❖❖❖

Śantivanam, February 6, 1967

[…] *This year I have found the return to Śantivanam too much of a burden. Uttarkāshī and the mountains have made too deep a mark on me. I mean that what I would like is either the genuine solitude that I have there, or else a chance of effective work in a receptive environment. But this half-*

Gandhi, nor Voillaume" (in reference to Voillaume's ideal of the Fraternity of the Little Brothers of Jesus).

way house, which Śāntivanam has been since the beginning, is useless.

[...]

Abhiṣiktānanda

❖❖❖

Harvard, February 14, 1967

Dear Abhiṣiktānanda,

Thank you for your letter. My mother died on the 2nd, the Purification of the Virgin, the Feast of Light. I left for Barcelona as soon as I arrived in New York. It was necessary for the whole family. My mother "relived" the whole book of Job. Quite extraordinary. I would like to tell you about it one day.

You see how we agree on cosmic acomism – the only true one?

Very disappointed in my brother Salvatore (matters of self-centeredness, envy and money).

Unfortunately I did not have much time to spend with Mme Stokes. John Cole came to see me at her house.

My regards to Fr. Dominique.

I well understand the attraction of Uttarkāshi. Don't worry, I'm not leaving India! The Ganges calls me. Everything here is wonderful, but I am not comfortable. It is all so perfect that each one is a self-sufficient, windowless monad. And my course so far is an unprecedented success. I would like to be able to write about it one day. I think it might give us a greater understanding, but I do not live to write. Speech is a sacrament, writing a technique. This is why I speak about the "Christian Interpretation of Other Men's Religiousness".[214]

Very bad news about the famine in Bihar – and not very reassuring about the elections.

---

[214] Title of the course held by Panikkar at the University of Harvard in 1967.

This here is the "opulent society". I feel lost. I act as if I were an Indian who has never left his village, but it is not an act: I am dumbfounded – and marked for life by India.

Yes, Lacombe's presence as chairman of my conference was annoying, but I think on the whole everything went well – also with Danielou.

I have just read *Car je t'aime, éternité* by J. Sulivan, a "laborer" priest I knew, but I still have not seen *Le plus petite abîme.*

Minoru[215] is here. I only saw him for an instant.

(cont.)

Saturday February18

The secularization and desacralization of Christianity is fierce here. You know Harvey Cox[216] – *The Secular City.* He is a professor here.

I have to hold a sort of Good Friday retreat for the entire faculty of theology (Divinity School). An Indian and Hindū professorhere considers my *Unknown Christ* as completely orthodox from the Hindū point of view; he wonders whether it is so also from a Christian point of view.

(Cont.)

February 22

I am reading *The Future of Belief* by Leslie Dewart.[217] Very interesting! I am not at this point yet – but the battle of India is waged here also.

Raymond

❖❖❖

---

[215] Minoru Hara, Japanese Indologist and scholar of Sanskrit and Buddhist literature and philosophy.

[216] American theologian of the Harvard Divinity School.

[217] Canadian professor of philosophy and religious studies.

Harvard, March 14, 1967

Dear Svāmi,

Thank you for your letter of 1/3.

Here at Harvard I am a monk. For example, my Tuesdays spent in silence, prayer and contemplation are purer here than in Vārāṇasī. Today, as is very often the case, I have not moved, or even left my apartment (one room). I live in solitude.

My course is going well and I would perhaps like to dedicate myself to it even more. On Good Friday I will hold a retreat at the Divinity School, something unheard of according to what they say in this environment, where piety is suspicious, confessionalism forbidden, faith outdated and the "scholarship" placed on the altar.

I have no contacts, so much the better! I am happy to be like this. Since my mother's death I have felt negative loneliness for the first time.

I would like to know what has happened in Kandy.[218] I hear that ICI – [issue] 1/3 – has published your photo and mine.

It seems that Ananda (Aguilar) cannot stay in Ceylon and will return to India. They have again called for applications for the teaching post at Varāṇasī, but I doubt they will give it to me.

I understand your yearning to escape. I miss India, but I live in total *śūnya*.[219]

I met again L. Dewart, the (lay Catholic) author of *The Future of Belief.* He's not bad, but still Greek and western. I convinced him, though, that there is a consciousness – and not a conceptual one.

The Church here, the churches, is the institution. It is the sign of life and also distinction.

Do you know R. Vachon[220] (La Salette)? An exceptional man.

---

[218] Roman Catholic diocese of Kandy, Sri Lanka, seat of the national seminary.

[219] Void, emptiness.

[220] Robert Vachon, Catholic priest of the religious order Missionaries of the Shrine of Notre Dame de La Salette, France, and one of the founding members of the Intercultural Institute of Montreal, which published many of Panikkar's articles.

Resos[221] means "prayers" or rather "the act of prayer".

Desig means desire.

My regards to Fr. Dominique.

The week after Easter I plan to go for a retreat at Mount Saviour Monastery OSB.

With a hallelujah—to the heart,

Raymond

John Cole appears to be very ill.

❖❖❖

Harvard, April 11, 1967

My dear Svāmijī,

I completely agree with your letter – with its spirit (I'm not talking now about SV or JN[222] – I will tell you about it) and your advice to me to live and die and not to do anything or found anything.

This is what in my vocation and in my meagre strength I try to do. This is why I have never wanted to found anything, neither with Fr. Barsotti, nor with Bettina, nor with anyone. Do you remember when you told me about a group in Varāṇasī? I have just finished a 10-day retreat at Mount Saviour Monastery OSB. Very good.

Always in abandonment,

Raymond

This is also the theandric and tragic personal line of Shanti-Uma-Mara, etc.

In the Spirit that blows.

❖❖❖

221 Çatalan.

222 Sāntivanam – Jyotiniketan.

Harvard, April 16, 1967
Third Sunday after Easter

My dear Svāmijī,

I need to speak – not to write; this time you are the victim. Yesterday from 7.30 to 12.30 at night—a "historic" conversation in German with Köster,[223] prof. of the N.T. here, and the famous Basel-born theologian F. Buri,[224] on my *Hinduism as a Religion,* my Christian belief regarding the myth of original sin and that of Prajāpati, etc., etc. It was a true revelation for them. You know Maritain's[225] influence on natural mysticism, which conditioned Lacombe, Gardet, Lubac,[226] Cuttat, etc. I tried to give a completely different interpretation.

Yesterday, again, from noon to 6pm—a charismatic meeting: a hundred nun teachers who during a 6-week vacation go to provide help and social service in one of the slums in Boston. I watched from a corner and kept quite. Two "negroes" and a local girl "informed" and "initiated" them into the environment and culture of these poor, black, Puerto Rican populations. Extraordinary! They preached evangelical simplicity and the freshness of immediate experience to these "beguines", who then asked questions. We must learn, listen, not preach; we must collaborate (even in abortions!), serve, simplify, not judge, not be surprised at anything, etc. Immediately there was a concelebration with the priest who arrived for Mass. The first part with all friends and then the priest's sermon and mine. The nuns began to pray and talk… There was singing with a guitarist. Sensational.

I got home at 2 in the morning. Today, instead of getting up at 5 am I got up at 5.45 because at 7 I had a parish Mass, sermon etc. A priest who is a tenant here offered to take me in his big car. He wanted to talk to me: 8 years in the seminary and 10 as a priest, but he is determined to leave the priesthood for reasons of celibacy. He would like to get married but

223 Helmut Köster, professor of New Testament and Early Christianity at Harvard Divinity School.

224 Fritz Buri, Swiss theologian.

225 Jacques Maritain, French Catholic philosopher, who was raised a Protestant, became agnostic and eventually converted to Catholicism.

226 Fr. Henri de Lubac, French Jesuit priest and cardinal, considered one of the most influential theologians of the 20th Century.

do it properly, without rushing, after a year or so, and he asked me what I thought and whether it would be possible not only to remain in the Church as a good Catholic, but also to "function" as a priest. A few days ago the student chaplain here left after a farewell sermon, followed perhaps by an abandonment of the priesthood... He wanted to be "honest" with himself. Now that he has made the decision to leave he is much more at peace, etc.

I could write 3 novels, as you see, just in one weekend.

Myself, I burn ... that is all!

I have been thinking about what you said regarding JN. As I have already written to you, I agree with you in theory and principle. But good is the enemy of best. You see your French essays, your correspondence, your Europeanism; I see my travels, the poverty of my languages, the impression of escape, etc. JN is English, etc. Solution? Do nothing until the conditions are right? Where possible, personal vocation – which is always linked to failure since, like existence itself, it is real in that it is bound to death (Enrique? Shanti? Mara? Uma? ... I know nothing about it all!), but here this is not possible as long as one remains aware of the hiatus, the inadequacy; isn't it better to get as close to the ideal as possible?

To you – and to me – this is clear, but should we not encourage and help the evolution and transformation of structures as much as we can? Symbiosis must be at all levels.

An old Chinese verse says, "the bird cries; the mountains are all the more silent".

Long interruptions for the visit of John Britto, who is finishing his thesis on Rāmānuja. It has evolved well.

In total surrender,

Always,

Raymond

I enclose a typical (but uncommon) "reaction" to the Good Friday retreat.

❖❖❖

Śantivanam, April 25, 1967

[...] I have just come back from Shembaganur. Tomorrow I will definitely be going to Pondicherry. This pace is too much for me.

Abhiṣiktānanda

...

❖❖❖

Śantivanam, May 26, 1967

[...] The mystery of realized interiority is the only solution for the Church in these times, because the disintegration is increasing dangerously and the tendency is to demythologize, remythologize, remain on the surface, anantarīkṣa, *rootless...*

...India is moving, the young clergy is moving. More than ever there is a need for discreet and humble leaders. Those who possess something must consent to be the leaven that apparently disappears inside the dough. An initiative by Europeans, which could seem to succeed in the beginning, would be the basic obstacle to real further development.

[...]

Abhiṣiktānanda

❖❖❖

Śantivanam, August 14, 1967

[...] Fr. Francis (Āchārya)[227] *is strongly urging me to act, to arouse opinion, to prepare and put forward new formulas which would enable the Indian Church to come out of its coma. But as everyone else is holding back, I*

[227] Belgian Cistercian monk (born J. R. Mahieu), later affiliated to the Trappist Order.

think that I also will go into hibernation – at Uttarkashi, for example. I no longer have the physical strength or vitality for such an enterprise.

[…]

Abhiṣiktānanda

1968

June 14, 1968
Abhishiktānanda
Uttarkāshi

Dear Svāmijī,

Just a word to tell you that I have written to Francis Åchārya accepting your kind invitation and assuring him that I will come to Bombay.

I will arrive in Bombay on Saturday 20th early in the morning (2:40am) and go to Vinayalaya.

Looking forward to seeing you again after such a long time and hoping to havc thc opportunity for a nice chat.

Yours always,

Raymond

❖❖❖

Gyansu, June 21, 1968

My dear Raymond

... The most urgent need in the Church today is precisely the realization that this experience is the very foundation of being. Everything collapses, and it cannot be otherwise. And if this realization does not spread among Christianswe can only despair of the future of the Church. The dislocation that is taking place right now will surpass anything history has ever seen. Theology of Faith, of Religion. This is the most essential thing, not the demolition of notions that have no value other than pragmatic.

I am just rereading Dewart. Wonderfully illuminating, although he perhaps identifies modern thought a little too much with a philosophy that is too specific to be "common". In the last chapter he plays with words: if Is *must be avoided in discourse about God – and this includes also God as non-being – it is impossible to say anything about Him and speak about Him: the silence of the Buddha! Possible, but also somewhat sophisticated in the order of Aristotelian-Thomistic notions! I would like, most of all, for a review of this book to extend this thought with a reference to the Vedāntic experience. Vedāntic (and Buddhist) experience is beyond any conceptualization, and this Dewart seems to reject. There is the act of pure consciousness, the source that can still be reached by the world through the* AHAM[228] *itself. But everything he says about Man's evolution towards deeper "consciousness" is excellent. He therefore goes further than Teilhard,[229] although Aurobindo[230] saw even deeper still, and it is this alone that will save the Church, if you know what I'm saying. The essential thing seems to me more and more to encourage those who "think" to open up to this fundamental plane of being. Only then will they be able to "see" without blinking the* saµsāra[231] *of all conceptual formulations throughout history. But certainly, in most of his book Dewart is an excellent awakener to this non-dualism of God and being (if you will).*

*I am happy that you are coming to Bombay.[232] This meeting could be very important. It is a matter of deciding the main themes to be worked out in the Church – to prevent it becoming "the grave of God"! Above all I should like to see some structures coming out of it which would be able to guide the "*aggiornamento*" – a "brains-trust", a study group, an official commission, call it what you will, but something with authority [...] Still better – and this could happen – a group of priests, not just specialist, but men determined to apply the new principles in their personal life and ministry, and to do so now. The other day I had a long talk with*

---

228 The Self. The I.

229 Fr. Pierre Teilhard de Chardin, French Jesuit priest, theologian and philosopher.

230 Śrī Aurobindo, Indian philosopher and poet.

231 The ever-changing phenomenal world and the cycle of birth and death.

232 The preparatory meeting at the National Seminar, which took place in Andher, July 28th.

Patrick [D'Souza].[233] *He would be the man to lead it* [...]. *Something on the lines of the Mission de France.*

[...] Here I am totally isolated from the world (I heard about the riots in France only through a letter from N.Y.!). Age makes itself felt, strength and vitality diminish year by year. It is time to withdraw. The calls that now come to me are coming too late. (...) The time for enthusiasm has passed.

Abhiṣiktānanda

1969

February 14, 1969
To Abhiṣiktānanda
Gyansu

My dear Svāmijī,

A meter of snow—the road is paralyzed here too. I am here with the "flu. I've been here since February 1st, but I have only left my room to go and teach across the street (and to the church). A hermit's life (sick for the moment, but I'm getting better).

I don't know if you like receiving letters from abroad. If you let me know I could also write to you from Vārāṇasī.

This time I am sending you an article of mine for publication before the All India Seminar. Since this is a sensitive topic I would appreciate your opinion, your comments, corrections, etc. To avoid postage costs you could send the text to Varāṇasī and your comments directly to me as soon as possible (if you have the time and opportunity, of course – otherwise just send me a line so I won't wait for your comments). This is a sensitive topic; it is important to say things well, but also not to hurt anyone unnecessarily. Thank you.

[233] Patrick Paul D'Souza (1928-2014), bishop of the diocese of Varaṇasi, to which Panikkar was to remain incardinated for the rest of his life. The two were united by a deep bond of mutual respect, friendship and affection.

I am thinking about you. In Rome I saw Scrima (and I am beginning to think you are right). The environment in general is very heavy.

No other news at the moment.

With all my heart,

Raymond

❖❖❖

Gyansu, 25 February, 1969

My dear Raymond,

Your letter arrived only yesterday. I am replying straight away. It is not at all difficult for you to write to me here nor for me to answer you from here, since your Indian name is clearly written on the envelope. I find your article excellent, although, as always, it is beyond the comprehension of the majority of potential readers! But it is still acceptable. Not too harsh, in other words. However, the word kairos will mean nothing to more than 10 people in India! [...] these are details. You will also be criticized, as is often the case, for only presenting the problems and not offering solutions. Rightly, people should be made to understand that the time has come to be themselves and not mere recorders or useful machines capable of doing exactly what has been inscribed in their mechanism, in the manner of animal instinct. No liturgical adaptation will be valid until the priest and the assembly have understood that mass is an act which must be performed anew each time. Changing the shape of the censer, offering flowers, or sprinkling the celebration with Oœ will not get us very far, and this is what discourages me about the current liturgy, so shallow both in its promoters and in its opposers!

I like the first part of your presentation, but are you not to a certain extent confusing the "incarnation" of the Church with "constantinization"? The Church could have incarnated in India without affecting the political structures, etc. In fact, while the Church has done practically nothing to incarnate here, it has sought extensively to constantinize (institutions, etc.), and if it has not succeeded it is because Indian society has not accepted the transplant (institutional, not spiritual) that the Church has sought to perform here. We must be realistic. Agra[234] *is one example that shows us that as a whole there is no awareness of the problems, even among intelligent people. A society cannot be transformed against its will except by totalitarian methods. The only useful method is, to put it in vulgar terms, innovation (communist cells). We must form within the Church "germinative" cells of tomorrow's Church. Achieve, through the seminary, the possibility of creating advanced groups which do not judge or condemn anyone but which go forward. This is the idea behind all my proposals for Andheri*[235]*. If we manage to obtain the study group and the pilot seminar, for example, the rest will follow in its own time. Why don't you finally settle down in India in this time of irreversible renewal, now that the ideas that ten years ago made us look crazy and dangerous have won their case throughout the Church? Beginning this autumn we will be in dire need of a pilot structure capable of running the show from a theological, spiritual and liturgical point of view. The KK Institute is solely intellectual. An ā©ram with real skills, which neither Fr. Mahieu nor Fr. Bede are able to provide with the very poor elements around them (they themselves aren't sufficiently free mentally and spiritually). Behind all this necessary renewal there is a difficult theological problem. You have come up against it repeatedly, and it is by no means resolved Is it resolvable?: the oneness of the Church in religious pluralism. When we express our convictions, it is concluded (with satisfaction or horror, as the case may be) that Christianity is relative and that there is no reason to preach Christ to Rāmaṇa nor to continue the sacramental practice for its own sake (I summarize, but you understand). The only way we can push for the Vedas to be accepted is by defining a solid Christian theology of the Vedas. The theological and spiritual basis for a much-needed renewal is lacking terribly. Hence the need to form groups, "cells" which will produce, germinate together this theology and this spirituality. Practically speaking, to do all this we would probably need two centres, one with you, the other with Klaus. Tony de Mello*[236] *(Andheri) has to be a part of it.*

234 The Church of Agra, in Uttar Pradesh, was built by the Jesuits in 1598, under the order of Muslim Emperor Akbar who, however, never converted to Christianity.

235 Refers to the Seminary in Andheri, Mumbai.

236 Fr. Anthony de Mello, Indian Jesuit priest and psychotherapist, writer of many spiritual books

I don't know any other men of great stature. If we attended the national seminar, we might perhaps find them. Bhatt would be an example of this. Among the women, Sr. Grant - there are some fantastic projects for renewal in her congregation. I will soon have an opportunity to discuss this. Articles like yours help to awaken people, but first of all we need to focus on the well-guided avant-garde intelligent spiritual groups. Only from these will come inspiration and renewal. I will leave from here between March 15th and 25th for Delhi, Jyoti, Ranchi and Allahabad and return between April 15th and 30th. Bettina, Térèse and Maria will be coming to Jn [Jyotinekatan] for holy week, I think. In Delhi I will go and visit Sr. Grant who, with Rodericks (and no doubt others), will be working until March on organizing the regional seminars in view of the national one.

My revised memorandum for Andheri will be published by P. Jonas, CMI, Bangalore, hopefully soon. Where will you publish your article? I think I will show it confidentially to Sr. Grant. (Before I send it to Vārāṇasī, as you have asked me, I will type out some copies). It could possibly be included as an afterword to the memorandum, ne pereat statim![237]

Think about all this and answer me as soon as you can. We must not miss the kairos, but trust in the spirit, moving at the same pace, neither ahead nor, most of all, behind (late). I had planned to leave on March 25th, but it seems Klaus would like to meet with me earlier to correct the draft of Rencontre[238] *in English. Better to write to me in April at Jn or if you are in a hurry c/o the Brotherhood, as the mail takes an awfully long time to leave from or arrive at Kareli.*

In Domino

Pray constantly for physical and spiritual strength.

Abhiṣiktānanda

❖❖❖

[237] "Lest it immediately perish."

[238] *La Rencontre de l'hindusme et du christianism,* later published in English with the title *Hindu-Christian Meeting-Point.*

Gyansu, March 8, 1969

Abhishiktānandajī

My dear,

Many thanks for your letter and your comments. I have just reread the article after your suggestions and will be sending it to Patrick [D'Souza] to use as he pleases. I think he had *Clergy Monthly* in mind.

You are right in your observations. It is difficult to avoid words sometimes if one wants to write briefly. Your point about incarnation and "Constantinization" seems to me very important.

In agreement with Patrick, you can use it as you wish.

I stayed only one day (round trip) in NewYork and it was impossible for me to see A. ST. [Anne Stokes]. A pity! During Holy Week I will spend some time at the OSB's Mount Saviour Monastery.

I am very glad to see how things are finally getting started in India. I received news from Varāṇasī that the meeting with Sivaram will take place in April. Klaus seems to be pleased with his meeting. I am very happy that your book is coming out in English.

Malenfant writes me very nice letters (for him, at least). Mons. Rossano[239] is almost convinced of our point of view.

I have written to Mara to get in touch with TH. and M. in Allahabad, especially if she has to leave India. I will think of you during your stay at Jyotiniketan.

Let us hope that the Seminary takes an act of faith in the Church. I agree about Bhat. I think you will go, at least for this "recruitment" (fishing, one might say), since I share your opinion regarding the future. You will have heard about the meeting of the Indian Theological Association in Ranchi. I think one more battle has been won.

[239] Pietro Rossano, Italian bishop and theologian.

The New York Times has covered the whole Illich affair[240]. I have immersed myself in the *Upaniṣads*, as my course and seminar are on the *mahāvākyāni*.[241]

With all my heart and in the light of Easter,

Raymond

❖❖❖

Jyotiniketan, April 6, 1969
Easter

I discussed at length in Ranchi, Allahabad and Delhi the possibilities of a pilot seminary, a study group and suchlike. Everyone is convinced. What we don't have are available men. We are at an impasse. If we had specific plans we could get them accepted in Bangalore. But the useful men are all busy...

... Amalorpavadass[242] reproaches me for keeping aloof, but how can I cover the enormous distances of India and make up for the letters that get lost?

[...]

Abhiṣiktānanda

❖❖❖

April 13, 1969

Dear Abhishiktānandajī,

Easter peace. Thank you for your letter from Jyotiniketan. I am thrilled about your festivities. You alone with a group of holy women.

---

240 Refers to an article written by Fr. Ivan Illich, entitled "The Vanishing Clergyman", in which he argues that the days when full-time celibate clergymen rule the Roman Catholic Church are numbered.

241 The great Vedic sayings in which the Vedānta doctrine is condensed.

242 Rev. Fr. Duraiswami Simon Amalorpavadass, Indian theologian who played a vital role in the revival of the Roman Catholic Church in India.

I think the atmosphere must have been truly Pentecostal. I am with you in spirit.

I spent Holy Week at the Monastery of Mount Saviour. I had a good time. Yes, I sent "The Alternative" to Patrick, but I've had no response. I hope he will do something with it.

I am so glad that you will be going to Bangalore for the seminar. It is needful. I am also convinced that your presence is far more important than mine. My job is to think about the theological implications and to inspire or stimulate people to build this theology that must be lived before it is written about. You know well that I am always willing and ready for anything.

The transformation of the Church takes place at a deep level and you can understand that any small changes in the liturgy will not stop us from acting deep down.

Illich was supposed to come here tomorrow, but he will come on May 10th—and still we know only the half of it. Unfortunately I didn't get to see A. Stokes, but I share her opinion that the situation here is quite bad (albeit providential).

Naturally, I plan to finish the Vedic texts this year. It will be my work when I return to India in July.

You know that we are in full protest here. I hope it is all very positive.

I don't think I have no desire to come and be in India.

Chettimathan is still here but you will see him in Bangalore. I have also seen Douglas Steere.[243] Next year he will travel through India and perhaps another meeting could be arranged.

How are Bede and Śāntivanam doing?

I think about you a lot. My book on *mahāvākyani* is not finished yet, but my course is going well. The *Upaniṣads* are truly extraordinary.

Always,

Raymond

❖❖❖

[243] Douglas Van Steere, American Quaker ecumenist.

Gyansu, June 25 1969

Dearest Raymond

[...] *I regard Bangalore*[244] *– and this is generally agreed – as a very important stage in the awakening of Church here. The Church realizing itself as the people of God, no longer only as the hierarchy.* [...] *Not a revolution, of course. Many of the contributions in the meeting were shoddy, made by people whose main goal was to be heard. However, reports and conclusions on the whole excellent, going far beyond the pettiness of the discussions. The conservative opposition was very talkative – as in the* [Vatican] *Council – but the votes showed clearly that they were not in a majority, far from it. The fundamental options were passed with big majorities even if it had to be through amendments. I left Bangalore feeling very optimistic. There is still much to be done; but we now have an excellent starting point.*

... Above all, as I constantly repeat, we need a renewed theology. The youth is calling for it, and needs it urgently to escape from the crisis. But here team-work is essential. Individuals alone are useless.

Despite the slogan "Work is prayer" a very strong emphasis was placed on real prayer [...]. *I got very large majorities for two amendments, one calling for āśrams of pure "prayer and silence', the other for a liturgical renewal in depth, drawing on the values of Indian interiority. Besides, in his opening address* [Cardinal Pignedoli] *placed unexpected emphasis on "the Indian Church" as above all a community of prayer, on monastic life and on small āśrams to be available in many places. Now that there are going to be such centers, I am sure people will come to them, for many are desirous of being initiated into this real Prayer.*

... I am enjoying my solitude after being on the road twice for six weeks already this year. I have no plans at the moment. I wish for long months of silence...

Abhiṣiktananda

❖❖❖

[244] The seminar was held at Dharmaram College, Bangalore from May 15-25. Abhiṣiktananda contributed largely.

July 10, 1969[245]

[...] *I have just received Concilium 46. I have read your article [Métathéologie ou théologie diacritique].*[246] *I at once began a long letter, but it soon turned into an article, and I don't know when it will be finished.*[247] *So just a hasty word.*

I am absolutely in agreement with your principles, those of Rahner,[248] *etc. However, this number of Concilium is more devastating than any of its predecessors. Total overthrow of formulas and structures. I agree that there is no way of avoiding it. But what a crisis! Comparable to the passing over of primitive Christian experience – expressed in mythico-apocalyptic terms and largely dependent on inspiration and prophetic freedom (...) – to its expression in terms of Greek knowledge and Roman law. What saved the Church then was the deep spiritual experience of the "Fathers". That alone made possible the faithful translation of the Gospel and Acts in terms of the four Councils.*

But that is not the point that interests me today. The disputes between Christianity and the modern humanist world are merely a local squabble. Christianity remains the only religious alternative to western humanism. That is why the protests, like the call to order, fail to touch our "depth" here. Paul,[249] *Bultmann*[250] *and Garaudy*[251] *belong to the same world. What is emphasized in your article – indeed this is your greatest contribution*

[245] From James Stuart's book, *Svāmi Abhiṣiktānanda. His life told through his letters*, ISPCK, Delhi 1989: «One of the very few theologians—perhaps the only one—who according to Abhiṣiktā addressed the problem was his friend Raymond Panikkar. They had exchanged thoughts for ten years. He had welcomed Panikkar's book, *The Unknown Christ of Hinduism*, and thought that his friend had written more courageously than he dared, for example, in *Sagesse (Saccidånanda),* ch. 5. The letter reproduced here shows his determination to pursue the truth wherever it may lead, no matter how unpalatable the conclusions may appear».

[246] "Metatheology or Diacritical Theology as Fundamental Theology" (1969).

[247] Probably the article, "Archétypes religieux, expérience du soi et théologie chrétienne" (1970), published in "Intériorité".

[248] Karl Rahner, German Jesuit priest and theologian who, together with Henri de Lubac, Hans Urs von Balthasar and Yves Congar, is considered one of the most influential Roman Catholic theologians of the 20th Century.

[249] Paul Tillich, German-American Christian existentialist philosopher, religious socialist and Lutheran theologian.

[250] Rudolf Bultmann, German Evangelical theologian.

[251] Roger Garaudy, French philosopher and politician.

to the international conference of theologians – is your constant reminder that there are other cultural-religious universes besides the Semito-Greek world of the Mediterranean. This is the representation that is so sorely needed in the new Commission, much more than Schillebeck and Kung. You are perhaps the only one who could have said the thing (because in the East also who is aware of the depth and gravity of the problem?.

The passage from Jewish to Greek Christianity involved a dangerous bringing to birth. It succeeded chiefly because there was no other religious alternative, and humanism, despite Seneca and Cicero, could not take the place of the "religions" for the common man. But here? There is an absolutely adequate religious alternative. Hinduism is capable of responding at least as well as Christianity to India's religious needs, even in modern conditions. But that is not all. In being born into the Greek world it was a matter of transmitting the Christian experience in terms of Knowing. Here it is a matter of expressing it in relation to the fundamental experience of the Self.

Can Christianity stand up to that? The whole salvation-history culminating in Christ presupposes a substructure of psychological dualism. India certainly accepts dualism as an aspect, a moment, in the quest for salvation. You have very well shown that Christ and I©vara [God manifested] fulfil an identical role in the two systems; but my conclusion from that is that, in an Indian interpretation of salvation-history, Christ shares the transitoriness of the world of manifestation, of māyā. Finally he disappears [...] He may be useful in awakening the soul- as is the gurū- but is never essential and, like the gurū, he himself must in the end lose all his personal characteristics. No one really needs him. [...] Whoever, in his personal experience has discovered the Self, has no need of faith in Christ, of prayer, of communion of the Church. (..).but a koinonia that is reduced to any kind of church, what sense can it have?(...)

The reformulation of the Trinitarian mystery is also on the agenda in Europe, and in the first place, the abandonment of all that implies triplicity. But here, much more than that is in question. What is the meaning of this unique Son of God? For an advaitin "anubhavī" [one who has experience of advaita] Christ can only be the ideal in human terms (i.e., at the level of manifestation), who has best actualized the mystery and the experience of the AHAM, which is not-two! [...] The Son, the universal mūrti [image] of God; the Sprit, the universal śakti [dynamic energy] of God. When the ātman-brahman is discovered in the sarvamidam [all that is] and in the depths of the phenomenal aham, there no longer remain any points of reference in the advaita of being, by which to set bounds to mūrti or śakti...

Will the transformation of Christianity into Vedāntin formulas leave to it any other reality than the (provisional) reality of the cults which have succeeded each other on the soil of Bharat? And if Christianity cannot be expressed in the religious-cultural terms of India without dissolving away, then it is not catholic. I do not see how one can escape from this dilemma. [...] All this is the result of your article, and indirectly of the others.

Abhiṣiktānanda

I may have to go to Delhi for a couple of days between the 20th and the 30th. If by any chance you will be going we could meet at the Brotherhood ...

❖❖❖

Vārāṇasī, August 4, 1969

To Rev. P. Le Saux

Gyansu

My dear Abhiṣiktānanda,

Here is my "argument" against Hacker, but this time without the contentious tone. I would like to publish this article soon. If you could give me your opinion, your criticisms, etc. I would be very glad. I would like the manuscript back as soon as possible.

Forgive me if I don't add anything else right now.

In union above intelligence,

Yours,

Raymond

❖❖❖

August 9, 1969

[...] It is this question of theology which most stirs me up at present. I regard it as the most pressing of all – first in India, and then for the whole Church. How can one bring it home to the would-be theologians and liturgists that in their articles etc. they only touch the surface of the problems? Who has the idea of a dialogue from within? ...

[...] It is only from long acquaintance with the Scriptural texts – and a corporate acquaintance – that a truly Indian liturgy will emerge. Nowadays people think that they only have to use the word saccidānanda etc. to make a prayer Indian!

[...]

Abhiṣiktānanda

❖❖❖

October 23, 1969

[...] Here is the important document of a project described in a letter to Patrick D'Souza and which could have been realized at Jyotiniketan.

❖❖❖

Jyotiniketan, October 24, 1969

[...] it is clear that catholicity has much to receive from India, and that it will happen not through svāmis but through the Christians of India. Up to now it has been a period of drought, but as with Elijah on Tabor, the little cloud heralds the monsoon. As long as that which is now about to germinate finds the right soil and a good gardener....

Abhiṣiktānanda

❖❖❖

October 29, 1969

My dear Raymond

I received your note to Zeither. The problem of the formation of the clergy seems to be attracting attention in general. I found here two questionnaires to be completed in view of the Bangalore meeting, which risks in any case being too numerous to be effective.

I am in the process of trying to understand the "secular priest", i.e. a man committed to marriage and a secular profession, who at the same time is in charge of the Christian community. My contact with Murray has convinced me at the same time of the sacerdotal value of the "couple" in the case of the married priest, and also of the terrible limitations imposed by the children on his freedom for the Kingdom and the apostolate. My experience is only of the "monk-priest', the only normal type in the Latin Church in recent centuries. Even with regard to this I am not sufficiently in touch with other people to be able to see what ought to be done in present circumstances for the renewal of priestly formation. I have insisted on the values of contemplation, of poverty, of initiation into Hindū tradition. But how? In fact, can this be carried out? Years ago, I proposed my "pet scheme" of a Pilot Seminary, but I cannot get further than general principles.

Your notes are too concise for me to be able to comment, and then in any case it would be a long article, so I don't see what use it could be right now.

I would like, nevertheless, to go back to the idea of the pilot seminary and put it into effect so that we might allow fundamental experiences.

Abhiṣiktānanda

❖❖❖

Gyansu, December 5, 1969

My dear Raymond

... To my translation of Prayer I have been recently tempted to add a final chapter, "In Spiritu et veritate",[252] *which would express in clear and non-symbolic terms the charge of the high explosive contained in this essay, demythologizing the language used through the book, and pointed (what else could one do?) to the experience of Rāmaṇa and Yājñavalkya*[253] *in all its purity. But who is ready for this strong dose?*

Yesterday I received an invitation from Canada, from a Christian yoga group near Montreal, for two or four weeks in June-July to give weekly sessions of initiation into Vedānta. They say that "yoga" (what do they mean by that?) is spreading more and more – yoga groups conducted by svāmis which are now leading Christians astray from their faith. "Christian yoga groups" which have fully made their own the Vedāntin experience (I am interpreting slightly) are needed to counterbalance this influence. Even though people quote Déchanet[254] *as an authority, they have the impression that Déchanet is too "sectarian" (to use our term) a Christian. This could be very interesting, but a journey to America would also mean a journey to Europe, and I should be caught up indefinitely ... On the other hand, I have grave doubts about the depth of all this. They want a Vedånta adapted for westerners, the sort of thing that is freely dispensed by the svāmi commercial-travellers in Vedānta. I have just replied that sessions of spiritual initiation into Vedānta lasting one or two weeks are for me absolutely inconceivable. In any case, the monk is not called to go running around the world.*[255]

252 This essay, entitled "Le chrétienen verité", is printed at the end of the French edition of *Prayer* (*Eveil à soi- éveil à Dieu*) and the Italian edition (*Risveglio a sé, risveglio a Dio,* Bergamo: Sevitium, 2011).

253 Yåjñavalkya was the great *ṛṣi* [seer, enlightened person] of the *Bṛhadāraṇyaka-upaniṣ ad.*

254 Fr. Jean-Marie Déchanet, Benedictine monk and author of *Christian Yoga*, etc.

255 Here we should include an important note, which was added by Panikkar himself: "Around 2 months after this letter we had a long conversation on this subject when he came through here (Varāṇasī). At times he was, on account of his lifestyle, not very knowledgeable of the modern-day human phenomenon in its entirety. I drew his attention to the fact (in itself worrying) that in Varāṇasī there were hundreds of young and not-so-young men who had come from Kathmandu or Rishikesh in search of a "path", a "*guru*". I asked Abhiṣiktānanada whether this phenomenon kept him awake

I confess, however, that I myself, more than anyone, find it difficult to see how this pilot seminary could be organized. To me it would essentially be an initiation into vedānta-paramārthal *through the Upaniṣads, etc. What ortho-doxy or what ortho-praxis would emerge from it? That is, what theology? What cult? What moral? What structures? Even more than the history of forms or demystification, how would the evangelical nucleus emerge? The good news would be something other than this infallible act... which is the act by which man owns his true identity in fullness and total freedom. I know that, as it says in Concilium 48,*[256] *Jesus neither teaches nor legislates; all that is theology and law derives from the impact of his* kérigma[257] *on widespread culture and psychology, but here again is the fundamental problem:* quid de Ecclesia?[258] *Without a doubt the Church is the only spiritual (or religious, in the best sense) alternative to the closed humanism of the West, but in the Hindū or Buddhist world of fundamental experience, what is its "utility"in carrying out this all-encompassing act of orthopraxis?*

Abhiṣiktānanda

❖❖❖

at night, he who was presicely called upon to be an *ācārya*. His very curt reply that he was not interested in practising a "cheap" *vedānta* showed how far-removed he was from the modern-day mentality—with the pace of life today, however, who is able, except on vacations, etc., to afford the luxury of long years of study and experience and in India? This in itself was a very complex problem. He was in a way wary of this new world, he felt he would never be a part of it. But did he have the right to turn away from it, to refuse a cry for help? Then he agreed to talk about it, and we came to a conclusion that put everything in balance: he would be willing to be an *ācārya* for international groups, in serious sessions held in India. His last reflection that "the vocation of the monk is not to run around the world", did not just come from him; an influential friend of his had specifically told him this, without, of course, taking intoaccount the heartrending cry for help that was directed to him or the *ācārya* aspect of his vocation. All this is the reason why I had insisted on this aspect in our dialogue".

256 Cf. the magazine *Concilium.*

257 *Kérigma* (Gr.):proclamation.

258 What about the Church?

Gyansu, December 11, 1969

Dearest Raymond

... The interest that I arouse is restricted to a very limited circle. My withdrawal to the Himalayas perhaps adds a mythical touch to my personality. In any case, I cannot imagine where you have "fished up" this idea of a commemorative volume.[259]

As I said to Murray, when he tried to get me invited to the West, it would be a betrayal of all that I stand for—solitude, silence and monastic poverty. I have no more sought solitude than Amos sought the role of a prophet, but once placed in that position, nothing else remains for me to be a hermit for good, and not a mere salesman of solitude and monastic life.

... Regarding the proposal of a pilot seminary... I am terribly overwhelmed by events. Some years ago I dreamed about this pilot seminary, with the idea that in a Gandhian type of āśram there could be an initiation into classical India, so vital for the development of the Church here.

But now we have to rethink the whole conception of what a priest is. While gladly accepting these new points of view, I feel myself absolutely out of my depth. I am incapable of the mental revolution required to share these new categories well enough to help others to find their way in them.

The monk represents the Eternal... but normally it is not at all his responsibility to show others how to experience the Eternal in the temporal... The perfect Christian monk, this is the myth, like that of becoming a monk to save oneself, such a common old argument, as if the desert were necessary for salvation. I do not think it is acosmism that is the myth; acosmism is projected onto the mythical background out of fear of the body, of the world, out of fear of losing one's identity, of a guilt complex. This acosmism seems to me to be the essential aspect of the monastic vocation. The staretz[260] *is the fruit of monastic acosmism, in Christianity as in Hinduism. But it is a fruit that is not sought after. Since it was introduced as an object of research and effort, everything is*

---

259 Some of his friends thought that the occasion should be suitably marked, but this aroused his vehement opposition.

260 Spiritual leader or holy man (in the Russian Orthodox Church).

falsified, "cosmism" gnaws at acosmism from within, like a worm eating away at a plant.[261]

Abhiṣiktānanda

❖❖❖

Varāṇasī, December 16, 1969

My dear Svāmijī,

Thank you for your two letters. I will reply to your very valuable critique of my article. Thank you very much. There are not many people here to talk about all these things. I must meditate on your words and I plan to do so tomorrow, but I didn't want to put off thanking you and writing to you immediately.

I will arrive in Delhi on the 30th; I think I will see James Stuart[262] and Murray too, and there is a lot of work I have to do (visas, etc). I will leave on the 31st morning for Europe. The only way we can see each other would be if I leave a day earlier, but it seems almost impossible. Here this time my life has not been very quiet, at least outwardly. How many times have I thought about Gyansu!

The *Gāyatrī*[263] and the Lexicon[264] will take up a lot of my time when I get back, but I think it's worth it!

It is absolutely right that you start publishing here in India. I will start doing it also.

---

[261] These reflections were provoked by reading Panikkar's article "The Problem of Monastic Aggiornamento", in Monastic Studies, 1969, previously published in Catalan, "La problemàtica del''agggiornamento' monàstic" in *Visioni attuali sulla vita monastica*, ed. G.M. Brasó, (Montserrat 1966) .

[262] Fr. James Stuart, Anglican priest and member of the Cambridge Mission Brotherhood in Delhi.

[263] *Gāyatrī:* famous verse from the *Ŕg-veda* (III 62,10) considered the sacred mantra *par eccellence.* Here Panikkar refers to the anthology *The Vedic Experience, Mantramañjari,* to which he initially gave the title *Gayatri.*

[264] Panikkar had planned to compile a dictionary, which, however, he never completed.

Talk soon. I hope to write you again this week,

Always,

Raymond

❖❖❖

Gyansu, December 19, 1969[265]

My dear Raymond,

First of all, Merry Christmas to you and to all those who are with you, Bettina, Carmen, Shanta, Maria, the Little Sisters, Uma and Nuccia, if by chance they are there too.

However, I am also writing to you about something serious, and it's a pity I don't have time to talk with you about it in person. You know what I did to help Murray stay here. In particular, I have sent him a Dutch (I think) priest who has a great desire for āśram life and would be excellent, I am sure, to help start an ecumenical āśram, while they wait for another Indian (Pinto) to join them, maybe next summer.

Well, today at midday I received a letter from Heather, on behalf of all three, which amounts to no less than blackmailing. The gist of it is this: If I do not take charge of the Poona business, which means, first of all, several months at the beginning and then a long period every year, and the promise to always on call, they will abandon Poona and leave India, leaving me to take care of it all.

I find this simply unacceptable.

1) I am not able to team up with Murray. We are both too terribly personal. Like you, I can help if needed, and I think I have done so more than it was my duty to do. But I cannot make any commitments to him. Besides, my ideal, though it is very close to that of JN, is nevertheless quite different. I would only agree to give up my present solitude if it were impossible for Indians, who are adequately qualified from the point of view of the

265 Abhiṣiktānanda deeply felt his isolation at Gyansu, where there was no friend at hand with whom he could talk things over. He could only write to Panikkar, who was soon to be leaving for Europe, and share his concern about this and other matters.

language (vernacular, if not Sanskrit), to present me with a truly workable plan in the Hindī-speaking country.

2) Poona is too far away from here. Unlike Murray (whatever he says) I don't have American money to pay for air travel from one end of India to the other. As I get older I am finding it simply exhausting to travel. My last trip in October left me worn out for weeks.

- 3) Poona is in Marathi[266] *country. It is absolutely impossible for me to dedicate myself to this new dialect. You will say: isn't it the same for Murray? Yes, but he has no choice, it seems. English will have to be the language of the* āśram, *and this itself reduces its possibilities. As I have said before, I will only leave my current solitude for something that is totally compatible.*

So it becomes clear that when Murray speaks of "joining" an ecumenical āśram, *it means that it is I who have to take responsibility for it. I cannot accept this blackmail. I will simply not answer, especially because I would not want them to receive my reply for Christmas.*

What Murray wants for the moment is simply that I go and spend at least eight days at Jyoti while this priest is there (January 4th to 11th), then wait at Jyoti or somewhere else while he goes to Nagpur, then Bangalore from the 15th to the 20th, and then that I accompany him to Bombay Poona to sort things out with the Anglican and Catholic bishops, and the matter of the āśram *(so that now I would be dedicating my whole life to the present and future JN).*

Under such conditions, the "poor" of JN can go and live an elegant life in Bankok or wherever they choose with the clear conscience of knowing that I deprived them of the means to live poorly and realistically in India.

– The problem of Canada has bothered me a lot these last two weeks. It is the price of a solitary life to not have someone nearby to discuss problems with. It is very likely that they will try again, unless one appeals to B. Griffiths (whom I was also thinking of inviting in May). At midday today a letter came from Fr. Dominique, who was absolutely categorical, in the sense of refusal. However, dear Fr. Dominique himself has also spent 4 months in Belgium for a family celebration plus medical treatment!

---

266 The language spoken in Poona (today Pune).

About all this, of course, we have no opportunity to speak before your departure. However, if you were to meet Murray, you might try to help him be a little more realistic and not shift his responsibilities onto others.

This is for you alone, of course.

Abhiṣiktānanda

❖❖❖

Gyansu, December 22, 1969

My dear Raymond,

Received your letter this midday. Thank you. So, it is absolutely impossible to meet up. Next year, then.

I enclose a copy of my reply to the letter from Jyoti. I wonder more and more whether behind all this there might be a subtle unconscious psychological reason: «Since we are no longer able to "teach our lesson" to the Church of India in the radical way performed at JN, we cannot stay in India. Or else we will be absorbed into a RC group, and then we won't have to take responsibility for our way of life that is so seemingly scathing towards the rest of the Church». I am so tired of their obsession with their own case, instead of asking "how can I serve the Church in India?" And as I said in my letter, since they will have to decide over the next weeks or months, all those involved in their "rescue"will have to adjust their calendar according to the needs of JN. As psychotherapists do, I have pushed in this direction. If the reaction is "bad", then things are clear. But I hope I am mistaken. I have also written to J. Stuart who, along with his confreres, though he loves Murray very much, is saddened by this all too frequent "judges of Israel"attitude among our friends at JN.

On another subject. As I already told you, I have finished translating Prayer. I have to send 3 copies to Europe (two for the German and Italian translations). If I have time I will send them to J. Stuart. I wonder if you might not be too busy to take at least one with you to Rome, the one for LE SEUIL.[267] *If you can take anything, please take that. Otherwise Malou*[268]

[267] Éditions du Seuil, publishing house in Paris.

[268] Mme Malou Lanvin, one of Abhiṣiktånanada's correspondents in France.

will bring the package or the rest in February or March. Au revoir.

You will see, next May I think, those people from Montreal who are keen to sidetrack me. Please tell them they have all my understanding for their efforts, but that to move from Gyansu to Montreal without any psychological shock would take six months of slow travel and readjustment.

In the Spirit.

Abhiṣiktānanda

❖❖❖

Gyansu, December 23, 1969

[...] Yesterday I wrote to you at Vārāṇasī a long letter about C. M. R. [C. Murray Rogers]. If you have received it, burn it. I asked you whether you would be able to take with you to Rome one or two copies in French of my book Prayer – one for Le Seuil, one for Brigitte;[269] *they will be at J. Stuart's. Thank you. Have a good trip, and Happy New Year! [...]*

Abhiṣiktānanda

1970

February 6, 1970

My dear Svāmijī,

Thank you for your letter of the 24th. Yes, I believe that monastic life is an anthropological dimension. I am glad you met Vachon, and very happy about your days in Varāṇasī. No, I would not want to push you to leave your solitude. My book was no more public than publishing your book. I say this to emphasize that I agree with Dominique, Thérèse[270] and yourself that your charisma and testimony are fine as they are and that you do not need to seek publicity. On the other hand, you have the gift of the pen and you should cultivate it. And so, as you do so wonderfully,

[269] Sr. Brigitte, German Anglican nun.

[270] Sr. Thérèse Lemoine, from the Carmel of Lisieux in France.

be a little at the source of different "movements". I still haven't received any word from Murray. Let's hope all is well. Saw A. Stokes. Her health has improved greatly since last time. We spent a nice evening together. Unfortunately I had a sharp pain in my stomach which prevented me from being more "sensitive". We got on very well. She is an exceptional woman and I admire her a lot. Here the interest in mysticism is growing. I will hold a seminar on this and next year I will give another more advanced one on comparative mysticism. Douglas Steere will come to Varāṇasī in December. What about putting him in touch with Dr. Mehta? Illich came by here. A little too argumentative, it seems to me. At the Monchanin Center[271] you are the great "myth". Good. I had a panel discussion on yoga and the Christian faith. The report on the discussion will be sent to you. Interesting from a practical and pastoral point of view...

Raymond

❖❖❖

Gyansu, February 24, 1970

My dear Raymond,

What a pleasure to receive your letter at noon today with Carmen's phrase "from the "monk" of Boston to the "monk" of the Ganges."

Is this the new monastic life you are hoping for there in Montserrat? There was also the Castelli Colloquium article on infallibility, very successful, it seems. From Switzerland Mme Odette Baumer has asked for your address in Germany and Italy. Not knowing your contact details, I told her to try to reach you through Castelli. In the end, she didn't have the courage.

After doing everything to avoid him, at Rishikesh I met R. Vachon with whom I spent several excellent evenings.... I'm afraid his advaita is still a little too rational, but he was certainly impressed. He told me that in the last weekend of February you will be in Montreal.

[271] Later became the Intercultural Institute of Montreal.

Spent 4 wonderful days in Varāṇasī, preparing the future with Thérèse. Very good meetings with B. [Bettina], *U.*[Uma], *Sh.*[Shanta], *Maria.*[272] *It was a bit sad since you had left just 15 days earlier. But you were too busy at the time for us to meet usefully. So the fundamental question remains, and you are one of the very few with whom one can try to keep it open... East/West? I very rarely come across any underlying propulsion towards the East, even in the best westerners. Fr. Henry O.P. sent me a questionnaire for Hindūs about "what I believe"; Outrageously western and absolutely incomprehensible here. Bettina, to whom I had sent it, had an even stronger reaction than me!*

Disaffection of the Church? If it were at least based on paramārtha![273] *Alas, it is often caused by falling back onto one's own tiny self! The Dutch provocation is serious, but even more characteristic is a speech given at IDOC,*[274] *Rome in 1969 by Rocco Caporale.*[275] *I am not unsympathetic towards this freedom movement, but one would first prefer to feel the Spirit within!*

I was glad to see Murray in Delhi at the end of January. Too little, because he spent all afternoon getting plane tickets from East to West for himself and his wife. We did not talk about the real problems. He will "forgive" me "for having left him", but he cannot understand me. From what I hear from other sources, I fear that the paths he has been following with his "potential companions" have by no means been crowned with success. Neither R.C. [Roman Catholics] *nor non-R.C. are interested in this strict and clearly outdated ecumenical formula. For his part, Paul Kumardas told me that he would gladly go to Poona as long as there are 3 or 4 Indians and there is plenty to eat (sic). I fear that in the end no one will agree to join the "three". It seems incressingly clear to me that the solution would be for them to very humbly start a small "urban brotherhood" in Poona, which would then develop spontaneously; but no one dares to commit to Murray in advance. Mehta wanted to hire me as "head" of his "Center for the Unity of Religions". On one hand, no one likes to get*

---

[272] Maria Bidoli.

[273] Supreme truth.

[274] International Documentation on the Contemporary Church.

[275] Renowned professor of sociology and anthropology and scholar of comparative religion.

involved with a "prophet" who decides only by pseudo-inspiration; on the other, I just do not see a path for me in there. I have tried – at Bettina's suggestion – to propose at least one interreligious meeting (a prelude to Yukti) *but he expected all or nothing.*

For 6 months I have been saying no to my friends: to you about the book, to Murray about Poona, to Vachon about Montreal, to Mehta about Delhi!

Fortunately I have Fr. Dominique and Térèse to remind me of the monastic needs of solitude, opportune, importune![276]

I am preparing a paper for Kursevy in May about Cosmic Awakening and Awakening in Christ. What can I say that is true?

In Spiritu,

Abhiṣiktānanda

❖❖❖

Gyansu, May 11, 1970

My dear Raymond,

Your latest news reached me through Anne Stokes in March. I often think about you, about your "involvement" in the terrible problems of the church in the USA, and my prayer is that the Lord will guide you and use you to guide your brothers (yatra-anutahsa puruṣāhyayamātmā... āvvih saṃnihitam guhācaram ...) Life here is very quiet or, as the Gītā says, neither the world disturbs me nor I disturb the world. The ICTA[277] seminar (on Christ the Revelator) at Kurseong has been postponed (since those invited to participate did not reply to the invitation). At the weekend I will go down to Rishikesh and Delhi for a couple of weeks. I will try to find out from Patrick D'Souza what is happening in the Church in India. Fr. Mayeul[278] holds meetings with Mahieu and Griffiths at Asirvanam[279] to decide on the evolution of monasticism here. He sends me questionnaires.

[276] See note 27.
[277] Institute for Councelling and Transactional Analysis.
[278] Fr. Mayeul de Dreuille, OSB.
[279] Asirvanam Benedictine Monastery.

They have established Samaj Monasteries in India (as if they were the monks of Bhard Sādhu Samaj). Patrick asks me what he could do.[280] *I have never met anyone in the central line, the only one that interests me. If someone appears later, it will be too late; my physical strength is greatly diminished and this "detached" life is constantly widening the "gap" between itself and the advancing branch of the Church. I learned from R. Vachon that your "total immersion week" was a great success (these Canadians have a knack with ideas) in Montreal. My conversations with R. Vachon, as nice as he is, have made me realize though how "lost"*

---

[280] Panikkar's letter of reply to his bishop merits inclusion here as it expresses clearly his own vision of the Church and the priesthood, a subject dear to both Panikkar and Abhiṣiktānanda: Varāṇasī, 17 August 1970

What do you expect of me?, Patrick (D'Susa) asks me.This is my answer:

"To be a man of prayer (not of authority or power), a Christian who is dedicated to people and not to principles (the Sabbath for men, not men for the Sabbath), and therefore that you concentrate first and foremost not on 'doing your work' or making sure 'the work is done', but on people, the true temples of the Holy Spirit, who are the living stones of the City of God, which is transtemporal; a living example of the simple Christian, who shows by the way he lives that it is still possible to be an Indian and also a bishop and a Christian.

... I expect reform from within, the organization without the structures, the bold steps needed for the innovation of life, which Christ asks of us. I do not expect grand deeds, pretentious declarations, but I do expect a practical and effective disentaglement from the institutionalized organization in order to liberate the living organism which still breathes inside it.

I am not concerned only with the serious reflection on whether the 'Cathedral' and the 'House of the Bishop' are in harmony with India and the Gospel, but also with the sober but decisive steps that must be made towards ecumenism and the collaboration of all men of divine will.

I expect that the dreams of Irenaeus, Ciprian, Ignatius and many others might once more be realized, but in a more universal and majestic context.

I expect you to not be devoured by administration, that you will appoint someone for such purpose and that you keep yourself free to truly vacare Deo et hominibus [be dedicated to God and to men]. *I do not expect (though it is my secret desire) that you will move out of the House of the Bishop and go and live among the destitute, but I expect blind faith to be still alive, and for everything which requires money for its realization to not be the direct and main affair of the emissaries of Jesus Christ.*

Theological language would accentuate the 'lex suprema, salus personae' *and would also speak first of all of the realistic humility that prevents us from believing that the salvation of the world depends on us or on the values or way of life that we represent, and thus from portraying the Catholic Church as if it were Noah's Ark, instead of Noah's Ark (in which there are animals of every type) as the Place of Salvation and, therefore, as the true concept of the Church.*

I would feel in that context. Several friends have reminded me (almost harshly) that it is in the Gyansu retreat that I am needed and nowhere else.

I have no news of Murray. He was supposed to spend a few days in Bareilly in May on his way from London to Tokyo. I was very disappointed and sorry about his attitude last year. John Cole leaves in early June, and will be in Delhi on the 10th.

I read in Rel. Soc.[281] *(March) an excellent article by W.C. Smith,*[282] *who happens to be in your department at Harvard.*

Give my thanks to your secretary for the information she sent me just before leaving Varāṇasī. I have just received it, while trying out my French version of Prayer.

In the feast of the Spirit. Let it blow!
And may we lose ourselves there from whence it comes.
It is that which is known by no one, much less those who profess to think about it.

Abhiṣiktānanda

❖❖❖

Gyansu, May 18, 1970

My dear Raymond,

Your February letter crossed with mine dated mid-May. I received the article at the same time. I had just enough time to read through it quickly before leaving for 3 weeks (Delhi). I had to send my Preface for Gnānānanda,[283] *which will be published this summer in Paris. Quite hard, and I have to reread it slowly to understand it well. The trouble is that the text*

---

281 The magazine *Religions and Society.*

282 Wilfred Cantwell Smith, Presbyterian minister and professor at Harvard Divinity School.

283 Book dedicated by Abhiṣiktānandaha to *Gnānānanda,* in which he describes his relationship with the *guru* of Tapovanam (near Thirupirapalli).

ends just when it is becoming more interesting. It is an approach to the fundamental problem, but it is not yet the philo-indio-logy of religion that you continually advocate. On the other hand, until the whole is capable of grasping the "Grund,"[284] *all this will continue to be misunderstood, because the religious taboo is still worth more than the slavery of the senses. Until the Spirit has been received,* "non potestis porta modo*"[285]! Who is Douglas Steere?*[286]*Mehta writes to me more and more. Spiritual calling, no doubt, metapsychic gift, sure, but also possessiveness and hypertrophy of the ego that become monomania. He speaks in monologues and repeats himself endlessly. He "curses" those who don't want to believe in his guidance, beginning with Indira and Chavan;*[287] *and he contents himself with threatening the destined of the world, for example those of the Church and Israel. You should know that he is the one who led the Six Day War, and that if Israel has not enforced its peace, it is because it did not follow the messages of Yeswar Place! I don't think I will even go and see him in Delhi when I'm there next week. Interesting especially from a psychological point of view.*

No sign of life from Murray. He does not and cannot understand. Alas, we are terribly limited.

I will be back hopefully by the 10th or 15th of June.

[...] Let me know your plans by return post so I know where to send you my thoughts on your text. I received your letter this morning, just before I left, so I will reply to you from Varāṇasī.

Even if I took your text with me, I wouldn't be able to write anything before 15/6.

– I know nothing about the Kyoto matter. I only heard about a conference that Murray is supposed to be attending in August.

---

284 Foundation.

285 Jn. 16:12: *adhuc multa habeo vobis dicere sed non potestis portare modo* ("I have yet many things to say unto you, but ye cannot bear them now.")

286 See note 216.

287 Indira Gandhi, Prime Minister of India, and Yashwantrao Chavan, politician and future deputy prime minister.

– About the meetings in Varāṇasī in December?! I know too well how much pressure you are under in that month, with all the work that's late.

I haven't received anything from Klaus.

Abhiṣiktānanda

❖❖❖

Indore, May 29, 1970

My dear Raymond,

Your letter—special delivery—was waiting for me in Indore last night, just as you should have received my letter sent from Gyansu a few days ago.

[...] It'll have to be another time.

This week in Delhi, extremely interesting, physically killed me (the plain, the sun, the crowds). I can't take this pace anymore.

[...]

[...]May the Lord ... dwell here with them, poor monks (so they don't get discouraged).

This is just a quick reply to your letter.

I arrived last night and today I cannot sleep.

[...]

[...]I have seen in the Examiner[288] *that Klaus*[289] *has gone, following after you, and soon Murray. You have all abandoned us. May the Lord grant to those who remain here their feeble powers, not to lose heart ...*

[...]

Abhiṣiktānanda

❖❖❖

[288] Catholic News weekly published in the Archdiocese of Bombay, India.

[289] K. Klostermaier had accepted a teaching post in Canada.

Gyansu, September 23, 1970

[...] I try to reduce to a minimum the journeys up and down to Rishikesh and Uttarkāshi; too expensive and exhausting ... More and more I am following the slow pace of India. This is why a quick one-day meeting does not agree with my psychology.

Abhiṣiktānanda

❖❖❖

Gyansu November 6, 1970

[...] The essential thing in this renewal of the Church is to have leader-animators, people who neither apply nor require formulas, but who draw from their own depths new methods to be discovered. It is by such animators that centers forinitiation, much more than training, should be opened. But again, who will animate these centers?

[...]

Abhiṣiktānanda

❖❖❖

Gyansu, November 23, 1970

[...]As I have written, I would have liked to combine everything so as to avoid expense and effort (I have felt, in fact, a sharp decline in my strength this year).

Abhiṣiktānanda

❖❖❖

Gyansu, November 29, 1970

[...]I do not want to try to plan any more programmes like last month. In attempting to fit things together and reconcile the irreconcilable, trying to please as many people as possible at the same time, I ended

by disappointing everyone. And all the more, because from now on I can no longer travel as much as in other days. Quite apart from the cost, I have felt too great a decline of strength this year to risk it again. So I am leaving things to work themselves out on their own.

Abhiṣiktānanda

❖❖❖

Gyansu, December 8, 1970

[...]It is hard to have to accept the decline of physical strength, the increasing difficulty of concentrating for any length of time; and without a very strong faith I am surethis would be absolutely unbearable. It is necessary to have discovered, at least in Faith, the satyasya satyam [the Real of the real], *of which everything is simply the sign.*

Here the cold is bitter, although my kutiya[290] *is much more comfortable now than it was in 1964. But it is my capacity to react that has diminished. I am well aware that I shall not be able to hold on here for many years – the Lord will provide in his own time, in his own unforeseeable way. What is most important is the request, coming to me both from young Europeans who come to India and from young Indian priests, to be more accessible. I do not believe at all in the renewal of the Church by the hierarchy,although some positions, like that of* [...], *are comforting; There is work at the grass-roots, which young priests could do, and they ask for help, I would venture to say both spiritual and* Vedāntic.

Abhiṣiktānanda

❖❖❖

Gyansu, December 18, 1970

This decline in health poses serious problems for me for the future. I hope the Lord will show the way in due time.

Abhiṣiktānanda

---

290 Small traditional Indian dwelling with thatched roof and mud walls.

1971

Hardwar, February 15, 1971

My dear Raymond,

I spent some excellent days with Fr. Oshida.[291] *A truly wonderful man, I am happy to have met him. From here I go back to Jyotinekatan. Murray wants me to meet Fr. Augustine.*[292] *Everything is lilā.*[293] *Excellent atmosphere in the* āśram. *That of Rishikesh is marked by seculars, the spiritual tourists of Europe. The exploitation of piety...*

Abhiṣiktānanda

[Below are a few lines in English written by Oshida to Raimon]:

My Immortal activity is Inactivity

For a few weeks now I have been experiencing what I should have experienced with and among my old friends. Many spheres and elements together—one of the funniest chings in the world. Right now I am wrestling with monkeys in these holy chambers of Śri Niranyananda. Tomorrow I will bc lcaving Hardwar with Svāmijī for a day's break in New Delhi. I wait for Poonja in Bombay. I often hear your name here among our friends and I feel that you are here. I deeply regret your absence. Mataji Pretash's pūjā[294] begins now.

Good health and rest to you.

Goodbye for a while,

Yours,

Shigeto Oshida.

❖❖❖

[291] Fr. Shigeto Oshida, Japanese Catholic Dominican priest and Zen Buddhist master.

[292] Fr Augustine Deenabandu, a Capuchin priest who left his monastery to join Jyotiniketan when he was in his 60s.

[293] *lilā*: game.

[294] Ceremonial worship.

New Delhi, February 16, 1971

Dear Raymond,

There's not much room left on Murray's aerogram for the letter I've been meaning to write for a long time...

[...]

Abhiṣiktānanda

❖❖❖

Harvard, February 20, 1971

Dear Svāmijī,

I am glad about your stay (euphemism for companionship, *koinonia* and friendship) at Joitiniketan and your words from Hardwar, which have reached me now.

How is your health? I am hoping to see Anne Stokes on her feet after having missed a trip to New York due to snow.

I think about you. I imagine the human quality of your meetings – without masks.

I am reading *Concordant Discours* by R. C. Zaehner, but I am afraid our differences will increase.

With all my heart,

Raymond

❖❖❖

Gyansu, March 12, 1971

Holy [Good Friday][295]

My dear Raymond,

Your letter was waiting for me when I got here on the 9th. I came back with Murray, who has obtained a 3-year permit in Gyansu. He will tell you his impressions himself. I dream that you too can spend a long time in silent retreat "on the banks of the Ganges". Sadly, since you always travel through India so quickly I don't know how you would find the time, especially as the 3 monsoon months are too harsh, and October too. The pressure of the January deadline is already hardly letting you breathe. In any case, I would avoid going to Varāṇasī during the monsoon. I met Patrik the other day in Delhi but I was only able to make an appointment for Varāṇasī after your return. In May I shall probably go down to Bombay/ Poona for the seminar of Indologist theologians, even though, after these two months of running around in the plains, I feel a great need for silence and solitude. Today is Holi, the celebration of Spring; the young men go past shouting in the street above, but fortunately they don't come here. Still too weary from the journey (bus, etc.) to sort out my ideas. What I would need are some long, peaceful days of conversation with you before I attempt to put in order – or rather, in harmony – the deep experience and its "expression". The Mediterranean expression is terribly unsatisfying. The one here is just as "misleading" when it claims to be more than just a Hindū finger pointing. And so at least an attempt of theology must be made ... or should the muni[296] just keep quiet and simply "be"? ... Here all these days free from all forms... An Oṁ which extends (expands) in a communion that accompanies a minimum of formulas.

> *Oṁ! That says it all, out of time and beyond,* sad asat[297]...
> *this Oṁ that awakens to the Self...*
> *Abhiṣiktānanda*

❖❖❖

[295] Abhiṣiktānanda had not been able to meet with Panikkar since October 1969.

[296] Lit. "silent", a term used for hermits, ascetics, monks.

[297] "Duality of being and not-being."

Harvard, April 13, 1971

My dear Abhiṣiktā,

I am replying to your March letter, which I have just opened now. No, in Varāṇasī I am peaceful – though active. In 1970 I spent 7 months there and in 1969, 8 months. I always think I will not leave India. I would certainly love to come and spend time with you in Gyansu– or you could come to Varāṇasī.

I think at the end of June I will be in Poona. De Nobili[298] have asked me to hold a course on Christian-Hindū theology, but I know absolutely nothing about the meeting of "Indologist Theologians" you mention. Could you give me some details?

Yes, you know I am a little worried about your health. We will have to think about it.

The situation here is impressively open. Do you know what it is like to see the good Jesuits and nuns at 5am on the rocks beside the sea, chanting OM before and during the sunrise?

Do you know of an Easter liturgy with the blessing and readings and acts of the 4 elements: Fire – love; Earth – religious vocation; Water – baptism, Christian vocation; Air – Spirit (as *inprāṇāyāma*[299]), etc.?

A good and Holy Easter, and let's try to keep our appointments.

I hug you very theandrically,

Raymond

❖❖❖

Gyansu, August 14, 1971

... As for his [Bishop Patrick's] projects and those of J. Dupuis,[300] *I am certainly very interested in them; however, I am afraid of discussing*

[298] De Nobili College, Jesuit formation house in Poona, today the largest in the world.

[299] Breath control technique originating from yoga practices.

[300] Fr. Jacques Dupuis, Belgian Jesuit priest and theologian.

them directly with P. [Patrick]; he might persuade me to accept certain responsibilities which for many reasons I dread. I would not want to play a merely marginal part in the project; so it may perhaps be providential that I am not discussing the matter directly with P.

[...]

Abhiṣiktānanda

❖❖❖

Gyansu, Christmas 1971

[...]

Yesterday I received and read Tablet.[301] *I frowned a bit at the negativity of the beginning but in the end I found the whole thing very fair. Yes, but it is precisely about the beginning that I want to write to you, since I am, in fact, absolutely in agreement with you. We marvel, we lament that India doesn't move a bit faster. But how could it move? The fact that it moves at all is wonderful. Who would be able to get it moving? How could those caught up in the "system" have the same vision of what should be? In Pauline terms, quomodo credunt si non evangelizantur[302]? In terms of the Katha-upaniṣad, "who could know "it" if "it" was not told to them by another?" So you, and me, just like M. [Murray], like K. [Klaus], what do we have to say? Have I retired to the Himalayas as you did to the West? Who stays in India to lead the movement? An Indian theology will never come out of our seminaries. Change them? Where are the elements? It would have required a chair at Vārāṇasī, Brindavan or Patiala, etc., with "disciples" who formulate theories on the fundamental problems. It would have required spiritual centers free of the burden of the institution, even the so-called monastic institution. For this reason it has never been possible to find the men and the circumstances... When one insists on a tenure with a high degree of accessibility, no one thinks about organizing it, and again I refuse to commit myself. This is an observation. We have*

[301] Refers to an article by Panikkar on the Nagpur meeting, published in "Tablet", a Catholic international weekly review.

[302] Cf. Rom.10:14: "how shall they believe in him of whom they have not heard?"

to get to the true core of the problem. If there is still no true Indian theology, it is not for lack of desire or possibilities, but of qualified gurūs *and properly organized research centers... Instead of saying that this is not the way, let us try and say what should be done so that things can move forward, not theoretically, but practically. Sometimes I suffer from anguish, and texts like yours in Tablet revive this anguish. Other times I am fed up with all that is institution and establishment of any sort, and I forget about saṃsāra, that of the Church and of all the rest, and take refuge in aham, which is acala*[303] *and nitya*[304]*...*

I have just re-read chapter X of the Gītā. *– Yes, but you see, the theological problems that all this poses have no answer on a conceptual level. They explode and annihilate each other on the level of experience. So is a true Indian theology still possible? One might dream of a Christian Śaṅkara, but the Upaniṣads ultimately defy any attempt to thematize. The Ganges is pure only at Gangotrī.*

Abhiṣiktānanda

1972

Delhi, February 15, 1972

My dear Raymond,

I have just come back from Ranchi (the Carmelites who have promising postulants) then Varāṇasī, at Bettina's request – following revelations about Poonja. Even for an Advaitin it is dangerous to play Kṛṣṇa's game (lilā)! Who can you really trust when it comes to Hindū gurūs!

I had the chance to meet up with Patrick, who was returning from Madras CBCI and leaving the next day for his Lenten mission tours. Two hours of conversation. He is annoyed, I know, but one must understand his position in relation to the mass of the hierarchy... The seminar programme... abandoned due to lack of personnel. Now he would like an āśram for jñāna, he says, complementary to the karma āśram of the sisters of Mother

303 *Acala*: the Immovable.

304 *Nitya*: the Eternal.

Teresa and the bhakti āśram of Īśvara Prasad,[305] *in which there would be special courses for initiating young priests into Hindū prayer and India's contemporary spiritual approach.*[306] *He would take charge of the house and the administration* [and he asked me] *to think about it very seriously. Fr. Dupuis, to whom I spoke about it here in Delhi the day before yesterday, tells me I should not miss the opportunity. I understand well, and better than others, the need for such an initiative, but for many reasons I would much prefer that the enterprise be taken on by others... All it would be is controlled freedom. How much I would prefer, if ever I had to do anything, to do it together with my Hindū disciples! Marc*[307] *tells me I should even stop writing and allow myself to be forgotten...*

I divide my time in Delhi: during the day at the Brotherhood for Sagesse *and in the evening at Shahdare with Ramesh.*[308] *On the 25th I am going to Hardwar and from 12/3 to 9/4 I will be in Poona.*

I have just seen Sita Ram Goil.[309] *He remembers you. It is good to meet up with certain Hindū friends. I have just heard in Varāṇasī about your stopovers and that you have arrived in Santa Barbara. I have also read 99 beautiful pages on sacrifice, 99 pages of Worship. Extremely good and readable translation!*

"Coupe de troupe" means that all signs must be overcome. The Self stands alone in kevala.[310]

In the joy of the Spirit always.

Abhiṣiktānanda

❖❖❖

305 Svāmi Īṣvar Prasad founded the KhristPanthi *āśram* in Varāṇasi.

306 *Jñana* (Path of Action), *karma* (Path of Devotion) and *bhakti* (Path of Knowledge) are the three Yogas cited in the *Bhagavad-Gītā* for the liberation of the human spirit.

307 Marc Chaduc (later Svāmi Ajātānanda) was a young French seminarist who went to India in 1971 and became a disciple of Abhiṣiktånanda, playing an important part in his life. After the death of the latter he disappeared in the Himalayan mountains, leaving behind his personal diary.

308 Ramesh Srivastava, disciple of Abhiṣiktānanda.

309 Indian historian, writer, publisher and religious and political activist.

310 Absolute, unconditional.

Gyansu, July 1, 1972

[...] This year's experiences have been intense. I feel a profound change. Yet this change makes one "foreign". How true the Upaniṣads are! But who [today] is willing to submit to the Upaniṣads with faith (śraddhā upaniṣadam upāsīta)?![311]

[...]

Abhiṣiktānanda

❖❖❖

Rajpur, October 18, 1972

My dear Raymond,

Your farewell letter on your departure from India reached me after you had already gone. Only now do I get word from Shanta, who tells me you are in Santa Barbara. I thought you were in Europe or South America. I was held up in Indore in April due to a small operation which, oddly, is still limiting me. I am afraid I will need an additional operation within the next month... Because of this I won't be able to go up to Gyansu for the time being. At least this allows me to turn down some invitations to seminars, which I only ever accept reluctantly. In any case, my time is not wasted here. Upaniṣad + *Gītā + Marc. At the moment I have two students from the Poona seminary, who are both very open. One is an intellectual who dwells on theological formulations. The other is a mystic who looks further. It seems that most of the seminarists throw themselves into the social sphere in order to avoid the basic problems, but the crisis is inevitable!*

311 [This is the end of the extracts of letters filed at HS (Hot Spring, the name of the house where Panikkar lived during his period of teaching at the University of Santa Barbara, California). We must realize that since Marc's arrival Abhiṣiktānanda's life changed both inwardly and outwardly. His correspondence with RP became more sporadic from this time onwards, while RP himself stayed in India for shorter spells (he wrote to him mainly during his stays in India). The correspondence between the two had already diminished following the National Seminar, mainly due to the fact that from then on Abhiṣiktānanda was in demand almost everywhere, and tried unsuccessfully, as he says himself, to satisfy everyone, while perfectly aware that his strength was visibly waning.]

Murray tells me he will be coming in December, on his way to Bangkok. Intrepid traveller... and enjoying it!

Marc will see Poonja in Hardwar, after which he will go to Benares. I await news with interest.

Sagesse will have to wait for J. Stuart's return in December. In any case, it's only a revamp of an old script. I would not write it now.

CBCI[312] *has appointed Fr. Albert CMI*[313] *as general secretary for the Commission of Interreligious Dialoguein Varāṇasī.*

Quid?

Abhiṣiktānanda

❖❖❖

Rajpur, December 18, 1972

My dear Raymond,

A collective wish for a Merry Christmas to you, Shanta, Bettina and Mary! If you weren't all so terribly busy, I would be very tempted to make a quick visit until Hanumanghat to wish you Merry Christmas in person. Murray will tell you about the wonderful week we spent together in Hardwar, Rishikesh and here. […]

I am thinking to make my way back to Gyansu this week, once I have finished with my Christmas mail and my proofreading of Gnānānanda.

Marc left for Binsar on 2/12.

A letter from Almora announced that he has arrived and entered silence. He will pass through Varāṇasī in January/February on his way to (or back from) Bodhi Gaya.

[…]

---

312 Catholic Bishops' Conference of India.

313 Fr. Albert Nambiaparambil of the Carmelites of Mary Immaculate (CMI).

Joy to all,

Abhiṣiktānanda

❖❖❖

Gyansu, December 23, 1972

My dear Raymond,

Reached Gyansu yesterday morning, and since yesterday evening I have at last got down to reading your paper from Jerusalem, "Supername".[314] *It is really "you" at your best. I will reread it all carefully, but before you leave India, I want to tell you of my pleasure at this paper. In philosophical terms (sometimes difficult) you give the proof of something of which I am more and more convinced: that the problem of the uniqueness of Christ is a false problem. For no more can the "Persons" in God create than created "persons" can be numbered.*

However, your conclusion does not tend still to resolve the problem from the Christian point of view. After having wrestled with the Angel for years, I am forced to accept that in practice, de facto, the whole so-called Christian approach to the "mystery" is just one of the approaches! A brilliant and sparkling līlā [game] *of "the One who plays among the worlds", the reflection in a given mirror of the* satyam[315] *who simply IS ... The point which the* Vedāntins *have for years been drumming into our ears with their over-simplified and condescending slogans ...*

I will write to you about that again when I can read it slowly and in detail.

Back to Uttarkashi yesterday, called urgently to the court about the theft of my typewriter, together with the thief (in chains, poor devil). The machine was there, but it will still probably take months and months before I get it back from the Police.

---

314 *Salvation in Christ. Concreteness and Universality, the Supername* (Inaugural Lecture at the Ecumenical Institute of Advanced Theological Studies, Tantur, Jerusalem), Santa Barbara, CA 1972. In *Opera Omnia*, Vol. III, Part 1, *The Christian Tradition,* Maryknoll, New York: Orbis Books, 2015.

315 Reality.

At Rishikesh I invited Chidānanda-jī[316] *to the conference on Worship in Rajpur in June and to the East Asia monastic conference in Bangalore in October. He accepted with pleasure.*

Again a Good Year to you and to your faithful collaborators.

Abhiṣiktānanda

1973

Gyansu, January 30, 1973

My dear Raymond,

Before I go down to Rajpur I wanted to send you this short letter. The reason I am going: J. Stuart is coming to spend 15 days with me to finish Sagesse *in English. On 20/2 Anne Stokes will be coming for a few weeks (she will leave N.Y. on the 19th). I will go and pick her up in Delhi and then take her to Hardwar, Rishikesh and Rajpur. I would like her to go to Varāṇasī after that. I will write to Shanta and Bettina and ask them to take care of her a bit. It will be good for her to see* de visu *your environment instead of having only hearsay and suppositions to go by. Because she has true affection for you she really wants the essential in you to transpire totally.*

I liked very much your essay on Silence and the Word. We intellectuals are victims of the Word and all too often we are only able to know, to recognise the S(s)pirit through the W(w)ord! Your article on the "Smile of Buddha" impressed Marc so much that he copied it. At Bodhi Gaya he met some Buddhist masters who honoured the Spirit without speaking, and he wrote to me that your "smile" is words! He will be back at the end of February and will try to stay.

(...)

[316] Svāmi Chidānanda Saraswati, President of the Divine Life Society, Rishikesh, India.

I have read and reread your "Supername". Many things in it fill me with delight, as I have told you. But I sometimes fear that the brilliance of the reasoning employed might be deceptive. And finally, whatever may be said on the penultimate page, it still remains an attempt at salvage, at restoring the situation! Or if you prefer, an attempt to lead Christians as gently as possible to accept that in losing their nāmarūpa they still keep everything!

As I wrote to you a month ago, beyond all our approaches, however subtly argued (the "who which", not the "what which"), all that is excellent, yet, yet ... when all that has to be restated in everyday language, we have to accept that it is all nāmarūpa -and to begin with, the idea of Salvation.

In the final pages you admit this yourself; "salvation" means nothing – nothing real – to the humanist, any more than to the Buddhist or the Vedāntin! There is a drive of the psyche, and to explain it the intellect elaborates a marvelous dream and imposes the mystery on the consciousness of a human group, and the collective psyche has the magnificent spectacle of the myth and logos ... and then we wake up. The dream is true in the drive from which it is originated and into which it is resolved, prabhava—apyayan![317]

The whole thesis of SAGESSE is outdated. I am in a hurry for it to be finished in English, because I feel too uneasy about it.

I had to tell you: my Mass this morning was a hymn to the Puruṣa. Everyone is the unique expression of this Puruṣā. And all that is seen in the world of nāma-rūpa, the Puruṣā...is the last stage (atman-brahman...). Then the awakening.

In this glory

Abhiṣiktānanda

❖❖❖

[317] The origin and the end.

Santa Barbara, March 1, 1973

University of California

Dear Abhiṣiktā,

Impossible to do justice to my mail. Bitter experience with the limitation of every technical aspect. Only the Spirit—or prayer—is everywhere.

Here among the students there is a great desire for true spirituality. I continue my life as a hermit – covert, camouflaged or perhaps lost – but happy.

I would like to know more details about Patrick's new program. I understand him, but it will be important to avoid taking missteps, especially if the aim is to institutionalize or whatever.

I am reading Marcel Légaut, *Introduction* à l'intelligence du *passé et de l'avenir du christianisme.* I also found some sentences that I had written around fifteen years ago or more, but there is the (French) genius of being able to express oneself. Nevertheless, I have discovered his myth.

Happy pilgrimage to Poona.

I have sent you some printouts to Delhi.

In union above Logos,

Raymond

❖❖❖

Rajpur, May 22, 1973

My dear Raymond

When I arrived in Rajpur there waiting for me was your letter of last November 4th, in which you announced you would be coming in December to Vārāṇasī... with your text for Damascus...

I came here for this School of Prayer which we have been holding now twice a year with non-RCs. The atmosphere is very good. It can only last for three hours due to lack of time, but even this is useful.

Uttarkāshi is going to become a problem sooner than I had expected. The new exarch of Bijnoor/Kotdwa, who henceforth has under his charge the four mountain districts, has begun to move. He sent two fathers to explore Uttarkashi. They came to ask me to put them in touch with the Malayali Christians working on the dam and were anxious to find out if I was well known as a Catholic priest! They want to install themselves first of all in the Headquarters District, so as to be able to contact the authorities easily – and one had thought that the Constantinian area had been liquidated with the Council.

Since they have parishioners ready, they will hasten to organize themselves into a double ghetto: an institutional Christian ghetto within charismatic Hinduism and a Malayali ghetto among the people of Uttarkāshi. In such conditions I shall have to think of finding a new place of refuge for the remaining years of my life in this ©arīram[318]*. Probably in the neighbourhood of Rishikesh or Hardwar. Nothing definite. More and more I am feeling so far-removed from this Church. The strong wine of* advaita *has dissipated all the flavors that once enthralled me...*

I plan to go back up to Gyansu in mid-June and probably come back down after mid-August before Marc leaves for France (unless he isn't able to get an extension and has to leave immediately). Yet another who has been so totally smitten by India that he is absolutely incapable of returning to his Lyon seminary or even another monastery. When one has tasted the real thing, what more do conventions have to say? He dreams only of finding a hermitage somewhere that is not being continually disturbed by the police.

I hope this letter of mine reaches you before you leave for Latin America. I think you will still be very busy this year finishing Gāyatrī*, and especially that you will only return to India much later.*

We will see whether there will be any chance to meet up; I would very much like to. I will probably have to go down after October 20th. I will also have to go back to Indore to see the results of last year's operation. In addition, I will have to be in Delhi in mid-December for the first winter session of our School of Prayer. When you get back you will let me know.

---

[318] Body, shell.

This is all from the outside.

In the communication of the Holy Spirit – the true non-dual communion...

Abhiṣiktānanda

PS. If on your return you need to send me a letter that requires a quick reply, you should send it to both Gyansu and Rajpur. There have been too many problems in the last few months with the sending of letters.

❖❖❖

June 23, 1973

Pentecost

Dear Svāmijī,

We are on the far side (or this side?) of words and I have heard very little about you this time. I have not seen Mme Stokes. So I am almost without any news of you, except for your last letter.

Patrick wants to appoint me as president of the theological commission for preparing the Synod. I think you will give us some ideas. One cannot always act marginally or on the sidelines.

Even if we consider the Church as a sociological group (I think this is what Küng[319] says), it is "our group" from a certain point of view.

I can go to Bangalore for the monastic meeting (or conference) in October. I think you will be going. Once the erected structures have been pulled down, we may, and must, build new ones – always provisionally, of course.

I would like to know how you are doing and if you are writing anything.

[319] Fr. Hans Küng, Swiss Catholic priest, theologian and author.

I understand that Marc cannot go back to the seminary – but I don't believe he cannot be radically reformed and this is only possible from within (not necessarily from an institutionalized "within" but a real one).

I will be here until the end of August.

In the Spirit of this Pentecost that is invisible and yet, for this very reason, more real than any *tamāśā*.[320]

All the best,

Raymond

❖❖❖

Rajpur, June 25, 1973

My dear Raymond,

I received your letter at midday today. I think you are alluding to the letter I wrote in mid-June before coming down from Gyansu.

In it I told you how the basic problem seemed to me to be increasingly existential, and how the institution is taking up less and less room in my life. I have past the age of action, and this pilot seminary that is being talked about more and more interests me less and less. Only one thing matters: awakening. And the Church is unfortunately far from this.

- On the 30th [there will be the] *ecumenical celebration of Marc's* saµnyāsa *in the Ganges by Chidānandajī and me in* advaita *of the monastic ministry... Whether here or in France, for several years he will only be able to live in silence and solitude. At 40 he will then see the next stage of his life.*

---

[320] *tamāśā* (Hindi): that which is coarse, ostentatious, showy; commonly refers to spectacle, farce, etc.

– Last week in Hardwar I met a Malayali who for at least 3 years has been living as a perfect and authentic sādhu, *going from* āśram *to* āśram *in Franciscan poverty. Deeply Christian, he constantly talks about Christ, but for 3 years he has had no opportunity to receive the sacrament. A blessed meeting.*

– Got kicked out of the Rajpur Center by Jai Singh, who is kicking out anyone who lives in the Center. The unwholesome influence of his wife, these people who create emptiness in order to assert themselves. Until an Indian replacement is found, the Center will remain dormant. I took refuge in Chet Singh (from where I am writing to you) below Rajpur, where I will stay whenever I am in the plains. But I have to try to find a kutiya *in Rishikesh now that the CMI are practically forcing me out of Uttarkāshi—aniketan!*[321]

I won't go to Bangalore in October any more than I did in March. Chidānandajī told me himself the other day (when I invited him) that it was not my place. True Indian Christian monasticism has nothing to do with the likes of Kurisumalai,[322] *Asirvanam, etc; these serve only to spread the monastic idea among Christians. The true monks are the Ekarasānandas*[323] *like the one I have just told you about. Also among the Hindūs, just this month I met some real mendicants, whom the common people regard as beggars, but who are much more genuine with their "gunny bags"*[324] *than the fine mahatmas.*

- I received some very important advice this year that I should avoid holding workshops, etc. The hermit's place is in his cell. A little hard to swallow, but isn't it true? Some would even like me to stop writing. And in fact, all that may still remain to be written is not at all writable. Everything appears vain once you have entered the fourth mantra of OM.

Nevertheless, to prepare for Marc's dīksa[325] *ceremony I read the Saṃnyāsa-upaniṣad and extracted a text (French/English), which I delivered the other day to Chidānanda. For me it was a bit like Josiah's discovery of*

[321] Homeless, wanderers.

[322] Kurisumala āśram.

[323] Ascetics like Svāmi Ekarasānanda, a renowned *sadhu* of the early 20th Century.

[324] Jute sacks typically carried by beggars in India.

[325] Initiation.

Deuteronomy. I had not realized what commitments of poverty and silence I had assumed by wearing the kavi.[326] *This is a very important text which would certainly be worth publishing, but who will take charge of it? I will finalize it anyway just in case.*

Structures of the provisional, you say (about the monks). But monasticism is above all charisma. The structures originate from the charismatic impulse of individuals, of true Indian monks. Conferences and seminars will be useless. Bangalore is too far to go by train, it is too tiring for me now. It was suggested that I go by plane, like for the seminar of Fr. Desrochers.[327] *To talk about true monastic or āśramic life (what I was asked in March) after arriving by plane is simply laughable. True monks do not fly, unless absolutely necessary. It is not based on chatter and discussions that reform will happen. [Saints] Benedict and Anthony went into the desert and Francis into the streets; they did not gather together the monks of the surrounding areas for a meeting.*

I think I will go back up to Gyansu between July 5th and 10th, providing the roads are practicable, because it's been raining so heavily for 15 days that I strongly fear everything will be blocked. – I should be in the lowlands again by the end of October. Sooner or later I will have to have a check-up at the clinic in Indore. In mid-December I should hold another so-called "school of prayers" with non-RCs; the one in Rajpur in May was excellent, thanks mainly to two young Englishmen and a Sikh colonel who were seeking to free themselves of their adhyāsa.[328]

So when are you coming back to India? I thought the courses were ending in June and that you would have to spend July and August in Latin America. And Gāyatrī? *Will it finally see the light of day at the beginning of the next* uttarāyaṇa?[329]

---

[326] Kavi (Tamil): saffron coloured cloth worn by Hindū ascetics.

[327] Fr. John Desrochers CSC, who was later to found the Centre for Social Action (CSA), the aims of which included the formation of socially aware and involved leaders.

[328] Superimposition of an attribute, quality or characteristic of one entity onto another entity.

[329] The northward journey of the sun, the path to be taken in order to complete the *devayana*, the path of the Gods from which there must be no return.

On August 15th I will have lived 25 years in India. What a blessing to have dared to take this step, though I could not know then what awaited me here. What awaited me was this marvellous discovery of aham asmi,[330] *so simple and so wonderful. Everything explodes, everything goes away and then what is left?* Etad vai tat.[331] *This, precisely this ... but there is nothing more to say ...*

What is this theological commission? Next year's synod of Rome? An Indian synod? But how can you direct this from Santa Barbara? I have no more ideas for reforms. It is all about leading towards the existential experience of the Self –svanubhāvam![332] *Everything else is chewing-gum for amusing the kids. Of course, everything is likely to explode when this thing gets around. Well. But who will explode?* Etad vai tat...

Joy of awakening.

On the back is the address of Mr. R. Chet Singh, but it is safer to write to me at Gyansu.

❖❖❖

Houston, July 30, 1973

Dear Svāmijī,

Robert Vachon is here. Let's talk about you. Received your letter telling me you are not going to Bangalore. There are many people in America who have never taken a train, but a plane—of course. There is a growing movement towards nature and mysticism.

I will not be able to come to India much earlier than Bangalore. I'll let you know my movements but maybe I could come up in November or December. I don't know yet. In India at least I would like to live freely and without plans.

I thirst for solitude – and also a little for rest – even though I continue with my 50% plan in America also.

330 "I am".

331 "This verily is that".

332 Experience.

The economic and political news that I hear here is quite pessimistic. I am referring to India. I haven't been able to see Anne Stokes since she came back from India.

There is something happening in the world – and also within ourselves.

I hope you are well and taking care of yourself.

In true friendship,

Raymond

❖❖❖

Houston

30-VII-73

chefbanzo.

Robert Sachs est ici. On parle de toi. Reçu ta lettre où tu me dis que tu ne vas pas à Bangalore. Il y a beaucoup de gens en Amérique qui n'ont jamais pris un train — mais, naturellement l'auront. Il y a un mouvement vers la nature et le mysticisme croissant.

Je ne pense arriver en Inde beaucoup avant Bangalore. Je te fixerai moi mes mouvements mais peut être je pourrai monter en novembre ou décembre. Je ne sais pas encore. Au moins en Inde je voudrais vivre libre et sans plan.

J'ai soif de solitude — et aussi un peu de repos — bien que je continue avec mon plan de 50% aussi en Amérique.

Les nouvelles économiques et politiques qu'on entend ici sont plutôt pessimistes. Je parle de l'Inde.

Je n'ai pu voir Anne/Hoke depuis son retour de l'Inde.

Il y a quelque chose qui se passe dans le monde — et aussi à l'intérieur de nous mêmes.

J'espère que tu vas bien et te soignes.

Avec ma vraie amitié

Ingo

California, August 20, 1973

ŌM

Voilà, your 25 years in India. It is life, that which we live, that counts. We thank you. In silence, because you did not want a book which, dedicated to you for your birthday, would have presented our ideas a little prematurely – although ideas are not the last word. I am leaving in a few days and could go to Bangalore before going to see my brother in Kerala.

I'll send word when I am in India.

A big thank you,

Raymond

❖❖❖

Indore, October 6, 1973

My dear Raymond,

... So you will go to the monastic summit in Bangalore [October 14th to 22nd]. *I do not believe that true monasticism can be cultivated here through institutions. It is only about charismatic vocations. On behalf of P.M., I have invited the president of Śivānanda,*[333] *Svāmi Chidānandajī, a man whom I love and greatly respect. He has promised me he will go if he is free. But he told me that it wasn't my place... This consoled me since I had rather rudely refused to attend, especially to arrive by plane and then bear witness to a poor and charismatic monasticism; in any case, my coronary attack instantly did away with any possibility of going.*

What should be told to them is what I wrote in the notice I sent in January: if a Christian in India hears the call of the "Desert" he must join together with unknown hermits in the Himalayas to receive the spirit of [Saints] Anthony, Hilarion, Arsenius and the others ...

Abhiṣiktānanda

❖❖❖

333 Ṣivānanda *āśram*, headquarters of the Divine Life Society founded by Svāmi Śivānanda.

ॐ Indore 8 Nov. 72

Mon cher Raymond

Merci de ton mot de Bangalore. Je me demande bien comment la réunion s'est passée en fait et je regrette bien que Swami Chidanandji n'ait pu y aller, car il me semble que les moines hindous chrétiens (juste des 'observers' de Shantivanam accueillis en dernière minute) et autres y étaient peu 'conspicuous'. Enfin, comme je te l'ai écrit, je crois que plus que jamais l'Esprit se libère des voies institutionnelles...

Ma convalescence est désespérément longue. Sans doute comme on le dit ici, l'attaque est elle tombée sur un organisme déjà bien fatigué. Ce sont des hauts et des bas avec pas de signes encore d'une remontée réelle. L'idée de Ranchi a dû être abandonnée, malgré le désir des Soeurs. Je n'en suis pas encore capable. Il y a plus de huit jours par exemple que j'ai été incapable de dire la messe. (chapelle pourtant dans la chambre voisine). Je regrette cette occasion manquée à nouveau de nous rencontrer. D'ailleurs les mémoires ne sont pas très brillants. Il s'agit bien de toucher le fond de son incapacité mentale et physique. Tout le revêtement de l'expérience que le monde a si merveilleusement tissé tombe en loques

et la nudité intérieure dont on a si merveilleusement parlé et écrit et pensé, se découvre enfin une pure réalité! C'est bien le but!

In Christo

[signature]

Indore, November 8, 1973

My dear Raymond

Thank you for your letter from Bangalore. I am wondering, of course, how the meeting actually went and I am very sorry that Svāmi Chidānandajī was unable to attend. Indeed, I have the impression that the Christian Indian monks (some observers from America who were sent in at the last minute) and others were not very "conspicuous".

As I wrote to you, I believe more than ever that the Spirit frees itself from institutional ways...

My convalescence is desperately long. Undoubtedly, as I am told here, the attack hit an organism that was already very weakened. There are some ups and downs but as yet no signs of a real recovery. The ruti idea had to be dropped, despite the wish of the sisters. I am not yet up to it. For more than eight days, for example, I was unable to celebrate mass (chapel in the next room). I am sorry that we have missed another chance to meet. By the way, the meninges are not very brilliant. And it is good to hit the bottom of one's mental and physical incapacity. All the covering of experience that the mind (manas) *has so marvellously woven falls apart, and the inner nakedness that has been spoken and written and thought about so wonderfully is revealed in the end as pure nakedness.*

God be praised for everything!

In spiritu,

Abhiṣiktānanda

❖❖❖

Posthumous Letters
FROM R. PANIKKAR TO ABHIṢIKTANANDA ON EASTERN AND WESTERN MONASTICISM[334]

Abyssus abyssum invoked
«Deep calls to deep at the voice of the cataracts»

Ps 42:7

The West calls the East
and they meet in the cataracts of the Word: *dabar, vāc, lógos*

Vārāṇasī, December 7, 1975
(Second anniversary of your Great Departure)

Dear Abhiṣiktānanda,

Do you remember? Some years ago I suggested that a "tribute book" should be published for your 60th birthday. At the time you made fun of the idea, so I didn't insist. Now I take my "revenge", though it will not be about one single book, but a series of texts from all over the world; showing that your 40-year-long dream will soon be fulfilled, confirming once more the parable of the grain of corn that has to fall to the earth and die to be fruitful.

---

334 Unpublished text from 1975, which appeared in abridged form in "Studies in Formative Spirituality", Duquesne University, Pittsburgh, vol. III, no. 3. (Nov. 1982). Also in *Opera Omnia,* Vol. I, Part 2, Maryknoll, New York: Orbis Books, 2014.

«An hour awaited for fifteen years!» You wrote to your family when, on the morning of August 15, 1948 (on the first anniversary of the Independence of India, although you did not seem to be struck by the coincidence), you reached the port of Colombo and went straight to Madras, entering your Promised Land, which you were never to abandon. Throughout the years you remained faithful to your calling, overcoming all the trials that India held in store for you. As early as 1947, you had written from your monastery of St. Anne de Kergonan to Father J. Monchanin in India about the possibility of joining him, or, anyway, cooperating with him in the spiritual bridge-building you both envisaged.

«Her call fills me with anguish», you said in a letter,[335] referring to the fascination that India had for you. This "anguish" indeed, is one of the words that appears most frequently in your personal journals throughout the years.

Dear Svāmi-jī, this is not a fictitious letter I am writing to you; it is real and genuine, a continuation of our long correspondence and a follow-up to the letter you wrote after deciding you would spend at least a month with me in Vārāṇasī. How I regret that we later had to cancel our plans because you were so tired «and still very weak»,[336] with no strength to undertake the journey. Two months later, in fact, you had passed beyond all earthly limitations, and my last letter to you arrived when you were no longer with us, in this time and this space.

We had planned to speak at length about so many common concerns—the Church, Christianity, Hinduism, the new generation of theologians, etc.—and there were so many problems that your spirit, lively and attentive as ever, wanted to share with some of your friends here, in the holy city of Vārāṇasi, this side of the River. Now you have crossed to the other shore, but precisely because we both believe that there flows the same River, I can write you a real letter, not a literary fiction or some sort of "supernatural" communication. Although an intimate letter addressed to you, it is also an open letter to all those who, directly or indirectly, know and love you. You have broken down the boundaries!

[335] Letter of August 18, 1947, in Jean-Michel Le Saux, Raimundo Panikkar, and the Abhishiktananda Society, *La Montée au fond du coeur: le journal intime du moinechrétien- sannyasi hindou, 1948-1973* (Paris: Oeil, 1986).

[336] Ibid., October 6, 1973.

I am still greatly moved by the reading of most of your personal journals. I only regret that those written after 1965 were destroyed, so that, except for some excerpts that have been saved, every reference to those years is secondhand. Doubtless it was a well-meant decision taken out of zeal, in order to protect your privacy, and maybe somebody else's; however, I am all the more sorry because it was done by a *saṃnyāsin* [a renouncer] who nevertheless thought he had a property "right" over those manuscripts, therefore a right to do what he liked best with them, namely to throw them into the Ganges. Why should we be afraid of our nakedness, hiding the dark sides of our existence? Or, on the contrary, the bright sides? Anyway, what remains of your private writings is rich enough to provide material for study, and for a possible book.

I will use your journals only to support what I want to express through this letter, which is in no way intended to be a study of your thought, nor will it try to follow your inner pilgrimage by analyzing your private papers. I know very well that those notes you used to write down were of use to you, and that you often played the role of the *pūrvapakṣin* [devil's advocate] with the sole intention of expressing a momentary mood. I hope that future studies will interpret those pages for what they actually are, in thc light of your whole life and works. Most of the quotations I use here were inserted after the first edition of my letter, after having read your journals, as a confirmation to what I had already written. The two quotations from Monchanin have been taken from his last book.[337] All the rest is based on my personal memories.

The Experience in India

We are grateful to you, dear Svāmījī. You were one of the most authentic "western" spirits ever to sail to our coasts in order to expose himself to the genuine "Indian" experience. You had a truly western character and a profound western formation. Only a man equipped with all the traditional western resources could have done what you did, endured the discouragements you met, and overcome the internal and external obstacles that stood in your way. I would like to emphasize this. Immediately before writing this letter, I went through your manuscript, *Amour et Sagesse,*

[337] J. Monchanin, *Mystique de l'Inde, mystère chrétien* (Paris: Fayard, 1974).

written in 1942 for your mother. It is a moving confession of your traditional Catholic faith, in the best sense of the phrase. It shows a command of scripture, tradition, and a deeply assimilated knowledge of theology that many a highly placed professor might well envy, and, at the same time, a mature fervor that only a true contemplative can communicate. He alone, who has assimilated tradition at its best, can go beyond it. Everything else is just amateur fantasies, with catastrophic consequences for both sides in the dialogue, as we have experienced so often: all those superficial "enthusiasts" hurt more than help both the western tradition they come from, and the eastern tradition they claim to imitate. But I imagine you would interrupt this digression of mine by waving your hand as you used to, a happy symbiosis between the Indian *mudrā* conveying indifference and patience, and the French gesture meaning "let it go."

As late as 1970 you were still saying, «The problem of *Advaita*-Christianity appears only on the notional level»[338] and, except perhaps for the last year of your life, you always faced this problem most intensely. We are grateful to you, because not only did you live your life *with* us, giving it away so beautifully, but you also lived your experience *for* us. The internal contradictions and rendering conflicts (*déchirements*, you called them) that beset you for decades helped us to see and to discern far more than any cheap synthesis or stubborn refusal could possibly have done. You became one of us; you lived for us a life that Indians alone might never have experienced in all its tensions and polarities. How often during your years of prayer, solitude, and meditation you used to complain that what you saw and suffered did not seem to be felt in its excruciating polarity, either by ordinary Christians or by the great majority of Vedāntins and even *sādhus* [monks]; for all of whom you coined the epithet *nāmarūpins,* those who restrict themselves to the names and shapes of things, to appearances!

Your distrust of concepts, of the mental, of entanglement in the *nāma-rūpa,* the name and form, your frontal attacks on theologians, philosophers, and all those you called *vivartavādins*[339]—all this is well known to those who knew you. You were a man of orthopraxis, rather than orthodoxy.

---

338 Letter of November 27, 1970, in *La Montée au fond du coeur.*

339 Those who share the limited idea of a world as an illusory transformation of Brahman.

Our gratitude is for your life more than for anything else. Only a few months after your arrival in India to take up residence in Kulitalai, Father Monchanin, whom you had joined, wrote:

«As the days pass in his company, I admire more and more the scarcely believable *convergences* of his views with my own aspirations. And this is all the more *striking* because on the humanist plane. . . we differ so much.»[340]

Indeed, a certain estrangement became inevitable. It was your fellow holy man Monchanin, or to call him by his Indian name, Parama Arūbi Ānanda, who, when you had lived a few years together, in late 1955, wrote,

«I experience a growing horror for the forms of muddled thinking in this "beyond-thought" which more often proves to be only "staying on this side," where everything drowns.»[341]

The Saṃsaric River

Your entire life, Abhiṣikta, was a desperate effort to cross this *saṃsāric* river [cosmic flow], which, for you, carried not so much the monsoon mud of matter, but the cold wintry waters of the mind. Many feared you would capsize in the crossing; now most concede that, in spite of whirlpools and storms, you did at the end really cross over and reach the land of nonreturn—because the only ones who return are those who do not attain the other shore, the *atīta* or Beyond, about which Monchanin wrote, in 1955, in the Preface to your book *Guhāntara,* which had to wait so many years before being published. You were fully aware of the difficulties. Years after Monchanin's death you wrote in a private letter that he "became more and more skeptical about the possibility of harmonizing *Vedanta* and Christianity."[342] But you added in your typical way in the same letter: *"and yet it moves!* or rather this will remain unshakable like Aruṇācala!"

But let us go back to your orthopraxis. Many people were put off by your sweeping statements, oversimplifications, and your judgments of others. They listened only to *what* you were saying; they did not understand you.

---

[340] Ibid., September 10, 1948.

[341] Ibid., December 17, 1955.

[342] Ibid., December 23, 1970, letter to Odette Baumer.

They dissociated your words from the man you were and interpreted your utterances within a "learned" framework, which was not in fact your context. They were attentive only to the *what,* disregarding the *who.* Some call this "objectivity," the "scientific attitude." I well understand your discomfort and irritation. You felt you were being reduced to lifeless "notions." For years you suffered from being regarded with suspicion by those who questioned your orthodoxy, always blind to your magnificent orthopraxis.

Do you remember, dear Brother, what happened on the morning of July 31, 1955, when you had already been to Aruṇācala and experienced the impact of *advaita,* and when you had already said and written so many daring ideas? Do you remember your distress in Bombay, in the house of a man who at the time tremendously influenced your life and used to insist on your "liberation" from Christian or any other kind of worship, when, while unpacking your things, you saw with dismay that the "ara," the heavy stone that serves as the altar, was slightly broken and that therefore you did not dare to say Mass? You went to confession and there learned of the privilege of the "antemensium."[343] Your *doxa* may have been in turmoil, but your *praxis* was of the strictest sort. Your asceticism, moreover, is not open to question. How often had I to say to all those "skeptics" in the fifties: You go and live the same kind of life, and then we shall speak.

Over a year later, when you were performing your marvelous *tapas* [ascetic practices] in total solitude, you could still write so candidly:

«This afternoon the hosts were damp, heated, stuck together, solidified, etc...» (We perceive your disappointment, but we wonder why you did not think about using the plain bread from the village.) «I had to write at once to Śāntivanam to get some others. Strange how the perspective of having to do without my Mass, should they not arrive in time, upsets me.»

Then you are unfair to yourself by adding:

> I believed myself much freer of the Mass than I really was. There lies deep within me a Christian *adhiṣṭhāna* [substratum] which is difficult to overcome.[344]

---

[343] A cloth in which a holy relic was inserted. Missionaries were allowed to use it instead of the "ara."

[344] Letter of November 22, 1956, in *La Montée au fond du coeur.*

Or, as you wrote three years before your death: «[I have] a visceral attachment to the Christian myth.»[345]

I do not want simply to recount anecdotes. What I want to say goes much deeper; it concerns what I believe to be your weakness *and* your greatness. Permit me to say aloud what we often discussed together alone.

I say "weakness," because what really worried you was orthodoxy and its proper formulation, whereas the experiential realm that you strove to expound is tainted the very moment you try to explain it. The innocence and therefore also the sincerity of thought is lost, since you cannot combine the two: the reflective preoccupation with orthodoxy and total spontaneity of heart. Besides, what you had at heart was inexpressible; and the fact that you wanted to express it in words, and others also wanted you to, just made the matter more obscure. Not only is a silence proclaimed as silence ipso facto distorted, but even a felt silence is no longer a silence. You wanted to make the *logos* [word] subservient to the *pneuma* [spirit], unlike most westerners, who have been attempting for centuries to encapsulate the spirit in the intellect. Deep was your distrust of "ideas" and "words," no less than your suspicion about the current christological statements, though you yourself were a man of Christo-spiritual depth as well as remarkably talented in writing, both in English and French.

Am I too bold in bringing Trinitarian subordinationism into the picture? The ancient subordinationists meant to subdue the Spirit to the *Logos;* you, exactly the opposite. Once at Śantivanam, your *āśram*, when Monchanin was still there, I vaguely recall feeling, but not daring to say, that the Saccidānanda *āśram* was not only named after the Holy Trinity in heaven, but also represented it on earth, Monchanin being the *logos* and you the *pneuma* —both springing from the same mysterious source, the Father— whether the *pneuma* was to be intended according to Latin or Greek theology *(Filioque,* or *per Filium).* In any event, a crypto-subordinationism was at work in either case. Were not the tensions in the *āśrama* reflection of that same old Trinitarian controversy? They were not merely psychological divergences: both of you were too deep and too genuine for that. They were theological polarities or, at least, options.

---

[345] Ibid., September 7, 1970.

Were you to live in the more radical Hīndū way, as the Spirit prompted you, or were you to accommodate yourself to the exigencies of the Logos, as Father Monchanin wished? An extraordinary challenge, and a striking paradox, for your Indian name refers to Christ (the Logos) and Monchanin's to the Spirit (*pneuma*): *complementum oppositorum!*

The Experience of Being

As this is my last letter to you, you will—I know—excuse these personal reminiscences, but I must not lose the thread of my discourse. Your most vulnerable point, it seems to me, was in the field of the *logos,* of doctrine, formulation, expression, word, language. You suffered from it and were distressed when, while you were still at Kulitalai, your manuscripts were negatively criticized and probably misunderstood by those considered to be great authorities on the matter. How could they understand your writings without *standing under* your own experiences? I must say, you reacted in a wonderfully humble way. The best evidence of it is that most of your writings did not see the light of day until late in your pilgrimage. Now they face the world as clear denials of what I termed your "weakness"—a weakness that you in fact overcame.

It was edifying to me (not without a certain joy in seeing you a bit less acosmic) to notice how carefully you chose the right words for your publications. You learned during the last ten years of your life that we write for others and to be understood by them. You took pains in correcting and revising your work again and again. I remember you telling me that you had to relearn French. Your published writings achieved a very precise expression; you had the tenacity of a Breton.

I named this tension "your greatness," and it *was* so, first of all because of its spontaneity and genuineness. There was within you, and in spite of you, an *elan,* an urge, a life, a spirit (either with small or with capital S, as you shrewdly pointed out). It was not so much to do this or that as a thirst to be, as you wrote in your journal: «To do? To do what? I am not here to do anything but to be.» This was your greatness, because you weren't aware of it. But the tension inside you was, too: a tremendous, unquenchable thirst to be. You did not let this "being" take care of itself; you *wanted* to be, you incorporated in yourself the best dynamism of the

West, your being could exist only *by being.* The will to be was so lively in you, and that's why you did not give up; you held out to the end. You insisted that one had to overcome the mental, and your very emphasis on this seemed a contradiction. You overcame the mental not with words, not by talking about it, but by your life, your true orthopraxis.

«To be, from God's point of view, is prayer,»[346] you wrote in your *mauna mandir* [silent retreat]. All that you wrote and said was validated by the witness of your life, and it was an expression of your being. That's why these expressions should not be divided from your being. They are not independent theological documents, nor isolated spiritual teachings. This, of course, is valid for every writer, and no text is completely independent of its own context, but it fits you particularly: you need to know the writer if you want to understand the written texts. There are some texts that, despite their dependence on a given context, try to express something that goes far beyond the actual milieu they come from. Most of your words were cries, interjections, and prayers coming from experience and aimed at experience, being repeated in the greatest range of tones. One of your last writings, published posthumously, put all the "blame" for this on the *Upaniṣads.* You wrote,

> The teaching of the *Upaniṣads* is not a matter of formulations—notions and proposition—which could be transmitted, that is, taught or received as such. Upaniṣadic formulations have no further function than to lead to an experience.[347]

You had suffered so much from "microdoxic" interpretations that you hardly listened when I argued that the same could be said of any living tradition and sacred text, including the Christian tenets and even dogmas, which are means, channels, *media quibus.* I remember how we once searched for a passage in St. Thomas Aquinas where he affirms that the "peaks" of sacred doctrine should not be imparted to everybody—an exact parallel to the word *Upaniṣad,* commonly interpreted as "secret doctrine." It was only much later that I found the passage quoted in a pamphlet by Svāmī Acyutānanda Sarasvatī, one of the few western Christian monks ever to have received an orthodox and traditional Hindū initiation while remaining

[346] Ibid., November 26, 1956.

[347] *Clergy Monthly* (1974): 474.

a Carmelite. I wish that his life were known to the world, and his example studied and followed.[348] Two people could not be more different than you were—a clear example of the manifold ways in which the Spirit works among humankind.

A year before your death, your *samādhi,* you applied this idea to Christianity:

> Christianity is first *upaniṣad,* correlation, non-direct teaching. Direct teaching only produces *nāma-rūpa.* Correlation sets the spark of *anubhava* [experience]; only this fulfills.[349]

Your writings were so sincere, your insights so genuine, your discoveries so true, that you found it difficult to think that other people could have reached the same type of conviction:

> The inner mystery calls me with excruciating force, and no outside being can help me penetrate it and *there, for myself,* discover the secret of my origin and destiny.[350]

And you continued in the same tone for several pages. Your sentences always bore the mark of personal epiphanies. That is the reason why it was easy to misunderstand them by ignoring their link with you, and you knew it all too well:

> There is always a risk of taking *ersatz* experience for experience. The way of *kevala* [solitude, oneness] is terrifying in its nakedness. ... The danger is to take the idea of *kevala* for *kevala* itself,[351]

you wrote that same day.

Let me deal a bit more with this dimension in your life of which you knew only the "other side," the negative one, without seeing its true greatness. To put it otherwise: your meeting with Nothingness, Svāmījī, did not happen in the often easy, shallow way of so many westerners

---

[348] Karel Soetaert, born in Belgium in 1912, became Father Lambert of the Mother of God when he took his first Carmelite vows in 1931 and Svāmī Acyutānanda Sarasvatī (with the distinction of Adhyatma Svarupi bestowed upon him later) when, in 1967, after twenty-eight years in India (during which time he acquired Indian citizenship), he was initiated into the *samnyasa* order of the Saraswati Dasanamis, while remaining an obedient and exemplary Roman Catholic Carmelite monk until his death in Alwaye (Kerala) in 1968.

[349] May 28, 1972, in *La Montée au fond du coeur.*

[350] Ibid., April 19, 1956.

[351] Ibid. (published in *"Esseulemen"* in *Intériorité et Revelation,* 130).

who, dissatisfied with their own heritage and enthusiastic about eastern glimmerings, swallow anything exotic and believe themselves to have already realized the supreme mystic experience just because they have forested the limits of their individual faculties. No; you offered all the resistance of a "Breton" soul to an ultimate intuition that would blur any final distinction between good and bad, God and world, being and Not-Being. To engage seriously in such an enterprise, requesting us to sink into the realm of nonreturn, it is not thesame as trying some *yoga, advaita* or tantrism. I am not questioning the sincerity of so many people following that kind of experience. I am just stressing the seriousness and pioneering character of your life, a total and absolute consecration to a life that, as you knew, would demand a real death—as the only, paradoxical condition for a true resurrection. If we die with the "hope" of rising, this is not a real death. Without the *lama sabachtani* [the words of Jesus on the cross, "My God, why have you forsaken me?"], there is no real death, hence no true resurrection. But this is not my point here. My point is best made by recalling two episodes in your life, both of which gave you a great deal of suffering and uncertainty, since at that time you were not conscious of the deep reasons coming into play in your spontaneous reactions, as always happens with any sincere attitude.

The first was a proposal made to you of a journey to the West to attend a conference—a serious one. A course was to be given on Indic spirituality, especially yoga, and you were asked to principal as an "expert," even a *gurū*. You could not deny the gravity of the invitation nor the possible good you might do. Moreover, you agreed with me that a visit to the West, the very first after your arrival in India, would give you not only insight into a changed West but a new perspective on India and her spiritual message. Yet you refused. I vividly remember our conversations and letters we exchanged on the subject. You felt in your heart of hearts that it would betray the plunge you had taken into an experience allowing of no return; instinctively you understood that you could not play with your own life and that, once you were dead to anything in space and time, you should no longer withdraw, going back to temporal "missions." Let me thank you, Svāmijī, all the more because my role of devil's advocate at the time was a strong one. You were right, you resisted playing the *jīvanmukta,* the accomplished saint, who can act in the *līlā, or* play, of this world as a *bodhisattva,* the enlightened man who stays in this world in order to save all the other beings. You did not accept to play such a role, and you were right, beloved friend. All of us now bless you for your "stubbornness."

The second incident was when you heard that some dear friends were planning to "abandon" India and pitch their tent elsewhere. Hardly anybody understood your burst of indignation and, again, it was my privilege to be your confidant and the outlet for your anger. You considered their leaving India a betrayal, a defeat, and even cowardice on their part. You were planning your own calling onto other people. For you, that *would* have been a betrayal, because of the depth and uniqueness of your life-and-death venture with Hindū spirituality.

You were not simply experimenting; you were totally committed. You could only leave India as you left it, by dying, to arise in the hearts and minds of those who, either directly or indirectly, will know about you. You yourself did stress, in fact, that your calling was unique, it could not be generalized. Proof of it was your total reconciliation with those same friends, the minute you sensed they were simply fulfilling another task, according to the mysterious laws by which life reveals itself in this *saṃsāra.*

Your greatness, Svāmījī, lay in your purity of heart, which led you to an uncompromising position. You did not spare even your best friends when they departed from what you thought—alas, "thought" (without the agreement of the party concerned, sometimes)—the right and proper way. A few months before your death, you wrote to me after refusing to attend a monastic meeting in India:

> It is not by way of verbiage and discussion that reform will come. Benedict, like Anthony, went into the desert and Francis into the streets; they did not gather together the monks of the surrounding areas for a meeting.[352]

You yourself were a gesture, a cry, a symbol. Now that you can no longer reply, except by sweetly inspiring us to study the meaning of your life in depth, I dare draw (if imperfectly) some outlines of your Self, that Self which for so many years you were unsure whether to consider *ahaṃkāra* [ego] or *aham* ["I"]. Imperfect as it may be, this sketch will perhaps encourage the publishing of better perspectives and more reliable portraits

[352] Ibid., May 25, 1973, letter to Panikkar.

by those who are maybe already working on it, but they currently have neither the time nor the wish to take part in an enterprise that must await its proper time.

Two Loves

Shortly after your arrival in India, you commented,

> I felt with joy the French atmosphere of Pondicherry. But now I have found myself "at home" again at Rue Dupleix, the Indian sector! I have two loves.[353]

Yes, you had two loves; and those two loves—for the Christian *mārga* [way] and the Hindū *dharma* [religion]—struggled within you during the entire twenty-five years of your life in India. Only at the very end, after your heart attack, or as you put it, the «Adventure of the Great Week»,[354] did the two seem to come into harmony. You wrote, then, of the flash that was the culmination of your life-quest:

> After a few days there came over me something like the marvelous solution of an equation: I had discovered the Holy Grail. And this I say to whoever can capture the image. The quest for the Grail is fundamentally none other than the quest for Self. Unique quest meant under every myth and symbol.[355]

Two months later you had drained the whole Cup. Do you know, Svāmījī, that *the* dream that C.G. Jung had during his only stay in India was of the Grail? Is this perhaps evidence of the integration of which I am speaking, the fact that, at the very end of your life, you too had recourse to that myth Jung himself called a "primordial European dream" (*ureuropäischer Traum*)?

For a quarter of a century you were haunted by the call of the abyss, by the *advaitic* experience that you sensed gave all the answers, because it eliminated both question and questioner. It was «the call of the higher abyss»[356]—as you effectively put it, playing on the paradox. Yet you

353 Ibid., February 20, 1949.
354 Ibid., July 10-18, 1973.
355 Ibid., September 11, 1973.
356 Ibid., July 21, 1956.

resisted; you did not dare take the final plunge, as you yourself wrote on several occasions. You preached it to others, you presented it as the "solution," and yet you doubted, you felt it to be a betrayal of your other love, not only externally, as far as western culture was concerned, but, more deeply, concerning the loyalty to that Christ whom you called *Sadgurū,* true Master (as you still remarked on March 23, 1970), although you could not dissociate Him from his geographical and historical milieu. You spoke of creation as «the fission of the One»[357] (for you felt creatureliness precisely as a fissioned particle) and you remarked, «Heaven exists for whoever desires it and Hell for whoever fears it.»[358]

Did you see that, as tradition requires, I preceded this letter with some words from the Holy Scripture: *Abyssus abyssum invocat,* as you used to sing at least once a week in the chorus or pray silently? The unfathomable depth of the Judeo-Christian tradition is crying out to the no less bottomless depth of the Indic wisdom. What these words convey is the abyssal nature of the encounter. You sensed so well that the fruitful *maithuna,* union, the only livable symbiosis, was not ultimately dependent on problems of technology, science, sociology, or philosophy, but on a mystical embrace in the depth of the abyss. Already it can be heard: the roar of cataracts, of living, of divine waters—the *āpodivyāh* of the two traditions. For you, the struggle was not justical dialectical or academic; your entire existence was at stake.

Like St. Paul, you were convinced that if Christ did not rise from the dead we were the most wretched of all living beings. You wrote,

> By committing myself totally to *advaita,* I risk, if Christianity is true, straying onto the wrong track for all eternity.[359]

Years later you were still repeating the same anguished cry:

> I am full of fear, plunged in an ocean of anguish which ever way I turn. ... And I fear risking my eternity for a delusion. And yet you are no delusion, oh Aruṇācala![360]

---

[357] Ibid., April 7, 1955.
[358] Ibid., August 2, 1954.
[359] Ibid., September 25, 1953.
[360] Ibid., November 27, 1956.

If *advaita* is true, you thought your entire life, and, what is more, all efforts and achievements of twenty centuries of Christian tradition to have been nothing but a bad, even pernicious dream. Your quest was for life and death on a cosmic level. Those who do not understand that the struggle is an ultimate one have no idea what the contemplative life means, what the fight against the devil means in the old monastic tradition: they have understood nothing about the life of the spirit. No need, Svāmījī, to defend you from all the dilettantes and *nāmarūpins* who wanted merely clear-cut standpoints, or exact formulas, at least.

The Mystical Poet

You were a poet, Svāmījī, and you knew it. Do you remember when I teased you, because in one of your books you referred to me as an artist "also"? In October 1956 you composed a beautiful hymn to Aruṇācala after the manner of the Song of Songs. But your inspiration reached a peak in the absolutely sincere poem that you composed from the *mauna mandir* some days later:

> You ravished me, O Aruṇācala, as a virgin to whom one speaks words of love and you left me there, like that before you.
>
> ...
>
> And I remain naked, lying right there, and I have no more strength to rise.
> I am clothed in shame,
> I dare not look at myself for all this is your work, O Aruṇācala,
> and I will no more think of you.[361]

You could not resist any more «the sundering call of my deepest being»[362] while on that same day you confessed once again your passionate love

---

[361] *Tu m'as violé,o Aruṇācala,*
Comme une vierge a qui on dit des mots d'amour
et tu m'as laissé là, comme ça devant toi.
...
Et je reste la nu, gisant, comme ça,
je n'ai plus la force de me relever
je suis couvert de honte
je n'ose plus me regarder car tout cela est ton oeuvre, o Arunāchala,
et je ne veux plus penser a toi.
Ibid., November 15, 1956.

[362] Ibid., November 24, 1956.

for Christ of over forty years, declaring in touching terms that you have been faithful to Him in an uncompromising and unflinching way. We should not, and do not, minimize your dark night and your subsequent purification, my dear brother.

It took years, however, to incorporate into yourself the *advaitic* experience. Sometimes it seemed that you *had* undergone it, and that your will was resisting it, but you knew that the true experience is irresistible and that you had not yet undergone it, since doubts were still creeping into your . . . what? Was it not the *mind* that was responsible for all this delusion? You used to retort, when you felt that I was making it too simple: Would not the entire structure of Christianity collapse? Or, at least, would it not lead to «the explosion of dogmatic, cultural, and sociological Christianity?»[363] «So what?» was my immediate, exasperated reaction. The fact that we were aware of such dilemma showed that we were not on the right path, and that neither a "yes" nor a "no" has any bearing on the real problem. A long story, Svāmijī!

The fascinating aspect of your growth is that it was not an academic or intellectual process, but a vital one. It was not a quandary of your mind but an aporia of your life. I argued that there exists also an intellectual experience and that we cannot throw away the mental without discarding what sustains it; that the great obstacle here is not so much the intellect as the will. This is where you were in truth a great westerner. «*Wollen ist Ursein*», the will is the primordial Being, says Schelling, summing up the western experience. This, however, is where you won. To undergo the *advaitic* experience in the Indian context had been done time and again (your cherished example was Rāmaṇa Mahārṣi), but to reenact the same experience with another type of "material"—that is, not with a different type of consciousness, since every mental construction is surpassed, but with another anthropological makeup—this was your contribution. What I dared call your weakness was, in fact, your real greatness. You needed to break with centuries-old mental and spiritual habits that lay heavily on your psyche. You had to do violence to yourself. That led me to see your uncertainty as a false problem and, as such, the cause of a useless

[363] Ibid., July 14, 1956.

struggle. Anyway, without passing through all these troubles, you would not have been able to help so many of your contemporaries.

Connections

In order to unite the western tradition with the *advaitic* experience it was not enough to undergo the experience; it was necessary that this experience consumed all western *upādhis,* or limiting adjuncts, that it transformed the traditional western approach to reality and exhausted it within this same *advaitic* intuition. I was tempted to make this too easy, perhaps because the Indic spirit had already cleared the trail, or because the westerner already foretastes it, or already has an intellectual glimpse of it. A mediator, not an intermediary, was needed, a person really at home in the two worlds. You yourself liked to quote, though in a higher sense, that famous verse of the tenth *mandala* [book] of the *Íg-veda:* that the *ke©in,* the long-haired ascetic, "bears the two worlds." You were such a *ke©in;* you were really led by the Spirit, and this is what, fortunately, you did not know.

We agreed that the central cosmological dogma of Christianity was generally relegated to the very end of the *creed* as an appendix: the resurrection of the flesh. We all know the possible Iranian origin of this tenet. Nevertheless, it is this ultimately divine destiny of matter that makes it more difficult to reconcile the Christian belief with an unqualified *advaita,* which would not allow for any pollution of the total purity and spiritual transparency of the *pāramārthika,* the ultimate level. You suffered the antinomy and refused to solve it by watering down the Christian tenet or by diluting the advaitic doctrine. I remember that, during our conversations, you would not accept my harmonizing explanations, lest you be disloyal to *advaita,* and at the same time you would not give up a certain belief in resurrection. You were never satisfied with merely intellectual answers. Unless you experienced, you would continue in your struggle. I know that toward the end this tension disappeared. Do not regret that you have written no theory on this, Svāmījī. Others will do it in your wake.

In 1956 you wrote of the «ever stated and never solved problem of the relation between the mystical experience of the Christian and that of the *Advaitin.*»[364]

---

[364] Ibid., February 6, 1956.

But three days later you wrote for yourself,

> It is false, absolutely false, to contrast Christianity with *Advaita*. Yet truth does not reside in an impossible synthesis of both but in a surpassing where both remain totally themselves.[365]

From then on you were directed toward that *dépassement*, that "going beyond." The search led you through many mazes, such as that of considering Christianity to be only at the level of appearance, or *vyavahārika,* and not at the ultimate level, or *pāramārthika.* This made you suffer deeply, for you were tremendously loyal to yourself. You considered that as long as you wanted to get rid of Christian cultic practices, you were not liberated from them and hence should not give them up. You did not take things superficially.

The Christian Eucharist was not for you another form of *pūjā* [cult]. You wrote of it: «The Eucharist puts at my disposal the total Incarnation »[366] and later, «The Eucharist is the fulfillment of the universe in God.»[367] This, however, did not deter you from saying,

> The Incarnation, supreme myth, manifestation in the cosmos of that interior mystery each Man carries in his very depths. Supreme sacrament, plenitude of all magic, of all theurgy, through communion in which Man reaches the depths of self. Christ, in truth, is the cosmic and social expression of what every Man carries buried in him.[368]

It was probably on the same day that, in a long meditation on *advaita,* you first hinted at a solution, an over-coming; but then you came back to your existential anxiety:

> There are two faces to Christ, the historic face and the meta-historic face. Christians celebrate the historic face. India and all cosmic religions the meta-historic one. Are these two not necessary in this world so that the praise and knowledge of Christ be complete? These two faces, anyway, are not opposed to one another. The historic face is the expression of the other one. And the *kevalinadvaita*is the plenitude of Christian worship.[369]

---

365 Ibid., February 9, 1956.

366 Ibid., June 12, 1952.

367 Ibid., April 15, 1956.

368 Ibid., February 1956.

369 Ibid.

Were you on the right track? A few days later, after an attack of influenza you wrote,

> Why not go beyond everything and remain plunged in the sovereign peace of *advaita?* However, Christianity claims that *advaita*is not compatible with it. And, in truth, true *advaita*makes the institutionalized Vatican Church blow up. What then? These ties that one has not the *right—or* perhaps the *courage—* to break and that are my anguish and kill my body more than any deficiency of diet, climate, etc. . . . This essential anguish at never being able to take rest or joy in all that used to be my rest and joy. . . Whoever once has felt on his tongue the taste of *advaita,* what nectar is left for him to desire? But from now on he must renounce nectar, whoever proffers it. From the two cups he cannot drink. This is the price of *śanti* [peace] and *ānanda* [joy].[370]

And yet with the ruthless honesty of a journal written only for yourself, you wrote in that same entry when you were examining the old, torturing problems as to whether fidelity to yourself obliges you to abandon the Church:

> As long as "desire" to leave the Church is in me, it will be the sign that the time has not yet come. This also goes for Âåntivanam. Desire is *rajas.* All is so natural in *sattva.* Can there really be a desire to be?[371]

Freedom

I wonder if you had in mind that *sūtra* of Patañjali[372] that affirms that freedom [*kaivalya*] resides in the identification between *sattva* and the *puruṣa* [primordial Man]? That is, that total purity, perfect solitude, absolute genuineness, can be attained only when our being succeeds in identifying our essence and our existence, as it were, or our humanity and our cosmo-psycho-somatic side. Only then can we act naturally and spontaneously, that is, perfectly freely. How far you are here from the puritanical attitude of those who abandon their native soil because they do not find it pure enough for the flower they expect to produce!

It would be fascinating to follow the internal travail of your life and find the milestones of your synthesis and harmony. You accepted with complete

---

370 Ibid., February 17, 1956.

371 Ibid., November 22, 1956.

372 The *Sutras* of Patañjali is a collection of Sanskrit sutras on the theory and practice of yoga.

earnestness both your *advaitic* Hindū experience and your existential Christian commitment.

As long as I call somebody brother here on earth, for whatever reason, I have the right to call Father the extreme depths of the *guhā* [*cave*].[373]

You wrote in moving self-defense. It was on this same date that you wrote,

> The Christian experience is truly the *advaitic* experience lived in the human communion.[374]

I can hear you accusing me of succumbing to the theologian's temptation and protesting that you are not interested in theory. I never believed you in this—and you were grateful for my disbelief.

Let me now try another approach that may serve to explain your innate distrust of entering into any philosophical inquiry.

The Inner Struggle

May I venture, dear Abhiṣikta, to comment on your inner struggle? Please do not misunderstand me. This is neither psychological analysis nor philosophical investigation. It is the tentative reflection of a friend.

Your struggle was not on the mental plane; it was not primarily intellectual. You used to say that you could not care less about philosophy. You wanted «to live the Gospel without theologizing.»[375]

I used to retort that this was already a philosophical statement. You smiled at me, made your typical gesture of "what can you do?" and we left it at that. Certainly your suffering did not spring from merely intellectual anxiety.

Nor was it a theological scruple. In the early days of your stay in India this might have been the case, but your inner freedom soon overcame any fear of a "*coups de* Denzinger" [the famous collection of Catholic dogmas]. Your fidelity to yourself and the Church had deeper roots than fear or concern about appearances.

---

[373] Ibid., March 8, 1972.

[374] Ibid.

[375] Ibid.

I believe that your struggle was a monastic struggle, specifically, a Christian monastic combat, *advaita* supplying only the outer garb, the terminology, and the occasion. Do you remember our long discussions on the way up to, and down from, Gangotrī? You described them beautifully in your book *Une messe aux sources du Gange,*[376] but did not mention the ultimate consequences that had emerged from our conversations. You perceived them as a threat to your ideas, and you preferred to accuse your own lack of courage, but that of course was not the case.

I argued that, taken to its ultimate conclusions, *absolute* monasticism was not human and certainly not Christian. Not human, because monasticism has an inbuilt claim to, and an irresistible tendency toward, absolute acosmism. Monasticism seeks to break all boundaries, the limitations of the body, matter, and mind, as well as of the spirit: it aspires to transcend the human condition and attain the angelic one, under the guise of "divinization" in Christianity, "realization" in Hinduism, and *nirvāṇa* in Buddhism. It is not Christian because such "perfect," completely logical and coherent monasticism stands in clear opposition to the Incarnation. Incarnation clearly stands for the divinization of the concrete, the limited, and even of matter and the body (since the *logos* became not only "flesh" but body), but without thc destruction of the latter, of the human, even of the corporal. On the other hand, "the *ke©in,* the radical monk, has no *pratiṣṭhā* [support],[377] which is more than just not having a pillow on which to rest his head.

I suggested further that the "trouble" did not lie in choosing either a radical or a mitigated acosmism, but stemmed rather from a lopsided insight, viz., a vision of reality as being only *nirguṇa-brahman* [Brahman without attributes] to the exclusion of the cosmos. You did not question the nature of the *Advaitic* Absolute, which leaves no room for the world, nor did we discuss in detail what I call the "cosmotheandric" intuition (a vision of reality as a constituent interaction among the Divine—infinity, freedom; the Human—conscience, will; the Cosmic—spatiotemporal matter).

In fact, we did not pursue the matter further. You knew, of course, that I was not against the monastic dimension in human life, but only against a

[376] Paris: Éditions du Seuil, 1967.

[377] May 4, 1973, in *La Montée au fond du cœur.*

certain absolutistic interpretation of monasticism. But I should not press my point here.

Monachos

In any case, *advaita* enabled you to make explicit the ultimate attitudes of this internal dilemma of monasticism. Your last disciple recalled, to both of us, your shock when, in Gangotrī, after listening to your eulogy of the acosmic life of total renunciation, the life led by the naked Hindū ascetic who remains there all the year round in total silence, I almost instinctively cried out, "Then why *not you,* here and now?" You felt sad, and so did I. You felt it was a lack of courage on your part not to live as he did, considering the garb you wore and the vow you had made. I, for my part, felt I had been wrong in being too "logical."

When discussing with Hindūsor Christians at a theoretical level, you could defend, and brilliantly, both *advaita*and the acosmic ideal of the monk. When alone and faced with realizing it in your own life, you felt the pain of being unable to live up to your ideal. This inability made you unhappy, humble, and distressed by the thought that you were not heroic enough to "take the last step." At the same time, I am sure you were convinced deep within yourself that by abandoning everything you would be abandoning reality as well, an act that, though logically justified, might be existentially destructive. In order to go beyond everything, you would need to leave reality behind you.

What people could not understand, what you yourself could not grasp, nor I formulate, was the inner struggle between the *ahaṃkāra,* the "old Man," and the *aham,* the "new Man." We toyed with phrases like "renouncing renunciation," "letting the ego disappear", "dying totally to ourselves", but you were not fooled by wishful thinking and mere mental flashes. Until and unless all of this had become part of your life, until it was "embodied" or "transcended" (strange, how these two words, at this deep level, are equivalent—does not the mystery of the Eucharist mean to eat Transcendence ?), you could not rest, at peace, with the joy you had felt at Aruṇacāla. That joy disappeared the moment you discovered yourself as a Christian, who must accept not only the concrete in himself but the limitations of history, which for you meant Church, Vatican, Organization, and so on. Your journals are sometimes pathetic in this regard and reveal you on the verge of a breakdown. And to make it worse, «I am alone, terribly alone.»[378]

What made you suffer was the radical existential dualism of the *advaitic* distinction between *vyavahārika* [the level of appearance] and *pāramārthika* [the level of reality and truth]. On that latter level nothing of the first could enter. In the same way, a certain traditional monastic spirituality so stresses the transcendence or otherness of God that it demands from you, in order that you may reach the Absolute, a total dereliction of the relative, a complete annihilation of all that you are and can be, of all your creatureliness. We were constantly passing from a Hindū terminology to a Christian one and vice versa. This reminds me of your remark:

> He who possesses several mental or religious or spiritual languages is incapable of absolutizing any formulation, be it evangelical, *upaniṣadic*, Buddhist, etc. He is only able to give stammering testimony to an experience...[379]

This in turn reminds me of the expression *in excessu mentis stare et videre* (to find oneself in mental ecstasy and [then] see), and *quidquid Deus non est: nihil est* [whatever is not God is nothing]—observations that do not come from Himalayan *ṛṣi,* bold mystics, or profound philosophers, but from the sober Thomas à Kempis.[380] Because you felt that in the Christian tradition this attitude, whether for theological reasons or for lack of fervor [*tapas*]or spiritual courage, was dying out orhad become sociologically impossible, you turned to India as the land in which monastic experience had been lived to the full. It is not for me, now, to speculate on historical influences, Jaina ascetics, Hindū *saṃnyāsin* [renouncers], and Christian monks, or to debate whether monasticism has its roots in human nature or culture. Suffice it to say that you felt the call of India not because you were Christian, but because you were a monk and wanted to be one completely and to the end. Am I right? Did you not write that *saṃnyāsa* "carries in itself its own death»?

378 Ibid., August 26, 1955.

379 Ibid., April 30, 1973.

380 Thomas à Kempis was a German-Dutch canon regular of the late medieval period and the author of *The Imitation of Christ*, one of the most popular and best known Christian devotional books.

For reasons that are perhaps too autobiographical to be expressed, I think, Svāmijī, I can understand the center of your life: it was your monastic vocation, your being a monk. You were tortured—as you often said—by the apparent incompatibility between Christianity and *Advaita.* Experientially and existentially committed to both, you could not solve the tension between the two, except perhaps at the very end of your life. Central to you was your monastic commitment. You wondered whether, out of loyalty to yourself, you should leave the Church; you hesitated to give yourself fully to *advaita,* but you never for a moment questioned your monastic consecration, including your way of life. This was the core.

In retrospect one sees the amount of egolessness that such a struggle implies. The tensions and polarities of two religions and civilizations, at the deepest level of their respective worldviews, were going on within you. Your support was your life of a monk, your commitment to the ultimate search, which led you to renounce anything else and overcome any obstacle. Many will find in you all the weaknesses of a mortal creature (how wonderful!), but we must pay tribute to that pure and clear gift of your existence which allowed you to become a *kurukṣetra* [battlefield] where the outcome of the war was still totally undecided.

Do you remember the preface to your *Gūhantara* where Monchanin, your Christian *gurū,* tries to defend you by saying that your intuitions are not of an Indological or philosophical or even theological nature? He goes on to state that the three traditional ways of western Christian spirituality (affirmation, negation, and eminence) offer guidelines for the understanding of your insights. He then discreetly suggests that the way of eminence, though often almost a reversion to the first kataphatic or affirmative way, is not subject to its limitations. He writes:

> The way of eminence is not a turning back, not an infinitization of the finitudes of the intellect. The way of eminence is a surmounting of the second degree, without ever denying it. What is denied is irrevocably denied.[381]

It is here, dear Svāmījī, that we can situate the existential gesture of your whole life. Your struggle, as I have said, was not a struggle of the mind, nor of the heart. Your mind was far too alert and clear not to know its

[381] Cf. Preface, *Guhāntara.*

own limits, your heart too pure and unselfish to worry about itself. Your *askesis,* in the classical sense of the word, your struggle, took place in the "*palestra*", in the arena of being, of life, of your own total existence. This is why we are all indebted to you: you lived that struggle for us.

A Unique Path

You did not remain at Gangotrī, and I did not, for that, deem you a coward. You did not remain in constant solitude either, and we are glad you did not. Nor did you solve the problem on the intellectual plane, and for this also we are thankful. It means that in this "space-between," in this *antarikṣa* where we live, we can still move and be, because life has not been identified with the consciousness of it or even with its intellectual or spiritual dimension. The real question and its answer reside on a deeper plane than any mentioned.

I should not use these pages to express my point of view about the monastic vocation, which is a constitutive dimension that every human being is called upon to realize to some extent. I should not reply to your objection that the absolute cannot be conjoined with the relative, that the *pāramārthika* has nothing to do with the *vyavahārika*—reality with appearance. We would run the risk of getting involved in a merely scholastic debate. You yourself "lived" the contradiction within yourself too thoroughly and too well to resort to other kinds of argumentation. You were far from acosmic, and this humanness of yours was by no means an imperfection or a fault. For it was this very warmth of your being and of your life that provided a solution, even after the recrudescence of your *saṃnyāsa* ideal. Let me explain it a little better.

A question keeps on echoing in me, Abhiṣikta, though I am not sure whether to put it to you, now that you can no longer answer. Anyway here it is, hopefully helping us to get a better understanding of you. After so much Freud, Jung, psychological analyses, critical approaches to religion, and—last but not least—the destruction of your last journals, the question gets even more embarrassing. So, excuse me if I express it candidly.

You wanted to find a monastery; you did not. You wanted to open an *āśrama;* you could not. You dreamed of Christian monks and solitaries in the deserts and mountains of Bharat, but the deserts remained uninhabited and the mountain caves untenanted. You desired to be a Hindū monk; you felt unworthy. You aspired to be a *saµnyāsin*; you remained an aspirant in your own eyes. Now it is not about "re-evaluating" all these statements, and discovering the "providential" way in which you succeeded, notwithstanding any apparent failure. This is not the point, here. I think that in the last period of your life you found a balance between incarnation and transcendence, the *vyavahārika* and the *pāramārthika*; a balance between extreme historicity (time is an indispensable factor of eternity if not "the real thing" itself) and extreme acosmism (time, space, matter, body are only obstacles, nonentities in the superior realm of the spirit). What you achieved is, to me, genuine *advaita:* the dynamic overcoming of all *dvandvas* [dualisms] without falling into monism, the existential overcoming of separation (sin) without pantheistic reductionism; in other words: authentic redemption. You acquired a deep human quality and a poise that radiated through the ecclesial milieu of India.

At the end of your life, you found a *śiṣya,* a true disciple. This reawakened your ideals, caused you to revert to the "fervor" of the cosmic monk; it reawakened in you your almost vanished dream, once so intensely felt, to live according tothe strictest standards of the *saṃnyāsa.* In the last article you published, dealing precisely with the *saṃnyāsa,* you wrote,

> The *saṃnyāsin* is essentially acosmic, as were the original Christian monks.[382]

Your responsibility toward your *secret* (disciple) made you stricter, more critical of any compromise with the world. Can you remember your sarcastic comments regarding the Asian Monastic Convention at Bangalore in 1973, the year of your death, an event in which you refused to participate? Yet—and here is the core of my question, here where all our categories collapse—you had just discovered a fundamental human dimension: fatherhood. The strictness of your abstract ideal softened in the love and warmth of that concrete encounter. Thus your fulfillment as a person was not reached through the fellowship of the brethren, nor through communion with new friends who understood and loved you, but

---

382 This is the text currently published in book form as *The Further Shore,* 13. The original says, "The *sadhū* is essentially acosmic, as was also the case of primitive Christian monasticism" (text of the article published in *The Divine Life,* September 1973).

in the depths of your own concrete, even corporal, self. Paradoxically, on the one hand you became sterner as to your ideal, even dreaming that your spiritual son would be able to achieve what you failed to; you become, once more, theoretically stricter, defending the purity of that ideal which was, perhaps, a projection of a psychological desire. On the other hand, on an existential level, you became "father", which is one of the most common experiences, and this time paternity made you more human, more concretely loving, with a love that had both *nāma* and *rūpa* [name and shape]. You were full of care, and even anxiety, for this child, and your acosmic ideal collapsed before the experience of being a father, rather than a master: "A human relation that reaches deep down to the most intimate depths of paternity,"[383] you wrote in a private letter. Here your theories collapsed. How wonderful is *Bhagavan* [the Lord] in all his works! Was this not the continuation of your destiny or rather the culmination of your life? It is also, maybe, a paradigm for our times regarding the excruciating issue as to where absolute perfection lies. Who wants a *moksa* [liberation] that is only escapism? Who wants narcissistic models of individual perfection? We shun caricatures of traditional types of sanctity, yet feel that holiness may well be the supreme value. But where is it? In what does it consist? You reached realization by becoming a father. You came to India to make Christ known to Hindūs, and were yourself converted to the supreme experience of Indic wisdom-*advaita:*

> I had come to make You known to my Hindū brothers. And it is You who made yourself known to me through their mediation, under the disturbing features of Aruṇācala.[384]

You became not a Christian *sādhu,* but a *saṃnyāsin* who found in Christ a living symbol, in as much as a *saṃnyāsin* can still operate on the symbolic level. You wanted to transcend all boundaries, and you believed that the ideal of *saṃnyāsa*was the only appropriate way. After years of doubts, internal ordeals, and purifications, you had yielded to a more human conception of it. And now you discovered a disciple who reminded you of your own words, who took you so seriously that, ashamed of your "laxness," you returned to an uncompromising theoretical acosmism. By then, however, it was too late for your weakened body and impossible for

[383] November 3, 1970, in *La Montée au fond du cœur.*

[384] Ibid., November 14, 1956.

your loving heart, because your disciple was dear to you in the way of the *bhakti* [devotion], which, so far, you had believed to be incompatible with the hardness and adamantine transparence of the *jñānin* [wise men].

You came to India as a monk, to find in India the ideal of the monk, and there, without ceasing to be one, you begot a son. You became not "abbot" of many but father of one, and though on a spiritual level, it was indeed a true paternity. What happened, Svāmījī? Did Aruṇācala play a trick on you once again? You became a loving father; you had fathered your own child. Everyone who visited you in the last months of your life can testify to the fact that you were another mantransfigured. We will not try to penetrate this last mystery of a human being.

I can only end as I began, expressing our gratitude for having come among us and our commitment to keep the flame, the *agni,* alive, the flame that devours everything, to the summit of Aruṇācala.

Allow me to finish in the traditional Indic way, Svāmijī. Our greetings are always warm and exuberant; but we never express a wish to see each other again, saying good-bye or *au revoir.* It would be like killing a friendship, denying the reality of an encounter, saying that the meeting had not been worth it so it was necessary to repeat it, since anything repeatable is not authentic.

Let me then discreetly disappear from the visible plain, as you did, and without saying anything enter the invisible sphere, where communion subsists and love does not require duality.

PS: The Example

This letter requires a *post scriptum,* which I would like to show you, Abhiṣiktānandajī, as you can still help us to put things right. It has to do with the paradigmatic value of your life. Or, more simply, it concerns a question: What value does your life have as an example for us? There is a methodological objection: isn't it too early for this reflection? Isn't it sufficient to honor the friend, the monk, and let people know his writings before trying to talk about your message?

I think the objection is valid. We should not hasten the rhythm of history. I will therefore not try to answer such an ambitious question. Nevertheless, the very fact that we do not think that it is enough to duplicate your manuscripts and circulate them among a few friends proves that, in one way or another, we do not only think of you as an odd fellow, who stops children playing and makes adults' heads turn, but that your impact goes beyond the influence of just some books or an inspiring memory for a very small group of dear friends. Yet the only thing that I can attempt here is to sketch some of the vectors to be checked by others and proved or disapproved by history.

Having had the privilege of being present at the birth or the consolidation of so many wonderful ventures in this country and elsewhere, I would like to formulate some hypotheses, although I may risk provoking critical reactions. Let me once again act as *pūrvapakṣin,* a sort of "devil's advocate," which was so often my role during our conversations: nowadays, who cares about monasticism?

A small elite may find your life interesting, even stimulating, but the majority of Christians will be indifferent. As far as the Hindūs are concerned, what will be the impact on them of your life, your ideas and your works? Hinduism is so rich in saints and *sādhus!* The fact that someone coming from another country and another tradition has followed their ancient way seems strange and a little anachronistic to a young India, which is rapidly growing away from the religious inflation of the past. Can we consider you a model to be imitated?

It is easy to give an antipragmatic answer or assume an "aristocratic" position, stating that we are not concerned with immediate results or tangible effects, but with truth and authenticity. It is too simple to neglect the importance of the social dimension and the ecclesial aspects because it is from its fruits that we will recognize the value of a human phenomenon; recognition has a public aspect.

Briefly and frankly: are svāmīs and *sādhus* still needed today? And does your life represent a model for India in general, for the Church in particular, or for some Hindū *sampradāya* [tradition], or is it perhaps something to admire but not to be imitated? More than once you told me that it is important that there be inaccessible snowy peaks. But the problem is precisely this: Are they inspiring heights, radiating beauty, or dark valleys of obscurantism? Is the *saṃnyāsin* an ideal to be imitated or an anachronistic figure to overcome? You felt the problem acutely and you knew well that not all are called to this life (whatever it can mean at this depth). It is not a way for all. This is certain. The problem is not so much to know if few or many are called to follow this path, as whether in our time this path is intrinsically valid—that is, if the human being, following it, can arrive at true fulfillment.

Neither you nor I are prepared to admit that human beings can be considered part of a mega-machine and "sacrificed" as a sort of castration of the person for the good of the community. The law of the cross does not consist in suffering, sacrifice, and asceticism as ends in themselves, but it indicates the way to enter the kingdom, to attain the fullness of life. In the same way, *vairāgya* [renunciation] is not a synonym of masochism, but it aims at the disintegration of all chains, obstacles, so that *mokṣa* [liberation] can shine in all its splendor.

In simpler words: Either the life of a traditional *saṃnyasin* is valid initself, or it has no reason to exist, and therefore it should be transformed without considering the stimulating effect that such an institution can have on the mind. Human manipulation should not paralyze the full development of a person for the love of the community. Furthermore, we cannot be satisfied with the purely subjective answer that some people seem to be very happy with their acosmic vocation. We are not questioning the right of the individual to follow what he thinks best. We are pondering on the pragmatic value of the traditional *saṃnyāsin* that you preached to us, Svāmījī.

Before continuing, we need to clarify a point to avoid the most dangerous misunderstandings for the life of a social group, something that would lead to a devitalization both of your "message" and of the creative tensions within the church, which I presume is still the main location of your example. I am referring to that pious "hypocrisy" that so often corrodes the spirit of a religious or nonreligious group and paralyzes the best enterprises.

It leads to this type of reaction: we try to tame Svāmījī, we adopt him in part, but only to the extent that he does not upset the thought patterns that are familiar to us, just as we accept revolutionaries in the social field only when they have been subjugated and put into the straitjackets of "microdoxy." We put a bit more devotion into our life (it does not disturb us) and also a bit more social interest (which can only be useful), but let us not take the prophetic cries too seriously, for fear that they convert us, completely upsetting our life.

We "interpret" the exaggerations of the saints so much so that we build monuments in memory of them, thus calming our conscience while we go about our business as usual. What would become of the church, if everybody was an acosmic *sādhu?* What would become of the country, if everybody was a radical social reformer? And of the world, if we were all uncontrollable saints? Thank God, we are on the right side, given that the Holy Spirit seems to do everything to avoid that hypothesis.

And so we continue happily to serve two masters. Will we not render a better service to the men of present and future generations, according to the two disciplines that you have lived—as a monk and as a *saṃnyāsin*—declaring without hesitation that your life is an example of what should not be done, rather than exalting in words your greatness and even admiring you as an inimitable model and limiting ourselves to that?

No! We should listen to your call to sanctity and consider your example of uncompromising faithfulness to your convictions, your behavior of total sacrifice. We should also learn from your inner conflicts and from your external battles. We should be moved by your life and not grow proud in your name, but sincerely humble ourselves in our name. All your limits, all your idiosyncrasies serve only to bring you closer to us and make you more human, less acosmic. I beg you not to take it badly, dear Abhiṣiktajī, if someone does not swear by your "ideas" and your vision of the human, Hindū, or Christian ideal. You did not simply limit yourself to communicating "ideas"; you tried to create the conditions for the spontaneous creation of an experience. And it cannot be denied that that experience exists!

This is not the moment to continue to discuss your conviction of the essential acosmicness of monks. We will consent to consider it as *question disputata* — and *disputanda*— open to debate. Would you admit with me that the acosmicness of monks is only valid if the Absolute is acosmic? But an Absolute that is not all-embracingis somewhat problematic! What is really important, however, is this total openness to the Absolute, this obedience to the Spirit, this inebriating awareness of the "*a Patre*" whose experience you lived so deeply.

As you wrote back in 1955,

"I am but in three Persons [...], yet subsisting in the second."[385]

Tavertet, February 7, 2005
Lent[386]

Dear Abhiṣikta!

Two years after your total resurrection I wrote a long letter to you You were alive for me. Tonight (or rather this early morning because I spent part of the day and most of the night reading the book by Shirley du Boulay), after 30 years, I am making another stammering attempt, because you are still living in me. Most probably I was one of your best friends. We never disagreed, so we didn't need to make "virtuous" efforts to overcome divergence of opinions as you had to do with most people — except perhaps with your disciples. It now dawns upon me that one of the reasons of our spontaneous friendship was that you never needed to play any role with me, or rather there was no role to play between us. I remember my rendering of that Gospel passage: «The Kingdom is (neither within nor among but) *between* you». I took you as you were and you took me as I was. We created a *between*, a communion.

I wish the brilliant author of your biography had never asked me to preface it. I finish reading her manuscript and I am … I cannot just say overwhelmed, impressed or moved. Her vivid narrative has allowed me to live a bit of my life again. Perhaps I should have stopped the sentence and not left it dangling but ended it with the "I am" that was so dear to you —though less to me since I existentially "discovered" the Trinity which is pure Relationship. The naked *am* (*Iahweh*) has ceased to be a symbol for me. The verb "to be" does not apply to the Ultimate Mystery.

The author's engaging description made me almost nostalgic for what could have become my life, but you yourself "rescued" me because,

---

385 Ibid., May 5, 1955.

386 Foreword by R. Panikkar to *The Cave of the Heart. The Life of Svāmi Abhiṣiktānanda.* Shirley du Boulay, Orbis Books, 2005.

as you so well describe in our pilgrimage to Gangotrī, the vocation of the monk is not that of the priest — although both (monasticism and priesthood) have suffered a tremendous erosion in recent times. Or is this the destiny of any institution? We agreed that *time* is brand new every moment. I remember that already before those days I had coined the word *tempiternity*. Shirley's description rekindled my memories and made me reenact those conversations between two passionate people convinced that we should deepen our lives (where the "Kingdom" is), because with mere "cosmetics" we would not contribute to the radical *metanoia* needed both for Hinduism and Christianity— as well as for the world at large. At the peak of your life you lived the mutual fecundation of both traditions in an existential manner.

You experienced, you struggled, you suffered to express your intuitions and get them across. It sounds strange, almost preposterous to confess that all that you say appears so clear to me that I wonder if it simply does not come from a higher source. In any case, the force of our vision and commitment was the same—although our language was slightly different.

You wrote to me from the Nursing Home in Indore in 1973 saying that, once you recovered, you would come to Vārāṇasī and stay with me. We had to catch up with each other after so long an absence. Alas, it was not possible. You left this body — and here I am, still. You may understand my feelings. Our relationship was *advaita* and this is why I cannot write just a Preface. I need to converse with you. Anything else would appear artificial to me.

I cannot write an "introduction" to your life. I would not have the necessary "objectivity". You are not an object for me. The only thing I can do, as I did thirty years ago, is to write a second and shorter letter.

To speak about the ineffable is not an easy task.

...

I shall not repeat what I wrote in that first letter to you. I am only underlying few aspects of your life just to add some minor strokes to the biography. I understand now better the significance of your stubborn existence with the hindsight of those past decades. Since your first youth you had one single aim: *ekāgratā*, we say in India — or "God intoxicated" as some people write. India was just a symbol. The *ātman* within you was "calling" you, we could say using a language dear to you.

"If the grain does not die ..." You have died to yourself, your beloved disciples have also disappeared (another symbol) but the earth has received you and the fruits are visible. The changes you dreamt for the Church are not all fulfilled, but they are no longer felt to be odd or seen as impossible. New "winds" are blowing —in spite of passing backlashes. You know that I had an indirect voice in some of the documents of Vatican II concerning the issues that were in your (and our) heart. Nobody will raise an eyebrow now when hearing that the Church is not identical to the Catholic government in Rome or elsewhere. The self-given title of the Church, repeated again in the Council, is precisely *sacramentum mundi* which, in the original language of the first Fathers, sounds even better and deeper: *Mysterion tou kosmou*, the Mystery of the Kosmos. To that *mysterium* was our loyalty.

I don't remember if we commented on the well-documented and courageous talk by Hans Küng at the Eucharistic Congress in Mumbai in 1964 when he forcefully asserted that it was high time that the Church (he meant the Vatican) disowned that old saying from the first centuries: "*extra ecclesiam nulla salus*" ["there is no salvation outside the Church"]. I quietly developed the same idea in my official discourse in which I stated that "the Christian has no monopoly on salvation". But I drew less juridical conclusions. I held that St. Cyprian's sentence was precisely the best description of the self-understanding of the Church — right or wrong. Many of the old Fathers of the Church believed she was essentially the place of salvation *tout court*. The idea was later obscured by the "politicization" of Christianity by its symbiosis with the *Imperium*. Before that time the main insight was theological and not political or even historical. If salvation occured in a temple, a synagogue, within a family or on a beach, there would be the Church: the place where the mystery of salvation occurs — wherever it may be.

We know that the Church is not the bricks of a building, but neither do our intellectual bricks make the Church. The "Body of Christ" (which was the normal meaning of Church during the first millennium) is not limited to the "members" of an organisation— respectable and even necessary as that may be.

Likewise we could say the same for Hinduism (if we disregard another passing backlash of a certain fundamentalism as a reaction against Christian colonialism); it is much easier for Hinduism to be tolerant because it has no fixed doctrine, although it also stands for a definite attitude. The power of the law of *karma* is visible not so much in the life of individuals as in the framework of history (as I had already written in an article I did show to you). If the danger of Christianity is "exclusivism", the danger of Hinduism is "inclusivism".

In our "All-India Seminar" of 1988 on *Sharing Worship* (*Communicatio in Sacris*) I did not dare to spell out what I had already written in 1973, that "unless there is *communicatio in sacris* there is no communication, but only an exchange of goods or words" — of banalities and irrelevant topics. Secularity has nothing to do with the desacralisation of human life—and of life in general. *Sacred Secularity* is a theme which we at that time did not pursue. Our task is not limited to the Christian Church. You slowly discovered that you could and should not abstain from sharing worship in Hindū temples.

Abhiṣikta! Your struggle and your sufferings have not been in vain. I have fond memories of our conversations and how skeptical you were finding me so optimistic when I was saying, for instance, that grammar was on my side in upholding that "monk" is the substantive and "Hindū" or "Christian" the adjective, so that it was not doing violence to language to say "Christian monk" or "Hindū monk", whereas it would be forcing the language to say "Hindū Jesuit" or "Buddhist Salesian".

You youself wrote that you felt you were too French and even Cartesian in your spontaneous approach to reality. It is all normal and even proof that you were not uprooted. We are all fruits of our culture—which is the natural springboard for transcending it. You were aware of it and this helped you to overcome some of your "scruples". But you were not aware that you were (as most westerners are) still a disciple of Parmenides, so that reality could not be contradictory. And here is your anguish at finding yourself to be Christian and Hindū, monotheist and *advaitin*. For me this was no problem at all, not only because I see no contradiction, but also because I do not identify reality with rationality. The real is not obliged to obey Parmenides and we do not fall into irrationality if we are aware of it. I think that the “double belonging” of which Shirley still writes is a false problem. I am as much son of my father as of my mother. Nowadays to be French and European would no longer be considered a “double belonging”. Your anguish came out of a dialectical thinking. Your greatness was that you overcame dialectical thinking, not by another way of thinking, through by a painful and excruciating experience. That experience was enormously fecund. You kept loyalty to two dialectically opposed world-views. We are grateful to you.

Dear Svāmiji! I cannot write about you. I can only write to you. I was not able to assuage your suffering. I was unable to convince you because you felt I was making it too easy. Now you do not need my words; but we still profit from your strugglings.

The obstacles lie on both sides. This should make us very humble. “Fundamentalism” (a word which we didn’t use) lies hidden in most religions. There is no point in discussing ideas, as you rightly said. What has immense value is your life. And you lived yours to the full.

Let me now fullfil my task of prefacing this beautiful biography. The author describes tackfully your doubts and your inconsistencies: you wanted solitude, but even when you could get it you went traveling here and there; you dreamt of a pure *saµnyāsa*, yet you fell short of the ideal; you wanted to get rid of all books, but you could not dispense with them; you wanted to be a *jñānin* and you discovered yourself a *bhakta*—and I could multiply the list. But let me defend you. I don’t think it is because of my love for you or that I am condescendingly excusing you. Certainly you were not consistent with your ideals. But they were your ideas and you sensed time and again that what is paramount are not the ideas, but life, experienced life. Your “inconsistencies” were the most consistent praxis of your experience. You allowed yourself to be led not by your ideas and not even by your ideals, but by the Spirit which “blows” when, where and *how* it “wills”. To that in-spiration you were loyal. Your greatness is that you were not conscious of it. It was not your will, but faithfulness to the Spirit that you interpreted as a weakness. I offer here a clue, a “hermeneutical” clue the philosophers would say, to evaluate your inconsistencies. Let me still qualify the metaphor. The Spirit was a wind which blew and directed you there where it found the least resistance, i.e. towards those flanks where you were weak. I understand why you became so annoyed by Cuttat's critical remarks. He was theoretically right. The danger of a certain *advaita* is that it does not give enough weight to love. But this was the weakness of a certain *advaita* and not your weakness. I don't know if I ever showed to you an article of mine, "*Advaita* and *Bhakti*".[387] You were a *bhakta* and by the same token a loyal *advaitin*. Yet this Introduction is not the place for further elucubrations.

You discovered your *bhakti*, again not as a theological reflection on the Incarnation, but as a lived and revolutionary experience in your encounter with Marc, your beloved disciple. You had also another devoted follower, Thérèse of Jesus, a Carmelite sister. With Marc your love knew no barriers. As I wrote to you in my first letter, you "discovered a fundamental human dimension: *paternity*". That love made you whole. I find a deep symbol in the fact that both Marc and Thérèse disappeared without leaving a trace. An acosmic spirituality disappears from this cosmos. But your love (*bhakti*) "saved" you. You experienced the reality of the Incarnation. I wrote in the beginning of this letter that the "Kingdom" is *between*. In that loving relationship *between* two people who had overcome their *egos* is the Kingdom.

I was not much younger than you then, but now I am much older than you ever were; perhaps this entitles me to be able to be a witness to your life.

I know most of the people mentioned in the biography. Many of them are no longer alive. The book is of an immense value because it describes you as what you were: a man of flesh and blood, an incarnated man and not just a "thinking rod". Writing about you also describes the situation not only of the Church in India but, indirectly at least, of the world at large.

Svāmijī, you were not an acosmic monk; and you are becoming a symbol for spiritual survival. Was this not the message of Christ?

R. Panikkar

---

[387] "Advaita and Bhakti. A letter from Vrindaban", first published in 1965, Brescia: Humanitas, now in Panikkar's Opera Omnia, Volume VI, Part 2, *Intercultural and Interreligious Dialogue,* Maryknol, New York: Orbis Books, 2018.

The Inner Journey of Abhiṣiktānanda
Odette Baumer-Despeigne[388]

To grasp the precise significance of the spiritual journey of Père Henri Le Saux, Svāmi Abhiṣiktānanda as he was called in India, Svāmijī as his friends called him, it is important never to separate his writings from his personality and the very special circumstances in which his life unfolded and, especially, to always keep in mind that he arrived in India fifteen years before the Second Vatican Council.

An excerpt from something he wrote in the 1950s sums up his entire journey:

> It is in the same measure in which one lives ones inner life, that one is ready to understand India and also to be understood by it. Conversely, to the same extent that one penetrates the secret of India, one is able to discover oneself internally and delve deeper and deeper into the mystery of the one, non-dual Self. In Hindū terminology, the Self can be related to the expression used by St. Paul: «It is no longer I but Christ who lives in me» (Gal 2:20).

I will attempt here not so much to talk about Fr. Le Saux, but to let him speak for himself, through his writings and especially his spiritual diary, the letters addressed to his Benedictine sister, his friends and myself.

With reference to all that he had written, Henri Le Saux once said:

> It is all biography... it all comes from the experience of this tension, of this comparison between Christianity and Vedānta [the teachings of the

388 After the death of Henri Le Saux, Odette Baumer-Despeigne was the custodian of his unpublished writings and especially his spiritual diary, which she dedicated ten years of work to deciphering and publishing.

> Upaniṣads, the sacred texts which form the core of the Hindū scriptures] that has beenat the center of my life since the periods I spent in the caves of Aruṇācala,[389] but everything has been rethought by the "mind" in the aura of a double culture. [390]

It is precisely this tension, this «coexistence of the Upaniṣads and the Gospel in the same heart» that lie at the origin of his extraordinary inner journey spanning a quarter of a century, in other words, the entire time he lived in India from his arrival in 1948 until his death in 1973.

Within him the encounter between two mysticisms, that of the East and that of the West, took place, not only on an intellectual level, in the context of comparative studies, but also at the level of personal experience, without ever slipping into syncretism.

His letters, and especially the diary which he maintained very regularly, allow us to follow the actual course of his spiritual evolution, as it gradually developed and approached what the Upaniṣads call the "Further Shore" – another term for the Real, or God.

Henri Le Saux was born in Brittany in 1910, the eldest of eight children. On his father's side he was a descendant of a line of seafarers; his mother's family originally came from Austria. His parents ran a grocery business in St. Briac.

While still quite young he expressed the desire to be a priest. At the seminary his superiors, finding him a bright student, wanted to send him to Rome for further studies, but he refused because he felt called to the monastic life. At the age of nineteen he entered the Benedictine Abbey of St. Anne of Kergonan, where he successively filled the posts of librarian and professor, first of Church History and then of Patristic Studies; when appointed "master of ceremonies" he took up his duties with immense enthusiasm, since he passionately loved the liturgy and Gregorian chant. Later he wrote to his sister, a Benedictine nun:

> You know I loved Gregorian more than anyone else, but now I have discovered a melody which is more perfect than any other melody: I

---

389 Arunācala is a sacred mountain in South India, identified with Âiva, the supreme Lord.

390 Letter to O. Baumer, January 23, 1969.

> lose myself in the silence of the OM – the sacred Vedic syllable, symbol of the Absolute.
>
> (July 6, 1973)

At the beginning of the Second World War he was mobilised. Taken prisoner in 1940 with his whole regiment, he succeeded in escaping by hiding in a field of corn.

His first writing, Love and Wisdom, a study of the dogma of the Trinity, dates back to 1942 and is dedicated to his mother. In the introduction we read:

> These pages contain simple personal, often extremely personal, reflections on the wonderful characteristics of divine love and wisdom... they proceed in a series of leaps in every direction within the ineffable reality that we would wish to embrace... Who, with a heart burning with love, has searched for the Word of Life in the Scriptures or in prayer and not found at least some traces of it?
>
> ... Books that do not convey this testimony are useless... I mean that here I have only given what was my own and have not repeated what is found everywhere else.

There we have an authentic portrait of our Svāmijī[391]: his "heart of fire" as he seeks God, and the clear assertion that all he writes is the direct reflection of his personal experience.

The call of India remained thirteen years in Henri's heart before he was given a chance to answer. In the meantime, he had dedicated himself to studying English, Tamil and Hindū scriptures, especially those of the *Upaniṣads*; he also followed a strictly vegetarian diet.

It was through a magazine article that he was put in touch with the French priest Jules Monchanin, who had already lived for some years in South India, where he had been leading «a life devoted to the understanding and service of India, guided by a single desire: to incarnate Christianity in the ways of life, prayer and contemplation characteristic of Indian civilisation.»[392]

---

391 As his friends called him in India.

392 Jules-Monchainin, *Mystique de l'Inde, Mystère chrétien,* Fayard, 1974.

He left the Abbey of Kergonan in 1948 and reached India on August 15. He was never again to leave his adopted country; he became a naturalized citizen in 1960. This did not prevent him from remaining in permanent contact with his original Abbey to the very end of his life.

With Jules Monchanin he went on to found the *aśram* of Śantivanam, "Grove of Peace', near Trichy, in Tamil Nadu.[393]

They built two huts beside the Kavery, a majestic river which is nearly one kilometer wide. The chapel, constructed on the model of South Indian Hindū temples, was inaugurated with a solemn Mass on the feast of St. Benedict in 1951.

They wore the orange robe of the Hindū monks and adopted Indian names: Svāmi Parama Arubianandam and Svāmi Abhiṣiktānanda.

In this lonely retreat they collaborated in writing a book which at that time – it was 1956 – was to cause a sensation: *Hermits of Saccidānanda, an Attempt at a Christian Integration of the Monastic Tradition of India.*[394]

Barely six months after his arrival in India, in January 1949, Henri Le Saux accompanied Jules Monchanin to Tiruvannamalai, at the foot of the sacred mountain of Aruṇācala, in order to meet one of the most authentic sages of modern India: Ârī Rāmaṇa Mahārṣi. This meeting was to leave an immensely deep mark upon his later spiritual course. In his book *The Secret of Aruṇācala*[395] he describes the meeting in these words:

> Even before my mind was able to recognize the fact, and still less to express it, the invisible halo of this Sage had been perceived by something in me deeper than any words. Unknown harmonies awoke in my heart... In the Sage of Aruṇācala of our time I discerned the Unique Sage of the eternal India, the unbroken succession of her sages, her ascetics, her seers; it was as if the very soul of India penetrated to the very depths of my own soul and held mysterious communion with it. It was a call which pierced through everything, rent it in pieces and opened a mighty abyss...

---

393 The *āśram* of Âāntivanam later continued under the spiritual guidance of Fr. Bede Griffith, a British-born priest of Anglican origin who became a Benedictine monk affiliated with the Camaldolese order.

394 Paris: Casterman, 1956.

395 Paris: Epi-Desclee De Brouwer, 1978; Delhi: ISPCK, 1979.

In his diary he noted: «The *āśram* of Rāmaṇa helps me to understand the Gospel; there is in the Gospel much more than Christian Piety has so far discovered».[396]

Between 1952 and 1958 Abhiṣiktānanda often came back to Tiruvannamalai, no longer on account of Śrī Rāmaṇa Mahārṣi, who died in 1950, but to stay for long periods in different caves on the mountain, to live there as a Christian hermit among Hindū hermits.

In March 1952 he confided to his diary:

> I am ready, if it pleases the Lord, to remain forever simply a genuine Christian *saṃnyāsin,*[397] in succession to my predecessor in this cave, Rāmaṇa, and so many others who have left all to consecrate themselves to the supreme Lord.

It is in this imposing, austere setting that from deep within him emerges the experience of the divine Presence, the ultimate oneness of Reality, of Being, which is at the heart of the Hindū mystical experience. And it is in this period that Abhiṣiktānanda receives all the great intuitions that he is later to develop, and which he refers to in his own words as follows:

> The only intuition that is beyond all conceptualization is: there is nothing that can be named between God and Man. I am not saying that God is Man, nor that Man is God, I am simply denying that Man plus God makes two.
>
> (June 5, 1957)

In other words, God and Man are not a pair of opposites. This is what is meant by the expression non-duality, in Sanskrit *advaita* (absence of duality).

He writes in his Diary on September 3, 1955:

> There is a fact that dominates everything: the religious experience that takes place on non-Christian ground, with an intensity never before felt, and along the same line as everything I had vaguely perceived previously. For me Aruṇācala is a birthplace. There, under the "guidance" of Rāmaṇa, I was born again. Against this all reasoning collapses … Then what must

396 November 14, 1952.

397 *Saμnyasin:* the renouncer, the wandering monk, he who has renounced all.

> be done? One simple thing: if the Christian mystery is true, it will be found intact beyond the *Vedantic* experience.

He would later say to me: «It is better still, I believe, to hold these two forms of a single faith, though they are in extreme tension, until the dawn appears». (1970)

What this birth "into truth" on Aruṇācala meant to him, he confided to Marc:

> He who receives this dazzling Light is petrified, torn apart, he can no longer speak, he can no longer think, he remains there outside of time and space, alone, in the very solitude of the Alone.

In his book *Saccidānanda, a Christian Approach to Advaitic Experience,*[398] Henri Le Saux describes his spiritual breakthrough in these terms:

> In my own innermost centre, in the most secret mirror of my heart, I tried to discover the image of Him who is "I am", of Him who lives and reigns in the infinite space (*ākāśa*) of my heart. But the reflected image gradually grew faint, and soon it was swallowed up in the radiance of its Original. Step by step I descended into what seemed to me to be successive depths of my true self – my being, my awareness of being, and my joy in being. Finally nothing was left but he himself, the Only One, infinitely alone, Being, Awareness and Bliss, Saccidānanda.[399] In his heart I had returned to my Source. *Tat tvamasi*, "You are That"[400] were the last words I heard before I fell asleep in the slumber of Being, before «I laid me down and slept»... (Psalm 3:5).

> He observed the image,
> in itself,
> but the image disappeared
> in the Self
> and all that remained of observing
> was the Observed!

In the same sense, St. Paul writes in a letter to the Corinthians: «Whoever is united with the Lord is one Spirit with him» (1 Cor 6:17) and as far

---

[398] Delhi: ISPCK, 1974, p. 172.

[399] Saccidānanda: «one of the best symbols of the innermost mystery of God himself in the spiritual vocabulary of India. But equally it signifies the mystery of the divine presence—the image of God—in the innermost sanctuary of Man's being.»

[400] *Chandogya-upaniṣad* 6, 8, 7.

back as the Book of Sirach in the Old Testament, its author glorifies the Most High saying: «Wherefore in sum, he is all … for he is great above all his works» (Sirach 43:27-28). For its part, the *Katha-upaniṣad*, written 1000 years earlier, asks: «How can he be apprehended except by him who says: "He is"?» (VI, 12).

*

These periods of immersion in the Hindū environment were also times in which Le Saux deepened his existential union with Christ, and represent a crucial stage in his spiritual evolution, as it was in the silence and solitude of his life as a hermit, dwelling in caves on the mountain of Aruṇācala, that he experienced his first great – and crucial – spiritual turning point.

In his diary entry of July 14, 1952 we find a clear echo of this:

> The realization of this all-pervading, all-penetrating Presence of God in my actions, as in my being, as in everything... *Satori*[401] illumination is the real Baptism, a new outlook on oneself and the world, not an intellectual knowledge, but an abyssal, cataclysmal transformation of one's own being.

During these solitary retreats he wrote his work *Guhāntara*, which translates as "he who lives in the cave'—not only of the mountain but also that found deep down in the heart, which he liked to call «the crypt of the heart».

Guhāntara, he wrote when he sent me his manuscript, «is the direct expression of those first glimmerings.»

The following is an excerpt:

> The Christian *saṃnyāsin* discovers with astonishment that when he buries himself in the caves of Aruṇācala he has penetrated to the very heart of Hinduism, and in reaching the peakof Aruṇācala he – Christian though he is – has realized the supreme ideal of Hinduism.

In 1954 he wrote from one of these caves on Aruṇācala to his younger sister the nun:

> You will see in my books when they appear, what I have learned here–to seek the Lord in one's own heart, not outside, not in memory, but really in one's own greatest depth.

---

[401] *Satori*: illumination in Zen Buddhism.

On August 3, 1953 he wrote in his Diary:

> Man's essential task is to find his true identity. Who am I? To become aware of what one really is, the total abandonment of the peripheral "me" to the inner Mystery is the sine qua non condition.
>
> Yet in reality it is not Man who reaches the Depths. It is the very Depths that are revealed in the dissolution of the peripheral "me', the ego.
>
> When Man penetrates into himself, into his bottomless Depths, all concepts, thoughts and reflection recede ... The more he sinks, the more the depths deepen ... As he penetrates these depths he feels first of all like a fruit that is peeled, its fleshy pulp is eaten, its kernel broken and its seed extracted to reveal the germ which cannot be reduced.
>
> And with each layer he removes, another layer appears, ever thinner, ever more adherent, like an onion. And a Voice calls out to him: Do not stop, remove the skin, go further down, immerse yourself in this ocean which to you seems bottomless, because it is only by sinking into it that you will discover the ocean floor, and the ocean itself, and you yourself as the ocean, because once you reach the inside, it is no longer inside. What would the inside be? If it were the inside of something, would it be the Supreme, the Nameless Being?
>
> (December 8, 1953)

Elsewhere [*Initiation à la spiritualité des Upanishads*] Le Saux writes:

> God can never be reached as an object, since an object is always a projection of thought. God is not a He that Man may talk about or philosophers and theologians discuss. God is a You, but a You that aspires to itself and to the elimination of the "me" that stands before it, since God is above all the "I" before which every "me" can only remain silent. This is the fundamental experience of the Hindū soul.
>
> Are not these depths of the soul that Man seeks to reach the mystery of Christ, of the essential encounter…? Christ is essentially the awakening of Man to his divine origin, his origin in Patre; the entrance of his self into the place beyond his own depths...
>
> (December 27, 1954)
>
> But the renunciation, the purification that this Awakening presumes is merciless.

In an earlier letter to this same sister (December 1953) he gives some details of his life as a hermit:

> Everyday at noon I make a little gruel of millet flour over a fire of some dry thorns kindled between two stones; morning and evening, a cup of tea.Sometimes I go for my dinner to the house of a Brahmin who has invited me, and then I am given a grand reception and treated sometimes better than I would have wished...

In December of 1955, Fr Le Saux was introduced to another Hindū Sage, spiritually very close to Rāmaṇa Mahārṣi, Śri Gnānānanda, who lived in his *āśram* at Tapovanam, not far from Aruṇācala. It was he who was to set the seal on Svāmijī's initiation into the spirituality of the *Upaniṣads*, in a sense at the heart of the mystical secret of India.

To his sister and to a friend[402] he explained:

> I have never found any man who impressed me as much as he does. The mysterious ways of Providence! In him I have felt the truth of *advaita*...
>
> (May 23, 1956)

During his stay with this Sage he noted in his Diary:

> I cannot escape the conviction that he is my *gurū*. I should need months, perhaps years of profound silence to determine my position in this matter which transcends the intellect.
>
> (July 3, 1956)

Long afterwards, in 1967, he wrote to me: «With Gnānānanda I had a marvellous experience of the transmission from *gurū* to disciple.»[403]

As Father Dupuis[404] was later to say: «For months and years, therefore, Abhiṣiktānanda has been involved with Hindū monasticism. He has encountered Hinduism at ritual level, penetrating into the core of the stone temples; he has encountered it in the hearts of hermits and *sadhū* seeking the Absolute, and has seen it at work in the true Hindū mystics whose teachings he receives. He is profoundly convinced that he has been called to something and all he has to do is heed the call. Thus he has allowed himself to be transported into the Hindū mystical experience, which he perceives as authentic. He owes it to himself in order to follow

402 Letter to Sr Marie-Thérèse and Fr J. Lemarié, March 25, 1956.

403 Cf. *Guru and Disciple: An Encounter with Âri Gnānānanda Giri,* London: ISPCK, 1974.

404 Fr. Jacques Dupuis, Belgian Jesuit priest and theologian.

his vocation, which he conceives as that of a Hindū Christian monk. He also owes it to the Church, which will not be able to fulfill its mission in India if it does not encounter India at these depths.» (*Interiorité*)

At the end of his stay with Śrī Gnānānanda, he noted in his diary:

> Once we understand from the Scriptures, from the teaching of the *gurū* and, above all, from our own beginning of experience that Reality is beyond all mental apprehension, there is only one possibility: to live in the state of essential relationship with the inner Mystery:
>
> I abide in this secret place in the depth of my heart, there –
> where all alone before God I am,
> where all alone with God I am,
> where all alone from God I am,
> where alone is He who IS.

Some months later, in order to integrate all that he had received spiritually from Rāmaṇa Mahārshi, Aruṇācala and Gnānānanda, he undertook a long and austere retreat at Kumbakonam.

There, shut up in an underground room at Mauna Mandir, he remained 32 days in total seclusion and complete silence. He had no book with him except his breviary; his food was handed in to him from outside. Once the Eucharist was celebrated, his sole activity, apart from long hours of meditation, was the writing up of his spiritual diary. Using school copy-books, he wrote 235 pages in his small and condensed handwriting.

Referring to Rāmaṇa Mahārshi and Aruṇācala, he made an observation which enables us to sense the depths at which the contact with them had changed his life: They have become part of my very flesh, they are woven into the fibers of my heart. (November 23, 1956)

Here in truth we touch the central depth of the interior drama which was played out in his soul, as he was torn to pieces between his loyalty to Christ and his overwhelming *upaniṣadic* experience of non-duality, the drama of the «coexistence of the *Upaniṣads* and the *Gospel* together within the same heart», which made him utter this sorrowful cry.

> I am afraid, I am afraid, an ocean of anguish wherever I turn. I am afraid of risking eternity for a mirage. And yet, no! You are not a mirage, Aruṇ ācala; and the light of dawn which has risen at the center of my heart

> is not false... Agonies which pierce me to the depths and make my soul just a cry of pain!!!
>
> (November 27, 1956)

Three days later he affirmed:

> Christ is my *Sad-gurū* – my true *gurū*" –and he makes himself the singer of the Presence of "this inner Mystery which Jesus called the Father, and of the relationship with the very heart of the Mystery, which Jesus called the Spirit.
>
> (November 30)

A year later this crisis came to a climax, prompting him to write:

> I often dream that I am dying, as it seems to me that there is no longer any way out for me in this life. I cannot be Hindū and Christian at the same time, and I can no longer be only Christian, or only Hindū.

So for long years Henri Le Saux – without allowing the slightest sign to appear outwardly – continued to be a man in torments, torn apart in the depth of his heart, until at last the light of peace and joy appeared in the serenity of the definitive awakening which followed his "great spiritual adventure", as he himself called the heart attack of 1973 which was to carry him off forever to the Further Shore.

*

With the death of Fr Jules Monchanin in 1957 a decisive turning-point appears in his life. The *āśram* monastery interested him less and less. Despite all their hopes, no Indian Christian came to join the two French monks. A number of people tried, but no one ever stayed on.

Now he begins to look towards the North and the Himālayas. He writes to his sister, telling her of his plans:

> Next week I plan to set out on a long journey in the North of India. I shall first visit Wardha, the *āśram* founded by Gandhi, then I shall go to Benares, and from there to the place of the Buddha's illumination, Bodhgayā. Finally, and most of all, I want to spend two months in the Himalayas and to see if it would be possible to establish a Christian *āśram* therein those places where there are so many Hindū monks.
>
> (February, 1957)

During this journey he wrote to her again:

> I have been making a wonderful journey... among the Himālayas... I have sometimes traveled by bus, but more often on foot, once for 40 km, then 50 km... It is marvellous to travel on foot like that. One is free... There is an enchanting solitude... You cross hills and valleys... follow the course of the Ganges... then descend with the river into the plains... I stayed for several days at Haridwar, just at this meeting point. It is a ceaseless pilgrimage. Thousands of people coming from every direction to bathe in the sacred river, and then to follow the Ganges up into the mountains... The Himalayas have conquered me!
>
> (April 1959)

In the following years, Father Le Saux was to return to the Himālayas many times, mingling with the uninterrupted flow of Hindū pilgrims who every year make their way on foot up to the sources of the Ganges, the Mātā-Ganga, the Mother Ganges.

In 1957 he travelled for more than 40 km on foot to reach first Badrīnāth, then Kedārnāth and lastly Gangotrī, the three sacred springs. Later he was to refer to the journey as «a tough but wonderful experience.»

In his way of life, Svāmi Abhiṣiktānanda was at times a Christian monk and at times a Hindū *saṃnyāsin*. «What is commendable is that he was able to establish a dialogue with Hinduism to the point of sharing the religious experience with Hindū monks. He was not satisfied with merely talking about Christianity and Hinduism or engaging in theological speculation on the hidden presence of Christ in India—he chose to live it all.» [405]

> «The wandering Indian *saṃnyāsin* is indeed very similar to the itinerant messenger of the Gospel. In fact, if we take seriously the rule that Jesus himself gave to his Apostles when he sent them out to preach the Kingdom, it is simply to sell all that one has, to not store up anything for tomorrow any more than the birds of the air do; to leave one's fields, house and family, take nothing for the journey and eat only what is given. [... The Hindū *saṃnyāsin* is] free from all anxiety or preoccupation, being without attachment of any kind, whether to things, places or people. Wherever he goes he is a stranger, and yet everywhere he finds himself at home, since he is sovereignly free in his absolute renunciation.»[406]

[405] Fr. Jacques Dupuis, Belgian Jesuit priest and theologian.

[406] *Saccidānanda, a Christian Approach to Advaitic Experience*, Delhi: ISPCK, 1974, pp. 8-9.

The great difference between the two types of monasticism lies in the fact that the Hindū monk, in his monastic profession, isfree from all rules, whereas the Christian monk is bound for life by the vows he pronounces.

Henceforward he was thus to divide his time between the South where he continued to maintain the *āśram* of Śāntivanam, and the North where he finally settled down for good in 1968. By then, Śāntivanam had been safely handed over to Fr Bede Griffiths.

Svāmi Abhiṣiktānanda then settled down in the heart of the Himalayas at Uttarkashi, the town of monks, the last major stopping place on the way to Gangotrī, the principal source of the Ganges.

From 1960, after obtaining his Indian citizenship, he arranged for the construction of a very small hermitage a few square meters in size on the bank of the Ganges, with a kind of rabbit-hutch on one side which he used as a kitchen. Upstairs there was a sort of attic which was reached by a ladder, in which it was impossible to stand upright. That was where each morning Svāmijī, seated on the floor in Indian style, celebrated the Eucharist, facing the sacred river which he could see through a small window set at floor level. These celebrations prompted him to say to his friend Fr Lamarié:

> Here, more than ever in the Church, Christ manifests himself as a priest according to the Order of Melchizedek
>
> (July 1965)

It was there that, little by little, the Indian liturgy was worked out, to which he made an active contribution in the course of the National Seminar of the Indian Church in 1969.

The photo featured in this book was taken by Prof. Panikkar, one of his closest friends, during a pilgrimage to Gangotrī. According to Hindū tradition, the priest celebrates with a bare torso, symbolizing the baring of the heart that the ministry requires.

The '60s were a time of numerous publications in French, which were later published in English:

Saccidānanda, a Christian Approach to Advaitic Experience (ISPCK, Delhi 1974); *Hindu-Christian Meeting Point* (2nd edn. ISPCK, Delhi 1976);

The Mountain of the Lord (CLS: Madras 1969); *Prayer* (ISPCK, Delhi 1967); *The Church in India* (CLS: Madras 1969).[407]

The French edition of Prayer, that little jewel of a book on true prayer, was only published in 1971 under the title *Eveil à soi-Eveil à Dieu* (Centurion: Paris).

During this decade his diary, as well as his letters, reflect his intense spiritual activity, his efforts to express to the best of his ability that which he perceived in the very depth of his heart, «the one intuition which transcends all conceptualization». Referring to these attempts he had already made, he commented in 1952:

> Any theologian who may chance to read these pages is requested kindly to regard all these "statements" as no more than working hypotheses...

And as he was later to say to Marc Chaduc and myself:

> They are vectors of free inquiry; the important thing is never to regard them as definitive or exclusive (September 1967).
>
> I am concerned with writing. The Mystery, when it is put into words, is too often comprehended in the form of a dream or an abstraction.

In a letter dated January 1968 he wrote to me:

> What is needed is that, based on what India gives us, Christians rediscover directly in the New Testament the values of interiority and non-duality and convey them to their brothers and sisters.

In his *Rencontre de l'Hinduisme et du Christianisme*, he explains these thoughts:

> The Christian must strive to recognize within himself, his innermost self, both the experience of the non-duality of being, which is at the heart of the Vedantic experience, and the experience of divine filiation, of the ineffable non-duality of the Father and the Son in the oneness of the Spirit, which is the constitutive of the experience of the Christian faith.

...

[407] Le Saux also published numerous articles in various magazines in and outside India.

As he wrote to me in 1966:

> I more and more believe that the deepening of the spiritual sense is the only remedy for the present crisis in the Churches. Christians and the world need to be re-taught that the "living and true" God is beyond the idea of God.

For many years he was thus seeking an ever more precise definition of that spiritual experience, as is shown by this passage from his diary entry of April, 1964:

> The Awakening to the Real is an awakening beyond thought, by means of and in the silence of the ego. The act of pure love is what awakens. Advaita, non-duality, is not an intellectual discovery, but an attitude of the soul. It is much more the impossibility of saying "Two" than the affirmation of "One". What is the use of saying "One" in our thought, if we say "Two" in our life? To say "One" in our life: that is Love.
>
> (April 1964)

In *Intériorité et révélation*, he meditates on the mission of Jesus:

> Jesus appeared in the world not to teach ideas, but to share an experience, his own experience, that of being the Son of God; and so through the power of his experience to bring them to realize and integrate with their total awareness that mysterious condition of being sons of God which is also theirs, a condition to which they are called by the Father with an eternal summons, a summons which cannot be distinguished from the very being of God.
>
> Christ is the perfect man, he who has fulfilled all his possibilities as a man, first of which, the highest, is his non-duality with God. "The Father and I are One."
>
> To call God Father, *Abba*, is in Semitic terms an *advaita* corresponding to the *upaniṣadic* experience.
>
> (January 1973)

Finally, to a friend in a monastery he sent these lines in 1968:[408]

> What interests me as the eternal value of Hinduism is precisely this: to find the truth lying beyond the eidos – the concept – not to remain the prisoner of concepts. Concepts are certainly valuable, but they are not absolute; they are linked to the evolution of human awareness. Therein

---

[408] Letters to Fr J. Lemarié dated August 18, 1959 and September 24, 1960.

> lies the whole problem that upsets theology... Would it not be good if western experience and its conceptualization were revivified by this transnoetic, or rather, this trans-intellectual experience? This is the one thing that interests me. To recover this experience at its very source, before it is conceptualized... What a great renewal of his experience of the Spirit it is, when the Christian has discovered this little spring that is beyond all... In spite of appearances, like you, I remain "Greek': my understanding molded by Scholasticism is really in agony before the problem posed by Hindū experience and Zen experience to Christian theology, a problem in which one gropes one's way and which sometimes brings one to a complete impasse. And yet, if Christianity is ever to pass beyond the world of Mediterranean culture, if it claims to be universal, it will have to face up to the irrefutable spiritual experience of Hinduism and Buddhism ... and integrate it.

But...

> Why seek at all costs to name the Mystery that is inside me? Under the name of Jesus I penetrated it wonderfully, and the heart of Jesus—my heart—appeared to me like the bosom of the Father. Under the name of AruṇācalaI penetrated it again and the light then was such that it dazzled me and all the names and forms which until this time I had distinguished under the guidance of my teachers vanished in the bright sunlight. But when the sun appeared, did the stars leave their place in the firmament? Did the moon halt its journey?
>
> Do not name, look, be dazzled, be ...
>
> Do not name it but be this Mystery.

It was not until 1973, a few months before his death, that he brought these reflections to a conclusion, as is clear from these lines that he wrote to me:

> He who possesses several mental or religious or spiritual languages is incapable of absolutizing any formulation, be it evangelical, upaniṣ adic, Buddhist, etc. He is only able to give stammering testimony to an experience. All formulations are nothing but humble, prayerful, contemplative approaches... The Council's acceptance of religious pluralism will overcome all the problems of the Church, but Christian thought must mature further if ineluctable conclusions are to be drawn.

*

Despite the great distances and the difficult, slow and uncomfortable means of travel, Svāmi Abhiṣiktānanda continually crossed India from north to south and from east to west, in response to the many requests which came to him from all sides to preach retreats, chiefly in the many Carmels with which the Carmel of Lisieux had put him in touch and to take an active part in the different efforts made by the Indian Church to adapt to its own particular situation the resolutions of Vatican II which resulted in the National Seminar of 1969. He very specially devoted himself to the renewal of spirituality and its expression in the liturgy, so that these might be more deeply rooted in the Indian tradition and might no longer be simply copies of those western forms which are so remote from the spontaneous expression of the Indian soul. In addition, he often shared his thoughts with the Jesuit Fathers in Delhi, Madras and Poona.

And what is more, he took part actively and frequently in ecumenical meetings, sometimes those between Christians belonging to different churches who wanted to deepen their knowledge of Hindū spirituality, sometimes between Hindūs and Christians.

Finally, he had to «come down to the plains» every time that he had to meet a foreign visitor, because Uttarkashi, being close to the Tibetan frontier, was then a prohibited zone for non-Indians.

In 1971 he stayed in Hardwar with a young Frenchman named Marc Chaduc (who would later become his disciple) and a Japanese professor from the University of Tokyo:

> I have spent some unforgettable days beside the Ganges – it is a great grace to be beside the Ganges. Twice we celebrated the Eucharist on the bank of the Ganges, another time on the mountain-side, facing the rising sun as it appeared beside the snow peaks. Our prayer rose up spontaneously, taking up and joining with all that was ever offered here in words and, equally, the holy silence of these places... there all signs merge in the Real.

In another letter he tells me of an encounter with Shigeto Oshida, a Japanese Dominican

> who, in marvellous harmony, lives his ancestral Zen and his Christian faith in full freedom in the Spirit and at the same time in transparent Christianity. At times serious, with the abyssal seriousness of Zen masters,

> and at times the full laughter of a child. The European is incapable of such harmony, his seriousness is too mental and his laughter does not plunge to the depths.

One has to have seen the condition of the mountain road, about 200 km in length, which descends from Uttarkashi towards the plains with the hazards of frequent landslides, falls of rocks and countless breathtaking sharp bends, in order to understand what these frequent bus journeys must have meant to him. Having reached the plains, he had to continue his journey on the hard wooden seat of a crowded third-class compartment and to remain stuck inside for periods which could last thirty, forty or even fifty hours! For many years Svāmijī had to endure this discipline, very severe for a western constitution, and which in the long run wore down his physical strength and severely impaired his health.

In 1970 he wrote to several friends:

> I am vividly aware of passing my 60th birthday, and my strength begins to decrease. I do not know how many more years I shall be able to live alone at Uttarkashi. *Dominus providebit…*

*

The year 1971 marked a new and very important stage in his spiritual journey. Some genuine disciples came to him, especially Marc Chaduc, a young Frenchman of whom he said:

> «In him I have found a true and wholehearted disciple; with two young Hindūs I have experienced from the other end what a *gurū* is.»

Svāmi Abhiṣiktānanda discovered spiritual paternity, and henceforth he was inseparable from his disciples.

As he wrote specifically to Marc:

> Seeing you as a son, I recognized myself. The act by which the father begets the child is inseparably the act by which the father contemplates himself.

In other words, an exchange takes place between them at the level of the foundation of being. In relation to this, in *Initiation aux Upaniṣads* he writes: «It is through his own awakening to himself that the *gurū* is able to open and awaken the disciple to himself."

More frequently than in the past he left his Himalayan hermitage in order to be with Marc and to pass on his teaching, either in the holy city of Hardwar or at Rishikesh, or again at Phulchatti, a small *ā©ram* hidden in the jungle upstream from Rishikesh.

Unlike his *gurū*, Marc, who had spent 4 years in a seminary in Lyon, would not experience any turmoil of conscience in relation to Christianity, being of a different generation, a different education and a different character. He breathed, so to speak, the experience of his *gurū*, put his trust in him and soon no longer asked him questions.

It was for Marc that Henri Le Saux wrote *Introduction aux Upanishad.* On another occasion he attempted to take stock of his own spiritual journey in order «to express the silence of the heart with words» and wrote in his diary in July 1971:

> Whether I will or not, I am fundamentally tied to Christ Jesus and so to the ecclesial Koinonia [communion]. It is in Him that the "Mystery" revealed itself to me, ever since my awakening to myself and to the world. It is through his image, his symbols, that I know God, and that I know myself and the world of men. Since my awakening to new depths of myself [the Self – ātman] here [in India], this symbol has become wonderfully enriched. Christian theology had already revealed to me the mystery of Jesus in the bosom of the Father: later India revealed to me the cosmic totality of this Mystery – the total revelation of the Mystery in which the Judaic revelation finds its place. The same Mystery which I have adored from the beginning under the symbol of Christ, also under the myth of Nārāyaṇa, of K®ṣṇa, of the Puruṣa. But for me Jesus is the *Sad-gurū*. It is in him that God has appeared to me, it is in his "mirror" that I have come to know myself in adoring, loving and consecrating myself to him.

In December of the same year (1971), he returned once again to one aspect of his fundamental intuition:

> The Gospel message is not bound to the Jewish world in which it was disclosed. Its universal and ontic value burns and melts the wax cells of the Judeo-Greek world in which this honey is stored. It is the very echo of the depths of the human heart, the message of love, of mutual giving, of relationship. The message of Man's divine state.

More than a quarter of a century was to pass before this intuition, which continued after the 1950s, would finally emerge among the Christian theologians of India and the Far East! At a meeting of the Southeast Asian Association of Theological Schools in 1980, in fact, the following words were pronounced:

> We must abandon the ways of thinking inherited from other cultures and other eras (Hellenic, Cartesian, Hegelian). The questions posed by our very existence as Asians could add new dimensions of truth to the understanding of the Gospel and forge a specifically Asian theology.

*

But let us come back to his *chelas*, whom he enfolds with not only paternal but also maternal concern, as is clear from his recommendation to Marc before leaving for a pilgrimage to Amarnath, in the high mountains of Kasmir: «Have you packed enough (woolen clothing) to wear?» Or, again, his suggestion a few weeks later to «avoid tension in your intellectual work (on the *Upaniṣad*) and eat until you are full—quantity must compensate for quality.»

In the spring of 1973 he wrote to Marc, expressing his satisfaction:

> I bought a new petrol pressure stove which works very well and cooks excellent *chapatti* [traditional Indian flatbread]; I did a huge amount of laundry this morning on the bank of the Ganges. All is well; my basket is full of fruit, the rose bushes are in bloom… I have just celebrated the Eucharist.

Svāmijī was not without a sense of humour. For example, to those who told him they did not understand the paradox he presented, he replied by quoting Psalm 40, «he who does not understand, let him ask the Lord to unplug his ear.»

Not a single detail of life escaped him, he shied away from nothing, he was interested in everything, he read a great deal, but essentially he always remained free from everything.

In May 1972 he stayed for around a month with Marc in the small *āśram* of Phuchatti, dedicating the entire time to the contemplation of the

Upaniṣads, the scriptures that through the years he continued to study deeply. It was at this time that this careful study began to flourish—or, rather, explode—into experience. Clearly, this is the same experience as always, but each time it is more profound.

«There is an infinite progression to these inner levels», he remarked.

As soon as he returned to Uttarkashi, he wrote to me:

> These were days of extraordinary fullness, a dazzling experience of the truth of the *Upaniṣads*, even though it was physically hard for me (the supreme *ātman-Brahman* correlation, that is, between the *ātman*, Man's innermost Principle, and Brahman, the Universal Life Principle, there is no duality). It is the whole deepest part of the soul that is lifted up, like when the swelling of the earth lifts and unsettles the ocean.
>
> It is too intense, feeling one is the presence of Truth. It burns! God is too bright a Light to be able to stand before Him; one vanishes into the Source.

A few days later he had his first attack of dyspnoea, which from then on would never leave him and which would develop into complications that would eventually lead to a heart attack in the following year.

He wrote to Marc:

> This morning during Mass the memory of the *Upaniṣadic* experience of non-duality was so strong that it brought on dyspnoea, which at midday is still continuing. Let us bless the Lord for everything, for deep inside us there is in front of us all the mystery of that which is in front and that which is beyond.

Despite this setback in his health he managed to oversee the English translation of *Sagesse chrétienne, Mystique hindou*, although at the same time he lamented:

> Why write again? What I have to convey can just barely be conveyed in words, not in books. The world is waiting for ideas and I would like to get across that what is needed is silence. The Spirit only allows itself to be understood by those who sit in silence.
>
> (Letter to M.T.)

Let us now briefly retrace the last stage of this extraordinary ascent towards God which was the life of Henri Le Saux, and which takes place between April and July 1973.

He was invited to participate in the Conference of Christian Monks and the Religions of Asia in Bangalore, and contributed with a paper entitled "The experience of God in the religions of the Far East" (cf. *Les yeux de lumière*).

Most of his time, however, was dedicated to the editing of *Saµnyāsa, or the Call of the Desert*, a study on the Upaniṣads that talk about the monastic path. This was in view of the upcoming monastic and ecumenical initiation of Marc Chaduc, which would be performed jointly by Père Le Saux, a Christian monk, and Svāmi Chidānandajī, a Hindū monk and President of the Śivānanda āśram of Rishikesh, on June 30, 1973 on the bank of the Ganges.

So it was that Marc, with his new name of Ajatānanda, «entered into the Christian and Hindū monastic line through a single act of the Spirit» (Letter from Marc to R. Panikkar, December 16, 1973).

This ceremony, so simple in ritual but so profoundly symbolic, deeply affected Henri Le Saux, who considered it as a chance for a sort of a "revision of life".

A few days later he dedicated to Ajatānanda a long poem which began with these words:

> So beautiful it was, the morning of 30 June …
> Your dikṣā[409] made me tremble
> to the very core of my being…
> taking me away from myself,
> losing me in infinite spaces,
> where I no longer know anything,
> where I seek myself in vain.

The days immediately preceding his heart attack on the 14th of July were spent by Svāmi Abhiṣiktānanda with Ajatanānda roaming beside the Ganges in the neighbourhood of a small Śiva temple lost in the jungle.

---

[409] *dikṣā:* initiation into monasticism.

Describing this time, Ajatanānda wrote to me:

> They were days when Svāmijī discovered ever deeper abysses of his soul... The inbreaking of the (Holy) Spirit snatched him away from himself and shone through every inch of his being, śarīram,[410] an inner apocalypse which at times blazed forth outwardly in a glorious transfiguration.» (December 1, 1974)

This intense inner experience came to its climax when a severe stroke suddenly laid him low in the street of a Rishikesh bazaar. In his own words, «It was an extraordinary spiritual adventure.» While physically helpless he remained perfectly lucid in mind and came with full awareness to the Great Awakening, and «having penetrated into his own source he recognized in the secret of his own soul the Mystery of God in his Epiphany.»[411]

Later on he described his experience:

> Seeing myself so helpless, incapable of any thought or movement, I was released from being identified with this "I" which until then had thought, willed, rushed about, was anxious about each and everything. Disconnection! That whole consciousness in which I habitually lived was no longer mine, but I, I still was.[412]

As soon as he regained the faculty of speech, his first words to Ajatānanda were, «It is beautiful, I can't tell you how beautiful it is! Just to open one's eyes, there where one is.»

Now he was able to quote literally the verse from the *Upaniṣad* which he loved so much and applied to the cosmic Christ: «the Man archetype in which every man is, inasmuch as he is Man.» (Diary, 1966).

> *vedāhametaṁ puruṣaṁ mahāntam...*
> I have known this great Puruṣa
> Who shines effulgent like the sun beyond all darkness.
> He who has known him
> goes beyond death.
> There is no other way.[413]

---

410 ©*arīram*: body, comprising the physical body and the mental faculties.

411 Op. cit., *Gurū and Disciple*, p. 65.

412 Journal, September, 1973.

413 *Svetasvatara-up.* III, 8.

At the end of August he wrote to a friend:

> The heart attack was only the backdrop to a marvellous spiritual experience. I then made the discovery that life and death are only particular situations, and the "I', the "Awakening', is not tied to them or limited by them. Of the two weeks spent in bed I recall nothing but intense joy. It was a tremendous surprise but also a unique experience. Awakening is a state of consciousness «in which the very terms of death and non-death have lost the meaning of opposites.» (Init.)

In a letter addressed to me at the same time he added:

> In this adventure I have discovered the Grail, and the Grail is neither far nor near, it is out of every place… the Awakening, and the search is over!

As soon as his condition permitted he was brought to Indore to the nursing home of the Franciscan Sisters who cared for him to the end with loving efficiency. It was in this hospital setting that I met him in October 1973.

All those who saw him (and I was one of them) during the months which preceded his Mahāprasthāna, his great departure, on the 7th of December, 1973, agree in their testimonies on the transparency of his whole being to the inner Mystery, the divine Presence, on the extraordinary radiance of his smile, of his countenance glowing with Light, and above all the singular expression of his eyes, wide open in wonder, which spoke so much to those who simply attended to him...

The pilgrim to the "Further Shore" had reached his goal, his whole being was now harmonized, unified, at peace; entirely faithful to Christ his *Sad-gurū,* and wholly immersed in the depths of his soul, in his "ground', he had "returned to his Source". His Christian experience and the *upaniṣadic* experience had flowed back to their unique Origin.

The Inner Journey of Raimon Panikkar

Milena Carrara Pavan

Biographical notes

Raimon Panikkar was born into a middle-class family in Barcelona, Spain, on November 3, 1918. As his father was an Indian of hind¥ faith and his mother a Catalan Catholic, he learned from early childhood to adopt, cultivate, and speak of both religious traditions, in which he always felt perfectly at home. For high school he was educated by the Jesuits and graduated with highest honours in 1935.

In 1935-1936 he started his studies in science and philosophy in Spain.

As a result of the outbreak of the Spanish Civil War and the impending danger to his family he was forced to flee with his sister Mercé and two brothers, Josep Maria and Salvator, to Germany, where he spent three years continuing his universitary studies in Bonn.

In the summer of 1939, Panikkar made a long and adventurous journey on bicycle through Switzerland and Italy, with the intention to return to Germany to complete his studies. However, the outbreak of World War II forced him to change plan and remain in Spain.

Shortly afterwards, in 1940, he joined an association of young people, which later took the name of Opus Dei, who aspired to live the Christian life to the full in their professional work within the Spanish society which had been devastated by the Civil War and was then lying in ruins. For the next twenty years Panikkar remained an official member of the Opus Dei society.

In 1941, Panikkar graduated with a degree in science from the University of Barcelona and a year later, in literature from the University of Madrid. He then continued his studies in Barcelona while working in the family business. In 1946, he received a doctorate in philosophy and literature from the University of Madrid; in the same year he was ordained a priest. In 1958, he obtained a doctorate in chemistry, again from the University of Madrid, and in 1961, a doctorate in theology from the Pontifical Lateran University in Rome.

At the end of 1954 Panikkar left Europe for India on an apostolic mission, and there, having left Opus Dei, he was incardinated into the diocese of Vārāṇasī and remained a priest of that diocese until the end of his life. He returned several times to Europe and travelled to many other countries.

From 1954 to 1967, except for many trips to Italy and other countries, he lived in utmost simplicity in two small rooms above a Śiva temple in Hanumanghat on the bank of the Ganges.

In 1966, Panikkar was called to Harvard University as a Visiting Professor, and from 1971 to 1987 he taught Comparative Philosophy of Religion at the University of California at Santa Barbara, spending a semester teaching in the US and the rest of the year in India.

In 1987, at the end of his university career, he returned to Catalonia and took up residence in Tavertet (Osona), a small town in the Pre-Pyrenees. Here he founded the center Vivarium, where he regularly held courses, seminars, and meetings on philosophical, religious, and cultural themes, and undertook in-depth studies of different religious traditions.

*

Having been educated in both East and West Panikkar was able to carry out in his work a constant dialogue among different traditions, ideologies, and beliefs.

Panikkar has published some seventy books, mostly in Italian, Catalan, Castilian and English, many of which have been translated into various other languages, as well as over a thousand articles. He has supervised some twenty theses from around the world, especially during his stay in the United States. Around seventy disserations have been written on his thought; these are now kept in the library of the University of Girona, to which Panikkar donated his vast library. In 1998, his *Opera Omnia* began to be published in Italian, followed by Catalan, Castilian and English editions.

Panikkar held courses in universities all over the world as well as delivered prestigious lectures such as the Warner Lectures and the Gifford Lectures, which were later developed into the book *The Rhythm of Being*. He contributed to the Classics of western Spirituality project, serving as editor of its last three volumes.

In addition to his intense and varied academic activities Panikkar was President of the Pipal Tree Association (Bangalore), founder and director of the Center for Cross-Cultural Religious Studies (Santa Barbara, California), and Vivarium, Centre d'EstudiosInterculturals de Barcelona (Tavertet, Catalonia). In 1960, he was one of the founders of Pax Romana, an NGO with consultative status at the United Nations, whose aim is to protect the rights and dignity of all people worldwide. He has also taken part in numerous international consultations for UNESCO and many other academic institutions. On two occasions he was a special envoy for the Indian government on cultural missions to South America.

Panikkar's long, intense life ended on August 26, 2010 at the age of 91. Part of his ashes was buried in the small cemetery of Tavertet, according to the Christian tradition, and part of them was scattered over the sacred waters of the Ganges, in keeping with the Hindu tradition.

Identity

To know the identity, that is, the deepest reality of a person, love and trust are needed, without which we cannot reach beyond the level of superficial or merely intellectual knowledge. Having had the priviledge of being close to Panikkar during the last twenty years of his life, working with him on the publication of his *Opera Omnia*, and translating and editing many of his books, I would like now to attempt to trace as best as I can his true identity.

....

Without doubt, Panikkar is one of the greatest thinkers of the twentieth and early twenty-first centuries. He was a philosopher, a theologian, an expert in three religions (Christianity, Hinduism and Buddhism), a pioneer of interreligious and intercultural dialogue, and so on. Those who were closely acquainted with him, however, know that more than anything he was a mystic who concealed his spirituality under an intellectual mantle. As he himself wrote for the Feast of Corpus Christi:

> Let my identity grow so I may be able to identify with my body and with all the earth and at the same time to distance myself from everything and not absolutize anything. I must begin from the experience of my own body, including headaches or something far more serious, which should not, however, bring me to despair. I will then discover that I am what I experience, but not only that, because what I am is "my" own being, and this being is my identity; "to be" is a verb and is not, therefore, reducible to either a subject or an object. If we let "our" being go through our body and also the "earth", then we will feel freedom within us. To live my identity, our identity, is *an* indescribable, amazing experience. It is the *advaita*.[414]

Panikkar dedicated his entire life, including his youth, to deciphering the mystery of existence, and tried to always be ready to offer help to those who were plagued by ultimate questions. As he said:

> Human life on a spatiotemporal plane is certainly a game, līlā, a game of human interaction, whose centre is tempiternal and mystical or completely mysterious, but in the guise of a social game. We must play the game honestly, but without allowing it to overwhelm or suffocate us.[415]

All of Panikkar's writings are autobiographical. They do not deal simply with a problem of the mind but with a concern of his heart and, indeed, of his entire existence, and which he strove constantly to clarity and analyze by studying in depth the problems of human life. None of his articles or books were written for the mere purpose of self-expression or to satisfy an urge to write. He never planned a piece of writing; everything he wrote was prompted by circumstances, urged by friends, requested by groups of people, or elicited in seminars.

If anything would make Panikkar suffer it was the pain of having to distill his insights into words; he had the excruciating conviction that everything he wrote had to be authenticated by the entire human experience. In

---

414 From his Diaries: May 28, 1964.

415 R. Panikkar, unpublished notes, February 17, 1976.

writing he struggled to express his thought as a practically universal consensus. The endless notes that accompanied his writings show how carefully he sought to keep alive the whole tradition whose insights he tried to communicate. He made an enormous effort to write neither as a westerner nor as an Indian, neither as a Christian nor as a Hindū, nor even as a man of his times. He tried hard to emphasise the eternal intuition that "the letter kills" and that the written word is not the exclusive ambassador of life to consciousness.[416]

In the first period of his literary activities, which began in the early 1940s, Panikkar's writings represent a dialogue between himself and the Spanish society after the Civil War and the Second World War. They were a plea for authenticity and for a more global vision of Humanity and Reality. He could not believe that right was only on the part of the victors. *Synthesis* was the title of his first major article, which inaugurated a new journal in Madrid.[417] In the early fifties he wrote an entire book on patriotism, which was at that time a rather dangerous indictment of nationalism – branding it as a heresy, and at the same time defending the need for concrete rootedness in and loyalty to one's own region, together with a universal ideal that can have no human limits.[418]

From the mid 1940s to the early 1950s, Panikkar devoted his energies to the study of three major problems, which resulted in three books. First, *Mysterium Crucis*, still unpublished, in which he attempts to connect the dogma of the Trinity with anthropology and cosmology, offering an integral vision of reality with the Trinity revealing the ultimate structure of Man and of the Universe. Secondly, *Cristianismo y Cristianidad*, which discusses the contrast between the Christian faith and Christianity, which would become a prophetic book for decades to come. Thirdly, *Introduciòn a la esperanza*, which attempts to explain how modern Man might live without either escaping from this world or blowing it up as an unjust society. Underlying all these concerns was the "nature" of the "supernatural." Is there any another dimension in Man which "saves" us from being crushed? Various circumstances prevented Panikkar from completing his trilogy on "nature", "human nature", and "supernature";

416 R. Panikkar, *Vita e Parola*, edited by Milena Carrara, Milan: Jaca Book, 2010, p. 8.

417 R. Panikkar, "Sìntesis. Visión de sìntesis del universo," *Arbor* (1944) 1, pp. 5-40.

418 R. Panikkar, *Patriotismo y Cristianidad,* Madrid: Rialp, 1961.

he only managed to finish the first part, which became his doctoral thesis in 1946 and a bulky book, *El concepto de naturaleza.*[419]

During this time Panikkar was also busy studying the nature of matter. This was the period of his involvement with questions of science and the philosophy of science. What Panikkar was seeking is not so much a "theology of science" as what he calls *theophysics,* or the divine, free, transcendent, and immanent aspect of the physical sciences.[420] Not science as a springboard to God, but science as a dimension, an aspect, an effect of that very mystery which, according to Thomas Aquinas, "all" or "some" would call God.

Throughout this period of his life Panikkar plunged himself continuously into priestly ministry, preaching retreats, hearing confessions, offering spiritual guidance, and taking part in new cultural and religious ventures. He did not have time to write treatises on spiritual theology. All he could do was to jot down random notes and prayers prompted by the most everyday circumstances, in the early hours of the day, before life began to stir around him. He called these notes *Cometas* [comets], a selection of which was published much later, when the particular events they referred to had already become history, both for him and Spain.[421]

The third period of Panikkar's life, from the early 1960s, was marked by his existential involvement in the religions of his ancestors, to which he belonged and which had nurtured him since his birth, and by an attempt to integrate them together. A number of articles and books date back to this period.[422] Gradually, timidly even, he went from seeking to make

419 R. Panikkar, *El concepto de naturaleza,* Madrid: Consejo Superior de Investigaciónes Cientìficas 1951, 2nd edition 1971).

420 R. Panikkar, *Ontonomìa de la Ciencia,* Madrid: Gredos, 1961.

421 R. Panikkar, *Cometas, Fragmentos de un diario espiritual de la postguerra,* Madrid: Euramérica.

422 These incude among others: R. Panikkar, "Die existentielle Phänomenologie der Wahrheit," *Philosophisches Jahrbuch der Görresgesellshaft*, (Munich, 1956), pp. 27-54; "Some Phenomenological Aspects of Hindu Spirituality Today," *Oriental Thought,* III, (Oct. 1957), pp. 157-191; *La India, Gente Cultura, Creencias* (Madrid: Rialp, 1960); *Die Vielen Götter und der eine Herr. Beiträgezumökumenischen Gespräch der Weltreligionen* (Wehhern: O.W. Barth, 1963); *The Unknown Christ of Hinduism* (London: Darton, Longman and Todd); *Kulturmysterium in Hinduismus und Christentum. Ein Beitrag zur vergleichenden Religionstheologie* (Freiburg and Munich: K. Alber, 1964); and *Religiòn y Religiones* (Madrid: Gredos, 1965).

Hinduism acceptable to himself and to non-Hindus to presenting it as a true religion, discovering in it the living, saving principle that Christians call Christ but which cannot be limited to a single name, for its true name is a "*Supername*,"a name beyond all names. This led him to declare himself both a Christian and a Hindu, according to the accepted, or at least acceptable canons of both traditions. This process, or rather, progress, can be traced from *The Unknown Christ of Hinduism* to *The Supername*, passing through his German and Spanish writings.[423]

This was by no means easy. He had no encouragement from any side. Christians looked down on him as a dangerous syncretist or an outright apostate. To have survived for decades in the fundamentalist climate of the Opus Dei appeared as something that could only be explained by an innocence bordering on puerility. Hindus equally mistrusted him, to the point where an incident arose which could have had more public consequences had he pursued it further. In 1964, he was denied the newly created Chair of Comparative Religion at the Banaras Hindu University for the sole reason that he was a Catholic priest and, as such, was deemed untrustworthy. The chair remained vacant for more than ten years. It was neither an intellectual decision nor an irresponsible whim that led him to declare himself both a Hindu and a Christian. It might have been a sense of loyalty to both of his traditions, perhaps also to his own father, who had died just one month before his first journey to India and whom he had literally abandoned in order to be ordained a priest. In fact, it was not a concious decision at all. Panikkar found himself not only psychologically receptive to Hindū worship but also religiously involved as a Hindū believer, without however intending to renounce his Christian faith. It was basically an existential process, which he attempted to express intellectually in many of his writings.

On Panikkar's activities such as fasting, religious observances, sitting at the feet of *gurūs*, living in temples and ashrams, making pilgrimages, learning from and discussing with people of other faiths, and so on, it

---

[423] This progress was adumbrated rather than clearly expressed twenty-five years later in the second, revised edition of *The Unknown Christ of Hinduism* (Maryknoll, NY: Orbis Books, 1973). *The Supername* was his opening lecture at the Ecumenical Institute of Advanced Theological Study, Tantur, Jerusalem, 1972.

is impossible to give a detailed account here, but it is certain that all of these activities have become part of who he was.

As for Buddhism, Panikkar was drawn to it only in the late 1960s. He did with it what he had done with Hinduism, that is, not experimenting with it but experiencing it. In short, the orthopraxis that had led him to both Christianity and Hinduism was now spontaneously bringing him to Buddhism, though he embraced neither syncretism nor eclecticism, charges against which he was forced to defend himself. Panikkar found himself having to re-enact what was for him the fundamental experience of the Buddha, namely, *śūnyatā.* The challenge for him here was atheism. His book *El silencio del Dios,* which had begun as *The Silence of the Buddha*, crystallizes his understanding and, in a way, acceptance of the *anātmavadā*, or the teaching of the not-I.[424]

Though he had long desired to write on Buddhism and atheism, this came about not as a result of his own initiative but as a response to a request to write on this theme for the four-volume encyclopaedia *L'ateismo contemporaneo.* "Buddhismo e ateismo" was in fact taken from *El Silencio del Dios*, which was originally intended by Panikkar as a meditation for himself alone.[425]

It was only then that Panikkar was ready to accept, in addition to Christianity, Hinduism, and Buddhism, the fourth tradition, namely, secularity, and became sincerely and fully secular. Events in his life at the time helped him take this momentous step. The center of his life was no longer Europe, as in the beginning, nor India, as later, but North America. Here his work was more that of a professor than that of a priest in the conventional sense of the word. Many of his writings, especially those written in French for the Castelli Colloquia in Rome, may be said

---

[424] The original Spanish text was published without a final revision while he was in India, and was consequently in need of correction. The first corrected version was an Italian edition, and it was not until 1996 that he was able to publish the new corrected, revised, and extended Spanish version, *El silencio del Buddha,* and the final Italian version, *Il Silenzio del Buddha. Un ateismo religioso* (Milan: Oscar Mondadori, 2006). The English version appeared as *The Silence of God: The Answer to the Buddha*, Maryknoll, NY: Orbis Books, 1970).

[425] R. Panikkar, "Buddhismo e ateismo," in: *L'ateismo contemporaneo,* vol. IV (Turin: Società Editrice Internazionale, 1967-70), pp. 449-76.

to express this effort to recover his naked humanness, as it were, without the qualifications of any religious tradition in the classical sense of the term.[426] It was at this time that he realized he had to face, perhaps for the first time, all the obligations of an average citizen living in the "world."

Bearing witness to this period of his life are two writings: *The Myth of Śunaḥśepa*[427] and *The Tempiternal Present*.[428] These two works are in fact related. In the first Panikkar discovered *Śunaḥśepa*'s vocation as the destiny of Man and his own karma:

> Only a total deconditioning can liberate us and others as well. Only prayer as an existential cry from the abyss of our precariousness will be vouchsafed. Only if led by circumstances and by others, only by being at the bottom of a ladder or hanging at the end of a chain will I justifiably live. Resurrection comes only "after" the death of the ego.[429]

The Tempiternal Present is even more personal, since it touches not only his innermost being but also the entire sociological situation of his life:

> If social revolution were the only way to help my fellow-beings to live a more human life, I should simply become an activist revolutionary; if proclaiming the Good News of salvation were the solution, I should become a preacher. I think that in this article I justify my cosmotheandric vocation, which I try to live the best I can – in spite of my conscious and unconscious failings.[430]

We should also mention the intense work which in his enthusiasm he had expected would take no more than a year but actually took ten years of his life. Through this work Panikkar was putting into practice something which he later called "diatopical hermeneutics." In spite of the abyss between Hinduism and the Vedas, Panikkar was convinced that there was in fact a deep bond between the two. Modern Hindus pay lip service

---

426 Many of these French articles were later published in English in R. Panikkar, *Myth, Faith and Hermeneutics* (New York: Paulist Press, 1979).

427 *Śunaḥśēpa,* son of Ajīgarta, is believed to be the composer of the Ṛg-veda hymns I, 24-30 and IX, 3. His famous story is one of the myths on the human condition.

428 "Le mythe comme histoire sacrée," in: *Le Sacré,* ed. E. Castelli (Paris: Aubier, 1974), pp. 243-315; "El presente tempiterno. Una apostilla a la historia de la salvaciòn y a la teologìa de la liberaciòn," in: *Homenaje a Karl Rahner*, ed. A. Vargas-Machuca (Madrid: Cristiandad, 1975), pp. 133-75.

429 R. Panikkar, unpublished notes, February 17, 1976.

430 Ibid.

to the *Vedas*, just as many Christians refer to the Bible without having much knowledge of it.

During the Christian reform that followed the Indian Independence in 1947-1950, which called for the indigenization of the liturgy with forms of worship more suited to India, Panikkar sought to propose a Cosmic Missal that may be used in the Christian re-enactment of the one single Sacrifice. He said:

> I soon realised that the best service I could provide was not an arranged translation of some *Vedic* texts for Christian use, but an independent scholarly work presenting the *Vedas* as they understand themselves to be (giant hermeneutical problems notwithstanding). *Vedic* Sanskrit is not classical Sanskrit, nor the *Vedas* just some *Upaniṣads* and well-known *Rigvedic* hymns. I plunged in that jungle and after having introduced and translated what I think is the most complete collection of the entire *Vedic* message I expurgated my comments from all *Vedāntic*, Christian, Greek and other ideas and reduced the text almost by the half so that it could be a text meaningful to our contemporaries independently of any religious or cultural persuasion.

What remained, neverthelesss, was a book of almost a thousand pages.[431]

Panikkar achieved such a degree of connaturality with the *Vedic* world that certain orthodox pandits even began to regard him as a reincarnated *rishi*. Although in practical aspects he was assisted by a small team of collaborators, this work was basically a spiritual experience for him.

Another paradoxical feature of Panikkar's life needs to be noted, nameky his love of silence and his deep involvement in the world. Panikkar loved silence and spent long periods in solitude. However, he never wanted a *fuga mundi* [flight from the world]; on the contrary he was aware of the suffering in the world and his involvement in the destiny of Mankind:

> What can I do? There is suffering in the world, there is injustice, hatred, exploitation. I am part of the majority of Mankind which appears to, or does, collaborate with a 'system' that is atleastpartially responsible for this state of affairs. (…)

---

[431] R. Panikkar, *The Vedic Experience. Mantramañjarî. An Anthology of the Vedas for Modern Man and Contremporary Collection* (Berkeley: University of California Press, 1977).

> I am trying to do what I can. Alas, perhaps a little in a low-key in these last years; but still the fire and the ideal are alive in me. If I leave the Church because it is rotten, refuse to pay taxes because the money goes to the military, or burn my passport because my country is unjust, unworthy or whatever it will not solve the problem. To leave the Earth because the air is polluted would not help either – even if it were possible. Non-collaboration with any form that we consider evil may be a powerful political tactic, but it may also stand in the way of other possibilities and place me in other equally compromising and unclear situations.

This is why he continually emphasised that the mystical dimension is necessary in order to live. "Only the mystic will survive" is one of his recurring phrases.

> When I get up before dawn and all is quiet around me, including the stars, I am not doing it to 'win heaven', accumulate merit or even simply get some work done. I am not doing it for work, but for life; I am doing it so I may live and live as authentically as I can. To live authentically means to be ready to die tomorrow without missing a thing. Perhaps the best book I could write would be a prayer, and yet I am afraid I will never write it unless I stop praying.

In 1987 Panikkar retired from academic life and moved to a small town in the Pre-Pyrenees, where he continued his life of contemplation and wrote many books: *The New Innocence, The Fullness of Man, Mysticism, The Dwelling Place of Wisdom,* to name a few.

In 1998, after three years of hard work dedicated to organising his vast literary production, work began on the publication of his *Opera Omnia*, first in Italian and then in Catalan, French, Spanish, and English. This represents the crystalization of his thought which conceals his mystical experience of Life.

The following text was written by Panikkar in response to my request asking him to tell me about his personal spirituality.

A Letter on "my" Own Spirituality[432]

Raimon Panikkar

July 1, 1996

Milena,

Many people have asked me to speak about my spirituality. I have always replied that it is my own self speaking, but not of "myself". I am a subject, not an object.

When I am pressed to do so, I reply that, if anything, I should write poetry: that would let me truly feel incarnated in my words—but unfortunately I do not possess a language of my own, despite knowing many.

Nevertheless, the countless lessons, conferences, retreats and sermons I have held, spanning half a century, have always reflected the spirituality that I live out, although on each occasion I have expressed myself according to the people I was addressing. Language is always dialogue.

But now *you* are asking me the same thing, and I feel I owe you an answer, however difficult and limited it may be, since you are my "favourite" disciple, as I told you on Kailāsa, to your great surprise—and also to my own.

The first answer I give you will qualify the question better. It is not a matter of *my* spirituality but, rather, of a type of spirituality (should I say Spirit?) that took hold of me—or maybe took shape in me.

---

[432] From *Pellegrinaggio al Kailāsa,* Raimon Panikkar and Milena Carrara, Sotto il Monte, Bergamo: Servitium, 2006; riprinted and enlarged in *Pellegrinaggio e ritorno alla Sorgente*, Milan: Jaca Book and Servitium, 2011; in English, *A Pilgrimage to Kailash*, Delhi: Motilal Banarsidass, 2018.

The second confirms the answer I have already given to others: my reflection on "my" spirituality is not "my" spirituality, but how I interpret it today. I feel that "my" spirituality is my life and that my life has unfolded, manifested itself and blossomed spontaneously—if you will allow me this poetic expression. The main "decisions" of my life have resulted mostly from my acceptance of circumstances which I have allowed—too passively, I admit—to condition it. I never planned to study in Germany, to be in Madrid, in Salamanca or in Rome, or even to go to India or to become a priest or a professor. I was simply consenting. Stupidity? Passivity? Blessed or unholy indifference? Weakness? A mere psychological attitude? I don't know. Perhaps I was centred and concentrated on a plan that went beyond these events? Probably a little of all of these.

Yet the fact remains that I have hardly ever analysed myself in this sense. Again, trust in divine providence or the inability to establish a goal in my life? I do not act according to a *telos, propter finem*, with the aim of attaining a goal.

Am I aware that the story of my life lends itself to being told either as an ingenious transformation in the light of external circumstances, or as a cowardly submission to the influence of others. Blessed new innocence or foolish naivety? Or perhaps both?

With that, I may have given you a summary and superficial image of myself, but I have not yet responded to your request.

So here is my third attempt to work out something that comes closer to an answer, however incomplete, to your legitimate question.

Without doubt, the spirituality that has shaped my life has taken on the triple form of *bhakti, jñāna* and *karman*, in other words devotion, knowledge and action, albeit with differing emphasis during the various different periods of my life.

To start with, let us say until my ordination as a priest in 1946, my spirituality was centred on the adoration of a personal God through Jesus Christ. Very soon after that, however, probably between the ages of thirty and forty, although this God continued to be personal, He started to penetrate everything; He was present everywhere and could not be reduced to a Supreme Being. The God of the mystics and also of philosophy (but not of such philosophers as Aristotle) convinced me more than YHWH. Despite the fact that I understood Pascal's reaction to certain "philosophers" in favour of the God of Abraham, Isaac and Jacob, the God of history was not my God. Perhaps my indic origins made me feel foreign to the cultural and religious current of the abrahamic traditions. "My" Christianity started to distinguish between faith and doctrinal statements. I did not identify my catholic faith with the western culture that transmitted it. I had the experience of a Christ who was not limited to Christians and even less to Catholics. Yet "my" Christ was actually the Jesus of the christian Scriptures—a Jesus Christ who in any case existed "before Abraham" and was the "alpha and omega" of the whole of creation.

This led me to a christocentric form of devotion. The Eucharist was the centre of my life and daily communion was a practice that I had followed since my early youth, until my second stay in India in 1964. For theological reasons I have always abstained from celebrating Mass alone.

I had the profound experience of the real Presence in the Eucharist, which slowly became the Presence of Christ, somehow different from the Presence of Jesus, though I only elaborated this theological distinction much later.

This devotion to Christ gradually led me to experience the reality of the Trinity or the central mystery of life. Here again, I developed the doctrine much later. Christ, the Son of God, the divine Incarnation, has no meaning outside the Trinity.

I cannot deny having had a deep filial devotion to Mary. An unpublished paper of mine, presented at the Lateran University in 1954, and which received the approval of my professor Pietro Parente, later to become a cardinal, upheld the theory of *Maria, Mater temporalis Dei*, meaning both "the Mother of the temporal God" and "the temporal Mother of God. I no longer remember the exact formulation.

Going back to my years in Opus Dei, it was like living in permanent ecstasy, beyond a purely temporal existence. This permitted me to endure the rigidity inflicted on me by that congregation. Outside observers attributed this to the fact that I was a philosopher living with his head in the clouds, unable to see reality. But in reality I lived on another level—which in those days was called the "supernatural dimension". In actual fact my doctoral thesis was on the "concept of nature" as the preparation for the reality of the supernatural, for which I felt an existential fascination.

My spirituality was centred on the adoration of the divine Mystery as the ultimate vocation of all intellectual creatures. This reminds me of Romano Guardini. The ultimate goal of a being is to sing "Glory to God". It was during those years that I believed I had completely died to myself.

Another aspect of my spirituality in those years, until my third stay in India, from 1964 onwards, is outlined in the paper I wrote in Spanish in 1950, *Mysterium Crucis*, which is still unpublished. Sacrifice is the essence of the Cross, which is the external revelation of the inner life of the Trinity, a mutual immolation of the divine Persons. In other words, only by completely dying to ourselves can we give life to the world, to reality, and therefore be resurrected.

Much later on, I found an equivalent intuition in the vedic doctrine on *yajña*, sacrifice. The world exists due to the self-immolation of Prajāpati. About one hundred pages of my book on the *Vedas* deal with this subject.

One of the two rooms I lived in at the Banaras Hind¥ University was used as a chapel and had a fresco that a friend of mine had painted by hand, bearing an inscription with a sacred text from the *Vedas* and the Christian Scriptures: "One and only sacrifice".

My first years in India helped me to deepen my vision of the sacramental structure of the world. My *Kultmysterium* is an expression of this intuition. I have re-worked a French translation of it in *Le mystère du culte*, and revised the unpublished English version that has been awaiting completion for fifteen years now. I regret that it may never be completed.

This sacramental experience helped me to understand the *tantra* as its homeomorphic equivalent. By this I mean that I discovered the indispensable role of matter and its essential cooperation in the *mysterium salutis*.

Furthermore, all this led me to experience not only the sacredness of matter but also the definitive nature of the secular aspect of reality. Another unpublished book of mine, with the revealing title *Sacred Secularity*, deals with this subject.

You must not think that I am talking about my books. I am telling you about my experiences. Actually, whenever I had an intuition I almost always started to write a new book, or at least an article, with the aim of checking, clarifying, deepening and eventually formulating my experiences—although I then gave them a philosophical slant, which I believe is an indispensable form of expression.

From this point it was only a short step to the intuition of the radical Trinity or theanthropocosmic (cosmostheandric) vision of reality.

Everything may seem clear and congruent. I can only say that these intuitions did not manifest themselves as deductions but quite spontaneously, as praxis had preceded theory by a long way.

In the appendix to my doctoral thesis I coined the word *theophysics* to express my intuition of the Divine that permeates every pore and corner of the material world, just as I had already seen—and written—that every being is a Cristophany.

I have spoken of *bhakti* and of *jñāna*, but I must not forget *karman*. I am not a particularly active kind of person, but neither am I a pure contemplative, detached from the world. Much later on in my life, I wrote a book about politics as a means of salvation, several articles on economics and also one about medicine – of course from an "ultimate" perspective.

My passion for justice was, and is, essential to me. Despite my intellectual tendency, I have always been against the "pure" contemplative, the *fuga mundi*, the acosmism of *saṃnyāsa.* I have defended (and justified) my lifestyle as a contribution to radical *metanoia*, of which our modern civilisation has a great need, using those talents that "God" gave me, which are not those of an activist. You already know my story about the *rabbi* of Vilnius.

I have described more than once the cosmotheandric experience and that of tempiternity. Both have had a real effect on my whole being, but they were above all intellectual experiences, rather than emotional or physical. The intellect is more than simple reason and the intellect, too, has its raptures and visions. Meister Eckhart is an example of this, but I could just as well mention Dionysius, Evagrius, the Cappadocian Fathers, or Śaṅkara, Abhinavagupta, Laozi and many others.

I cannot recall when I first had the experience of *advaita*- which, together with the trinitarian experience, is perhaps my fundamental experience. They certainly go back to when I was very young, however, perhaps long before I had heard the name *advaita*. I can only say that it is one thing not to be convinced by monism or dualism, and another to "see" the *advaitic* nature of reality. This vision cannot be rational, because reason cannot understand without unifying. I can understand that God and the World cannot be one or two, but I cannot grasp them together rationally.

The rational alternative to the monism/dualism dilemma is dialectics. Yet, as I have always claimed, it is not necessary for the structure of reality to be dialectic. The *advaitic* experience transcends reason: it is the vision of relationships as constituent of reality. God and the World are not two foundations of reality, rather, it is the relationship that is real. God and the World are only real in their relationality. This can only be expressed with a paradox: when I see the World I see God; when I see God I see the World; I see one as the real dimension of the other. I cannot put them together, as they are distinct, but I cannot separate them, they are not two—as in the Trinity. This is more than a perception of the divine aspect of the world or of a conviction that Creator implies Creation. In Christian terms it is the "taboric light" that makes the apostles see the divine aspect of a man and the human aspect of God. Christ, fully human and fully divine, is for me a paradigm of the *advaitic* vision.

You asked me about my spirituality and here I am going on about my experiences. But "my" spirituality is experiential.

Let me try again. If I were to summarise "my" spirituality, I would define it as cosmotheandric experience.

I can start by quoting the passage from St John (10:10): «I have come so that they may have life and have it to the full»—that is to say, in its fullness. I can then relate this to another passage from the Prologue to the *Gospel of St. John* (1,4): «In him was life, life that was the light of men» and this light is God.

I have led various retreats on the "silence of life", which is not a life of silence but the silence of Life itself "before" it bursts into Word. This Life is the Divine, as it is called by the mystics of many traditions.

But I am circumventing the answer again. I could distil my spirituality, without defining the word for now, in three points.

1. The experience of the *theos*, that is, of the infinite and of freedom.

No limit comes from God, no boundary; no constriction is divine. If the so-called "commandments" were not liberating (as one Psalm says) they would not come from God. It is a spirituality that expels fear. "Do not fear" is the *kerygma* of the risen Christ.

If the Divine is infinite and free there is no law, no *Torah*; there are not even the commandments *strictu sensu*. It is fine to be oriented, to receive suggestions or advice, but to follow a commandment simply because it is an order is not ethical or even Christian. If your thoughts are impure, if you are cross-eyed, if you look at a woman with lust... "Hypocrites!" said Jesus. Hypocrisy was the only sin he seemed to censure, because it condemns itself.

I also go so far as to not accept the *metaphysical* validity of *physical* laws. This is consistent with my intuition of the *creatio continua*, which contemporary physics is now more willing to admit as plausible.

A spirituality of freedom is not anarchy, nor is it monarchy. God is not a Power, a Supreme Being. St John wrote that in the beginning was the *logos*. The *logos* is not the Beginning. It was there *in* the beginning, but it was not *the* Beginning. Here is *advaita* again, and the Trinity.

Freedom requires our responsibility—our ability to respond and not only to react. Re-action is not free: it is an anti-action. A free response is not conditioned by premises or circumstances. We must not and cannot judge others; rather, we can and must judge ourselves, as is so emphatically expressed in a non-canonical sentence by Jesus: «Man, may you be blessed if you know what you do», that is to say, taking responsibility for working on the Sabbath (cf. also Luke 6:4).

The secret lies in the strength of a word that I have not yet pronounced, and that "moves the sun and the other stars": love.

Any action moved by love is authentic and brings with it forgiveness where required, as shown by the moving story of Mary Magdalene.

Authentic love is free. It has no other motivation; it is not driven by a reason or a goal. It is above volition, because one cannot love by order, not even by the order of our will.

Thus a requirement of this spirituality is pureness of heart.

I believe it was above all the experience of freedom that led me to experience God. I am aware that it might also have been the experience of beauty, of goodness or of truth. In any ultimate experience one is able to touch the Divine. Perhaps I prefer freedom because it "embodies" better what I have defined as cosmotheandric experience. I do not know.

For many years a phrase of Job's accompanied me: "Take the path of no return". Does that mean trembling when I behold the infinite? Do I need someone to tell me not to be afraid? It is not the infinity of the spaces, as it is for Pascal, but the infinity of reality, the lacerating experience of divine infinity, the abyss of freedom.

All men follow their own path, their own authentic (divine) nature and the impulses of their own pure heart. In spiritual life there are no prescribed formulas, instant recipes or ready-made highways to heaven.

2. The second pivot on which this spirituality rests is the experience of *anthrôpos*, that is to say of consciousness.

"*Ko 'ham*, who am I?" asks the *Veda*. "Know thyself", said the Delphic Sybil. "Know the strength of Man", says the *Tao te ching* (XXVIII), albeit in another context. To eat the fruit of the tree of knowledge of good and evil is forbidden because it is simply objective knowledge, says the book of Genesis. But closer to the centre of paradise grows the "tree of Life". Life is conscious life, the consciousness of Life itself, the *logos* of the Trinity, the *sat-cit-ānanda*, the salvific *gnôsis* of many traditions, *upaniṣ adic*, neo-platonic and evangelical.

"Be aware! Know! Be attentive! Reawaken! Realise! Become enlightened!"... are all expressions of this second dimension of spirituality. "Be yourself" says the last line of Plato's last letter.

It is a serene and sober spirituality. It does not disdain the critical power of the intellect. It combines and eventually unites knowledge and love.

This spirituality is not based on the *siddhi* or paranormal powers or supernatural phenomena, though it does not deny these aspects and is certainly not the prerogative of any elite.

In saying this, I stress the apophatic dimension of this spirituality, because it is actually the intellect, or pure consciousness, that leads us to that infinite *docta ignorantia*, cloud of unknowing, beam of darkness, *sadāsata nirvācanīya, neti neti, wu wei, mu*... of many traditions.

In the same way, love has no reason, it is free and does not have a why. This awareness is pure grace, it has no other foundation; it is an *Ungrund*, an abyss, as many masters have said.

Without doubt mystics can describe the periods they have passed through, recount their experiences and discover a hierarchy among themselves once they have reached the summit. But alas for the true pilgrim if each stage is not the last one, if each step is not the final one, as if God were only on the summit and not equally close to everyone and present in the pause between each step. What I maintain is that every spirituality is unique: for the pilgrim each stage is final and each step is the last.

Spiritual life has no charts or maps. Each path is unique, just as each person is unique. If even the single leaf is different from all other leaves, could we be so uniform and homogeneous that we are only numerical cases in a general scheme?

Let me reiterate. Man is an intellectual being, a conscious and self-conscious creature. Blind faith is not even faith. The "second eye" is indispensable for a truly human spirituality. I said that one must follow one's own heart, a pure heart. But a heart without a head is not even a heart, just as a head without a heart is a dead thing.

But I hear your reproof that I cannot get off my high horse or come down from the pulpit. I will try to be more concrete.

My spirituality is therefore presumably a human spirituality, obviously not in a humanistic sense but probably more in the sense I attribute to the experience as the "Son of Man".

3. My third point is the overwhelming discovery that we are *kosmos*- in other words matter. I *am* body, I do not just *have* a body. Space and time are not just the external framework within which we move: they are part of our being. We are essentially spatial and temporal. The earth is not simply our medium or *habitat* for the moment. We are earth and we are terrestrial. Adam means the "earthly one".

It is easier to save the soul, to cultivate a disembodied (or non-existent) spirit than to lead the whole man towards his fullness and salvation.

Furthermore, I am convinced that an incarnate spirituality is a pressing need in our times. In Christian terms, I would say that it is a matter of living our own resurrection, here and now. I will omit the problem of life beyond death.

*

Now I would like to speak to you about resurrection. I have already told you that the so- called resurrection of the body is not an event in a historical future. It is commonly said that it is an eschatological fact, but eschatology does not mean the end of temporal history, rather it means something ultimate and definitive. I will never forget an experience I had back in the late 1940s. It was the experience of the mass as a tempiternal act and as the actualisation of personal resurrection from that very moment. It is the experience of "eternal life" here and now, in a *here* and *now* that is more, not less, than space and time. If every moment is unrepeatable, it is unique, and if it is unique, it is incomparable (because it has no parallel). This led me to live tempiternity not as moments that last forever, but as moments that in their very temporality are charged with eternity. Sometimes they are special, interior moments, full of emotivity, and could be called ecstatic. At other times they are ordinary and banal but full of the awareness that they are unrepeatable. But I feel that by speaking about this I am disfiguring what I want to say. Ineffability is not a "trick" for hiding our imperfection; it is the empty "space" through which the Spirit blows. Forgive me if I am unable to describe it better.

The body is far more than just a tool. It is something divine, a temple for the Holy Spirit, to quote the Scriptures.

The integration of the earth into our spirituality is what I have called *ecosophy*- and you already know what that means. It requires a new lifestyle and a new notion of civilisation. This is where the power of spirituality can be seen in creating a culture. We are earth, part of the earth, working together with the earth to create "new heavens and a new earth". Matter is not just a simple object for man. Ecosophical consciousness implies anthropological change.

Man may be called the "king of creation" as long as his regal role is not separated from the priestly one: man is the mediator between heaven and earth, the *pontifex*, the bridge between the divine and the cosmic, he who participates in both these natures in personal union.

Now you may tell me this is pure speculation. I will answer that I hold a vision in myself, an experience, and add that I am giving voice here to an ancient song of humanity, albeit in new terms.

So I am defending a cosmic spirituality, which is also hinted at in christian Scripture when it speaks of "the final goal of all things" (Peter), of the "recapitulation of all things in Christ" (Paul), and of "God all in all" (1 Co 15, 28), etc. These and other phrases have nourished my spiritual life; they have resonated within me and have become experiential.

This is where human love reaches its apex. Human love as the concrete expression of divine love—and divine love as embodied in human love. Once again we are faced with an *advaitic* relationship: they are neither two nor one.

The two "principal commandments" are *one single* commandment, because they cannot be separated. One cannot love one's neighbour with constant, full love without at the same time loving God, because my neighbour is not always loveable. One cannot love God if one does not love one's neighbour because I cannot know what love is if I do not have the experience of human love. Divine love would be a mere abstraction. It is written that we should love our neighbour as we love ourselves, but what is *closer* to us, more of a *neighbour*, than God himself?

It is here that the spirituality that I think of as mine finds its place; a spirituality which integrates the cosmic with the divine; a spirituality in which human love is the likeness of divine love, and divine love is a human love that has broken through the boundaries of our contingency. Many mystics say that it is love that unites us with God, but this love of God must be human love if it is to be love *among* human beings—and not just a purely mental projection or abstraction.

Now, let us return to your request that I talk about myself and not about my ideas, though of course they are a result of the experiences I have lived through.

I lived for many years without paying attention to my body and subjecting myself to the typical penances of a certain kind of ascetic spirituality. I do not wish to talk about my *tapas,* both out of modesty and because I think it is no longer relevant. I do not regret that practice, although I probably would not repeat it now.

I feel that I am part of the Earth, being earth and dust myself, as Ash Wednesday reminds us. I feel that my destiny is the same as that of the Earth and, albeit without pantheistic feelings or "immense consciousness", I feel connected to this cosmos. I must immediately add that this cosmos is not exclusively matter, nor is it only temporality. I experience the Lord's Prayer as an *advaitic mantra*: «*sicut in caelo, et in terra*» (Mt 6:10).

***

You also asked what the meaning of life is for me.

The meaning of life is Life, life itself. Life is life whether one discovers this or that meaning to it or even no meaning at all. But my life, even if it is not my property, is ontonomically linked to the meaning I discover or attribute to it.

I can understand that this may seem a bit like what you somewhat disdainfully call "philosophizing". But in fact—believe me—it is the expression (the translation into words) of an experience, or better, the experience of the whole of "my" life, because it is what I have passionately sought for throughout the whole of my existence.

When I say "sense" I do not mean just meaning (conceptual or notional), but also sense as when one speaks of the "senses", or the sense of direction and above all the ultimate awareness of life.

Basically, the *sense* of my life is the experience of my life—an experience which, as you well know, is inseparable from its (my) interpretation.

The Mystical Body (of Christ, of Buddha, of *karman*, or of human solidarity...) is a reality.

You will say that I am an incorrigible philosopher, but the question of the meaning of life is the crucial question of philosophy, and if I want to make myself understood I must explain the meaning of the words I use. You are very intuitive and sensitive, and it is my task to anchor these gifts on to a more solid foundation, but not to the detriment of your gifts and without turning you into an "intellectual" with the meaning that you attribute to this word.

A metaphor, I would say almost a universal one, is that of the pilgrimage, the passage, the *pascha,* through the *agro* of time and space. Man is a pilgrim, a *homo viator* towards God, towards *ātman*, *nirvāña*, nothingness, the future, realisation, enlightenment, heaven (happiness), truth, goodness, beauty... *Homo viator* is a powerful expression for me—and you know what *viaticum* is.

The destination of the pilgrimage is not the Mecca or Jerusalem, Kailāsa or Varāṇasī. The destination is the next step, both the same as and different from the one before. The pilgrims who do not make it to Santiago de Compostela are still pilgrims.

We are living in a civilisation of "means". Everything seems to be "a means *for*": making more money, reducing effort, moving faster, producing more, being more perfect, climbing higher, reaching another level..., and so on. For me, this is not the meaning of life. Life is not a question of living faster or better than others. The faster one lives the less one lives, because life does not lie in its end but in its present (which I call tempiternal). The more one depends on others, the less one is one's own master.

In other words, the meaning of my life lies in living it, and living it step by step, with each breath. In the indo-european languages "to breathe", "to live" and "to be" belong together etymologically. *Homo viator* is not antithetical to *homo faber*, because along the way one can rest and one can do – where doing means creating and partaking in creation. *Otium et negotium*, as the ancients used to say.

For me the *terrain* is not a "vale of tears", a *kurukṣetra*, a wrestling field with everyone against everyone or against me or against nature (whether to conquer, dominate or exploit it), but nor is it a paradise, a flower-filled valley where rivers of milk and honey flow. There is everything on the land of men. Along the path one will encounter a bit of everything: flowers and thorns, heat and cold, days and nights, friends and enemies, good people and bad people.

But you asked me about the maning of life and now I can feel you impatiently wanting to ask me about this pilgrimage and how far I have come.

My answer is that I introduced the metaphor not in order to elude the question but to focus on it, and to indicate that I could interpret it with more than one language or means of expression. I think I could give you a Hindū answer, or a Buddhist one, or others too. One must not absolutise anything.

I would, however, like to give you an answer which interprets the metaphor in Christian terms, being the one closest to my heart and perhaps the one I know best.

"I am the *way*"—that is, the path—said Jesus; and he added that he was the path of *truth* which leads to *life*. The meaning of life is to *walk* in *truth* towards *life*. As you can see, I do not separate Jesus' sentence into three parts (the way *and* the truth *and* the life), I rather interpret them as a whole.

So I could say that the sense of life is to follow Jesus Christ, but this Christ accompanies the two pilgrims from Emmaus for quite a way, and then, when he is finally recognised, he disappears. He leaves us with total freedom and total responsibility, he does not even want to be imitated—at most he wants to be eaten so that we become one with him.

The Christian pilgrimage is not towards heaven: «Men of Galilee, why are you standing there looking up into heaven?»... On the earth we must walk, and with our own feet. *Resurrexit, non est hic!*— «He is risen, he is not here», in no kind of "here", in no place outside of us. Christ does not proceed like a standard bearer; he hides within us and leaves us free.

With this, I will repeat what I said at the beginning. The meaning of life is Life, my walking towards Life, attaining Life by living each step. This life is the so-called "eternal life", infinite life. And so this life is not found at the end of life but in life itself, in every moment of our life, in each step of the pilgrimage.

So how can we find Life in life? By living life. But what does "living life" mean?

To live life means to live it for itself and not for something else. Life is not a means. Thus we should not live life *in order to* be happy, *to* go to heaven, *to* reach a certain goal. This would mean passing life by and prostituting it, degrading it to a means for achieving an end. There is therefore nothing surprising about present-day neurosis, about the disease of activity as a way to escape oneself, the alienation of our very lives. We want to go to the moon, or often to travel only so as to escape ourselves. To live *this* life *for* another life is a blasphemy against the Creator of this life.

Now you ask me, less rhetorically, what is the human activity that has no other end whatsoever, but is an end in itself. In the West, from Plato onwards, there is an answer: *bios theoretikos*- contemplative life, though this does require some comment. We can also express it as contemplation and love. Contemplation means resting in the knowledge of truth, and love means union in the enjoyment of the truth. Both could be perhaps summed up in *gaudium de veritate*, the joy of truth.

When love is pure it is an end in itself; one loves because one loves, just as one lives because one lives. Life itself is its own "reason why". Without life there is no "reason why".

"This is eternal life (infinite life), that they may know You and him whom You have sent" says Christ in the language of his people.

Loving contemplation is neither spiritual egoism nor shutting oneself up in an ivory tower. On the contrary, he who is in the *gaudium de veritate* is truly free and is not afraid to commit himself to the search for the kingdom of God and his justice.

You will say that all this sounds Christian. That is true: it is Christian language describing a universal truth, and thus we see in Christ the symbol of this fullness of Life, which for me represents the meaning of life.

I could add that the meaning of life is union with God, the divinisation of Man, transformation in Christ, but in that case I would be talking to you about the *doctrine on* the meaning of life and not *about* the meaning of life.

If living life is life, and life is an end in itself, there can be no means for living it, because the means would presuppose the life itself whose meaning is being sought.

Doctrines aim at sense: they describe it, express it and translate it, but they are not sense. Sense manifests itself to the third eye. Meaning stems from the sight of the second eye, while it is the first eye that gives rise to the question: I *feel* myself live and ask myself what this living is. *Vita viventibus est esse*, wrote the mystic Thomas Aquinas, inspired by Aristotle. And the being of the living is love. I have said that the meaning of life is to reach and discover the fullness of man, therefore our fullness. This fullness consists in realising the triple dimension of body (cosmos), soul (humanity) and spirit (divinity) and partaking in the *perichôrêsis* of the whole of reality.

Life is a gift; to live life is a grace.

Glossary

āśram (Hindi): commonly refers to the home of a *gurū* and his disciples or ascetics.

acala: unmovable, unchangeable.

ācārya: master, teacher, spiritual guide of an *āśram.*

adhīṣṭhāna: substrate, foundation, base.

adhyāsa: superimposition of an attribute, quality or characteristic of one entity onto another entity.

agni: fire.

aham: personal pronoun "I'; *aham asmi*: "I am".

ahaṃkāra: "the sense of the 'I', principle of individuation which generates the sense of I-ness.

akhaṇḍa: without parts or distinctions, absolute.

ānanda: bliss, joy without an object).

aniketana: homeless.

antarikṣa: the intermediate space between heaven and earth.

anubhava: direct experience.

anubhavī: one who experiences the *advaita.*

āpodivyāḥ: divine water.

apyayan: end.

Aruṇācala: "Mountain of Living Light", sacred mountain in Tamil Nadu, associated with Śiva.

asparśa: without contact [with the phenomenal world], without support, absolute.

atīta: trascendent, the Beyond.

Bhagavān: Lord.

bhakta: he who follows the path of devotion.

bhakti: devotion to, love for the Divine.

bhāṣya: commentary.

bhavan: building, structure used for meetings, gatherings, entertainment, etc.

bhikkhu: Buddhist monk.

bodhisattva: one who has achieved enlightenment but remains in the worldto save all other beings.

cela: disciple.

darṣana (Hindi): beholding of a sage or saint.

dharma: religion, harmony, expression of the Oneness of Being.

dīkṣā: initiation, consecration.

dvandva: pair of oppostites.

eidos (Gr.): idea, form, appearance.

ekāgratā: One-pointedness of the mind; concentration; close attention.

etad vai tat: "This verily is that".

guhā: cave, grotto, secret place (human heart).

guṇa: qualities or attributes of being

gurū: spiritual master, he who eliminates ignorance.

hṛd: heart, the spiritual centre of being, site of *jīvātman.*

jīvanmukta: saint, one who is realized, liberated in this present life.

jñāna: knowledge, wisdom.

jñānin: sage, one who knows the Truth.

kaivalya: isolation, total liberation.

karma,karman: action, the result of actions (good or bad) performed in a former life, which determine one's future life.

kavi (Tamil): orange/saffron colored robes worn by Hindū ascetics.

kenósis (Gr.): annihilation, emptying of oneself, overcoming of one's *ego*.

kérygma (Gr.): message, proclamation (of the word of God), from the Greek *keryssí* (to proclaim), corresponding to the first level of the evangelical teaching.

keśin: long-haired (*keśa*) ascetic.

kevala: the unconditional state of being liberated.

koinínia (Gr.): community, communion.

kurukṣetra: battlefield.

kutiya (Hindi): small Indian house with thatched roof and mud walls.

līlā: game; the game of the Lord within and through the Universe.

maṇḍala: wheel, visible horizon.

mahātma: a great soul; title of respect.

mahāvākyāni: the great *Vedic* sayings in which the *Vedāntic* doctrine is condensed.

maithuna: fertile union.

mārga: way, path to realization.

maunamandir: place of silent retreat.

māyā: metaphysical ignorance, illusion of mortals.

mokṣa: liberation (from the bondage of the cycle of birth and death).

mudrā: symbolic gesture of given states of consciousness.

mūrti: image in a temple, form, icon.

naiṣkarmya: realization through renunciation of the fruits of action (which do not create further *karman)*

nāma-rūpin: those who limit themselves to the names and forms of things, to appearances.

nāmarūpa: name and form.

namaskāra: salutation (prostration before a deity).

nirvāṇa: pure transcendence.

nitya: eternal, permanent.

OṀ: sacred syllable, symbol of Brahman.

paramārtha: supreme, absolute, unconditioned Reality.

pāramārthika: plain of reality and truth, ontological reality, ultimate level of reality.

prabhava: origin.

prāṇāyāma: control of breathing, yogic practice.

pratiṣṭhā: support

pūjā: ceremonial worship, often in front of a sacred fire.

puruṣa: universal Man, the archetype of Man.

pūrvapakṣin: sort of "devil's advocate", interlocutor.

rajas: one of the three guṇas,which drives activity, desire, passion.

ṛṣi: seer, sage, wise man; the poet-sages to whom the *Veda* were revealed.

saccidānanda: *sat* (being) +*cit* (awareness) +*ānanda* (joy, bliss), one of the most profound Hindū intuitions concerning God, with Trinitarian references which are traced in the book by Abhiṣiktānanda of the same title.

sādhaka: one who is dedicated to following a chosen path.

sādhu: monk, sage, he who has achieved perfect realization.

samādhi: state of meditative consciousness,also death and tomb.

sampradāya: tradition

śarīra: body (physical, spiritual)

sarvamidam: "everything is this".

sarvodaya: universal elevation or the progress of everything.

sattva: being, existence in itself, wisdom.

saṃnyāsa: total renunciation, the last of the four traditional life stages.

saṃnyāsin: he who has renounced everything, Hindū monk, ascetic, hermit, often a wanderer.

saṃsāra: the impermanent phenomenal world and the cycle of birth and death.

śānti: profound peace.

staretz: holy man (in the Russian Orthodox Church).

śakti: dynamic energy.

śiṣya: disciple.

śraddhā: faith, the active trust (in Gods or in the rite itself) required in every act of worship; confidence (in the teachings of the *Veda*).

śunya: void, emptiness, nothingness, structural condition of reality and all things; represents the ultimate reality in Buddhism.

śunyatā: emptiness, the non-consistency of illusory things.

sūtra: aphorism, thread that binds together different things.

svāmi: monk of a particular confraternity, also Master.

svanubhāvam: direct experience.

tamas: one of the three guṇas, that which corresponds to obscurity, darkness.

tamāśā (Hindi): spectacle, entertainment.

tapas: ascetic ardor, austerity.

upādi: something to which one clings.

uttarāyaṇa: the northward movement made by the sun to complete the *devayana*: the journey of the Gods from which there is no return.

vāyu: air, wind.

viśiṣṭaadvaita: qualified *advaita* which maintains duality between the soul and God, according to the teaching of Rāmānuja.

vivartavādin: those who limit themselves to the notion of a world conceived as an illusory transformation of Brahman.

*viveka:*intuitive discernment, especially between what is real and what is not.

vyavahārika: empirical reality, the plane of appearance.

yajña: ritual *Vedic* sacrifice performed in front of a sacred fire.

Bibliography of Abhiṣiktānanda

Ermites du Saccidānanda: un essai d'integration chrétienne de la tradition monastique de Linde (in collaboration with J. Monchanin), Tournai: Casterman, 1956.

Guhāntara: au sein du fond (written 1953-54).

Sagesse hindou e mystique chrétienne: du Vedanta à la Trinité, Paris: Centurion, 1965.

Saccidānanda: a Christian Approach to Advaitic Experience. Delhi: ISPCK, 1974. (Author's revision of the original.) Reprinted with additions, 1984, 1990.

Tradizione indù, mistero trinitario, Bologna: EMI, 1988.

La rencontre de l'hindouisine et du christianisme, Paris: Le Seuil, 1966.

Hindu-Christian Meeting Point—within the Cave of the Heart. Bombay 1969. Reprinted with author's revisions, Delhi: ISPCK, 1976, 1984.

Une messe aux sources du Gange, Paris: Le Seuil, 1967.

The Mountain of the Lord: Pilgrimage to Gangotri, Bangalore: CISRS, 1966; reprinted, Madras: CLS, 1967. Reprinted in *Gurū and Disciple,* London: SPCK), 1974. New edition, printed separately, Delhi: ISPCK, 1990.

Una messa alle sorgenti del Gange, Brescia: Morcelliana, 1968.

Alle sorgenti del Gange. Pellegrinaggio spirituale (Quaderni di Ricerca, 46), new edition by Milena Carrara and Espedito D'Agostini, Troina: Servitium, 2005.

Prayer, Delhi: ISPCK, 1967. Reprinted, 1969; revised edition, 1972, 1975, 1979. Reprinted, London: SPCK, 1972, 1975; Reprinted, Philadelphia (Westminster Press) 1973; reprinted, London: Canterbury Press Norwich, 2006;

Prayer: Exploring Contemplative Prayer through Eastern and Western Spirituality (Revised and enlarged edition), edit.by Swami AtmanandaUdasin, foreword by Rev. Dr. James D.M. Stuart, Delhi: ISPCK, 2015.

Eveil à soi—éveil à Dieu: essai sur la prière, Paris: Centurion, 1971; reprinted, Paris: Le Seuil, 1984, OEIL,1986.

Prayer (new edition, translated from *Eveil),* Delhi: ISPCK, 1989.

In Spirit and Truth (translation of "Le chrétienen verité" revised by the author, 1972), Delhi: ISPCK, 1989.

Preghiera e presenza, Assisi: Cittadella, 1973.

Saccidānanda: A Christian Approach to Advaitic Experience", Delhi: ISPCK, 1974.

Risveglio a sé, risveglio a Dio (Quaderni di Ricerca, 51), Troina: Servitium, 2011.

Gnānānanda: un maitre spirituel du pays tamoul, Chambery: Présence, 1970.

"A Sage from the East: Sri Gnānānanda" in *Gurū and Disciple* London: SPCK, 1974. *Gurū and Disciple: an encounter with Sri Gnanananda, a contemporary spiritual master* (rev. edition), Delhi: ISPCK., 1990, 2000; new and enlarged edit.by Swami AtmanandaUdasin, pref. by Swami Nityananda Giri, Chennai: Samata Books, 2012.

-*Gnānānanda. Un maestro spirituale della terra Tamil.* ed. Stefano Rossi, Troina: Servitium, 2009.

-*Gurú y discípulo. Un encuentro con Sri Gnanananda Giri, maestro espiritual contemporáneo.* Pequeña Tierra, 2017

The Further Shore (containing "Sannyāsa" and "The Upanishads—an Introduction"), Delhi: ISPCK, 1975. Reprinted with addition of "The Upanishads and Advaitic Experience" and poems, 1984.

-*Initiation à la spiritualitédesUpanishads: "Vers l'autre rive",* Sisteron: Présence, 1979.

- *L'altra riva*, Milan: Servitium, 2018.

Souvenirs d'Arunachala: récit d'un ermite chrétien en terre hindoue, Paris: Epi SA, 1978.

- *The Secret of Arunachala,* Delhi: ISPCK, 1979, 1988.Revised edition, 1997.

- *Ricordi d'Arunachala. Racconto di un eremita cristiano in terra hindu*, ed. Stefano Rossi, Padova: Ed. Messaggero, 2004.

Les yeux de lumière: écrits spirituels présentés par André Gozier et Joseph Lemarié, Paris (Centurion) 1979. Revised & enlarged edn, Paris: OEIL, 1989.

The Eyes of Light, Denville, N.J.: Dimension Books, 1983.

La contemplazione cristiana in India, Bologna (EMI) 1985.

Intériorité et revelation: essais théologiques, Sisteron: Presence, 1982.

La montée au fond du coeur: le journal intime du moine chrétien—sanyasi hindou 1948-1973. Introduction et notes de R. Panikkar. Paris: OEIL, 1986.

-*Ascent to the Depth of the Heart. The Spiritual Diary (1948-1973) of Swami* Abhiṣiktānanda, Delhi: ISPCK, 1998.

-*Diario spirituale di un monaco cristiano-samnyasin hindu (1948-1973)*, ed. Milena Carrara, Milan: Mondadori, 2002.

Bibliography of Raimon Panikkar

As the publication of Raimon Panikkar's *Opera Omnia* has now been completed, which includes all his books and most of the articles, a list of the titles of the books composing the various volumes is given here.

Volume I, Mysticism and Spirituality

The New Innocence, New York: Cross Current, 1977

A Dwelling Place for Wisdom, Westminster: Louisville 1993; Delhi: Motilal Banarsidas, 1995

The Experience of God, Minniapolis: Fortress Press, 2006

Myth, Faith and Hermeneutics, New York: Cross Cultural Studies, 1983, (Ch. 9) *The Experience of God,* Minniapolis: Fortress Press, 2006

La gioia pasquale - La presenza di Dio – Maria. Milan: Jaca Book, 2007

Blessed Simplicity, New York: Seabury, 1982

Spirituality, the Way of Life, Maryknoll, New York: Orbis Books, 2014

Volume II, Religion and Religions

Religione e Religioni, Brescia: Morcelliana, 1964

Volume III, Christianity

Humanismo y Cruz, Madrid: Rialp, 1963

The Fullness of Man. A Christophany, Maryknoll, New York: Orbis Books; Delhi: ISPCK, 2006.

Volume IV, Hinduism

The Vedic Experience. *Mantramānjarī,* University of California: Berkely and London 1977; Delhi: Motilal Banarsidas, 1989-2004

Il Dharma dell'induismo, Milan: Rizzoli, 2006

Maya and Apocalisse, Rome: Abete,1966

L'utopia concreta. L'astuzia di Indra, Milan: Jaca Book, 2016

Volume V, Buddhism

The Silence of God, Maryknoll, New York: Orbis Books, 1989

Volume VI, Cultures and Religions in Dialogue

Pace e interculturalità, Milan: Jaca Book, 2002

The Intrareligious Dialogue, New York: Paulist, 1978-99; Bangalore: ATC, 1984
L'Incontro indispensabile, Milan: Jaca Book, 2001

Myth, Faith and Hermeneutics, New York: Cross Cultural Studies, 1983 (Ch. 8)

Volume VII, Hinduism and Christianity

The Unknown Christ of Hinduism, London: DLT, 1964; Orbis 1981; Bangalore: ATC, 1998

Le mystère du culte dans l'hindouisme et le christianisme, Éditions du *Cerf*: Paris 1970

Volume VIII, Trinitarian and Cosmotheandric Vision

The Trinity, Bangalore: CISRS; Madras: CLS, 1970; London: DLT § New York: Orbis 1975

La realtà cosmoteandrica. Dio-Uomo-Mondo, Milan: Jaca Book, 2004

Volume IX, Mistery and Hermeneutics

Myth, Faith and Hermeneutics, New York: Cross Cultural Studies, 1983 (Ch. 1, 2, 3, 4, 13)

Worship and Secular Man, London: DLT § New York: Orbis, 1973-75

Lo spirito della parola, Bollate: Borlinghieri, 2007

Volume X, Philosophy and Theology

The Rhythm of Being, New York: Orbis, 2010

Maya e Apocalisse, Rome: Abete, 1966.

L'esperienza filosofica dell'India, Assisi: Cittadella, 2000

Jacobi y la filosofía del sentimiento, Buenos Aires: Sapientia,1948

El concepto de naturaleza. Análisis histórico y metafísico de un concepto, Madrid: CSIC, 1951

Volume XI, Sacred Secularity

The Cosmotheandric Experience (Part II), New York: Orbis, 1993

Il daimôn della politica: agonia e speranza, Bologna: EDB, 1995

I fondamenti della democrazia, Rome: Lavoro, 2000

Concordia e armonía, Milan: Mondadori, 2009

Cultural Disarmament, Lousville: Westminster/John Knox, 1995

Volume XII, Space, Time and Science

Ontonomía de la ciencia. Sobre el sentido de la ciencia y sus relaciones con la filosofía, Madrid: Gredos, 1961(introduction)

La porta stretta della conoscenza. Sensi, ragione e fede, Milan: Rizzoli, 2005

Index

Names

A

B

C

D

Places